South-East Asian Social Science Monographs

The Malaysian Economy

The Malaysian Economy: Pacific Connections

Mohamed Ariff

SINGAPORE
OXFORD UNIVERSITY PRESS
OXFORD NEW YORK
1991

Oxford University Press

Oxford New York Toronto
Delhi Bombay Calcutta Madras Karachi
Petaling Jaya Singapore Hong Kong Tokyo
Nairobi Dar es Salaam Cape Town
Melbourne Auckland
and associated companies in
Berlin Ibadan

Oxford is a trade mark of Oxford University Press

© Oxford University Press Pte. Ltd. 1991

Published in the United States by
Oxford University Press, Inc., New York

ISBN 0 19 588564 3

British Library Cataloguing in Publication Data

Ariff, Mohamed 1940–
The Malaysian economy: Pacific connections.— (South-East
Asian social science monographs).
1. Malaysia. Economic conditions
I. Title II. Series
330.95951
ISBN 0-19-588564-3

Library of Congress Cataloging-in-Publication Data

K. A. Mohamed Ariff, 1940–
The Malaysian economy: Pacific connections/Mohamed Ariff.
p. cm.—(South-East Asian social science monographs)
Includes bibliographical references and index.
ISBN 0-19-588564-3 (hard cover):
1. Malaysia—Economic conditions. 2. Malaysia —Commerce.
3. Malaysia—Foreign economic relations. 4. Malaysia—Foreign
economic relations—Pacific Area. 5. Pacific Area—Foreign economic
relations—Malaysia. I. Title. II. Series.
HC445.5.K14 1991
330.9595'054—dc30
91-11186
CIP

Printed in Singapore by Kyodo Printing Co.(S) Pte. Ltd.
Published by Oxford University Press Pte. Ltd.,
Unit 221, Ubi Avenue 4, Singapore 1440

To the memory of my beloved father

Foreword

As is well known throughout the world, the Asia–Pacific region has experienced tremendous economic development over the past few decades. These successes have, on the whole, been achieved through a combination of correct macroeconomic policies, an emphasis on private-sector development, and increased international trade and investment linkages. Hence, to a large extent, the countries in the Asia–Pacific region have prospered by integrating their respective economies. Although there is no 'typical' country in Asia, Malaysia presents an excellent example of an export-oriented, natural resource-based economy with an enterprising and well-educated work-force. Combined with prudent government policies, these characteristics have been ingredients of great progress in the economic arena over the past few decades, and the results are quite typical of many Asian success stories. Malaysia's economic performance in recent years has been surprisingly good; the rebound from the collapse of commodity prices in the mid-1980s has been speedy and robust. Along with the Asian Newly Industrialized Economies and Thailand, Malaysia has become part of the group that the OECD calls 'Dynamic Asian Economies'. Forecasts for sustained growth and development in the 1990s suggest that Malaysia will continue to be one of the world's most exciting economies.

Throughout recent years, Malaysia has been looking East. Its trade with and investment flows from the Asia–Pacific have been increasing significantly, while its interaction with Europe has diminished. Hence, in the light of these developments, it would be useful to explore Malaysian links with the Pacific, as well as examine what the future, albeit uncertain, holds.

This is exactly what Professor Mohamed Ariff has done in the present volume. Well known for his work on the economies of South-East Asia, and of Malaysia in particular, he has embarked on this task at a very opportune time: the current GATT Round is slated for completion in December 1990; the unification of European economies in 'Project EC 1992' is well underway; ASEAN is at an important point in its history, focusing more on economic imperatives; protectionism in and conflict among the developed countries are on the rise; and a new fledgeling 'Asia–Pacific Economic Cooperation' organization is in the process of taking shape. As Malaysia is one of the most open economies in the developing world, the direction and intensity of these events are of great concern to the nation, and Malaysia's role in the new international economic environment, by itself and through ASEAN and APEC, is important to the region.

Professor Ariff undertook much of the research for his book as a Research Fellow in the Development Policy Program of the East–West Center in the 1989–90 academic year. The East–West Center is a public, non-profit educational institution established to promote better relations and understanding among the nations of Asia, the Pacific, and the United States through co-operative study, training, and research. The Development Policy Program is broadly concerned with the international economic relations and development prospects of the countries in the Asia–Pacific region. Research on ASEAN and its member countries is an important focus of the Development Policy Program. The fellowship programme serves to bring Asia–Pacific scholars to the East–West Center, where they interact and co-operate with resident scholars in order to stimulate thoughtful and useful ideas and research. During his stay, Professor Ariff contributed substantially to Development Policy Program research through seminars and discussions. I also believe that Professor Ariff benefited from his stay at the Center; his book is concrete proof of this.

The present volume is insightful, well thought out, and rigorous. It serves as excellent background material on the characteristics, strengths, and weaknesses of the Malaysian economy, and presents a thoughtful assessment of Malaysia's new role in the region and, indeed, the world. In short, it should be required reading for all serious students of the economies of Asia.

Honolulu, Hawaii   DR SEIJI NAYA
July 1990   Vice-President
                                                        East–West Center

Preface

THIS book is written with a wide audience in mind. It is targeted at researchers, students, policy-makers, industrialists, traders, and all those who have academic/professional/commercial interest in the Pacific region. Given the wide spectrum of readership aimed at, special care has been taken not to be too technical. But, as many would understand, technical jargon is simply unavoidable in an exercise of this kind.

An attempt is made in this volume to examine the importance of the Pacific region to the Malaysian economy. Particular emphasis is placed on the contributions of the Pacific to Malaysia's trade expansion and industrial development through foreign investment. Trade in manufactures and direct foreign investment in the manufacturing sector have been singled out for a closer look. In addition, the book also traces the trends in the Pacific, discusses the possible impact of such trends on the Malaysian economy in the years ahead, and draws policy implications for the 1990s and beyond.

The main message conveyed through this work is simple and straightforward: the Pacific influence on the Malaysian economy is profound and is growing increasingly stronger, as Malaysia has been gravitating away from the Atlantic and towards the Pacific. The book draws attention to the opportunities that the Pacific can offer, which Malaysia cannot afford not to take advantage of, as well as to the dangers and pitfalls a Pacific bias would entail, which Malaysia should guard against. Although the future looks very uncertain, there is little doubt that the Pacific dynamism will prevail. The book underscores the need for Malaysia to play a proactive rather than a reactive role in the Pacific process.

It is a pleasure to acknowledge the assistance of many individuals and institutions in the preparation of this book. This monograph was written while I was on my sabbatical leave at the Resource Systems Institute (RSI), East–West Center (EWC), Honolulu, Hawaii, USA, between October 1989 and July 1990. I am grateful to the University of Malaya for granting me leave of absence and to EWC for awarding me a generous fellowship. As a Research Fellow at RSI, I had full access to the excellent infrastructural and research facilities, including the Data Bank, at EWC. I gratefully acknowledge the financial assistance provided by EWC for obtaining additional data from the International Economic

Data Bank of the Australian National University in Canberra. I am particularly indebted to Dr Seiji Naya, Vice-President of EWC and Director of RSI, for inspiring me and encouraging me to undertake this project.

I wish to express my thanks to all those who provided comments on draft chapters. In this regard, special thanks are due to Dr William James, Dr Michael Plummer, and Dr Manuel Montes for their constructive criticisms and helpful suggestions. I am particularly grateful to Professor Heinz Arndt for going through the entire manuscript diligently and meticulously and for his valuable comments which helped improve the quality of the final output. Needless to say, I alone am responsible for any errors and omissions.

Numerous individuals provided valuable assistance in the course of my research. Help provided by Mr Wesley Oasa and Ms Janis Togashi, Project Assistants at RSI, in the preparation of tables and charts, is gratefully acknowledged. I would like to record my thanks and appreciation to Ms Ann Takayesu and Mrs Eileen Chong at RSI who took care of my fax needs. I also owe many thanks to my colleague, Mr Tan Eu Chye, at the Faculty of Economics and Administration (FEA), University of Malaya, for his help with data and other research materials. Reference must also be made to the word-processing service provided by Ms Rohinee Serisena of the faculty.

A vote of thanks is also due to Mrs Mendl Djunaidy, Program Officer, RSI, for the excellent administrative arrangements, including housing, which made .my sabbatical leave in Honolulu pleasant and comfortable. I must hasten to add to all this my profound thanks and appreciation to Mr Michael Manson, Assistant Director of RSI, for taking such good care of me when I fell ill in Honolulu in December 1989. Finally, I acknowledge the support and forebearance of my family, without which this study could not have seen the light of day.

University of Malaya   MOHAMED ARIFF
Kuala Lumpur
October 1990

Contents

Appendices

Tables

Maps

Figures

Abbreviations

ADB	Asian Development Bank
ADC	Advanced developing country
AIC	ASEAN Industrial Complementation
AIJV	ASEAN Industrial Joint Ventures
AIP	ASEAN Industrial Project
AJDC	ASEAN–Japan Development Corporation
AJDF	ASEAN–Japan Development Fund
APEC	Asia Pacific Economic Cooperation
ASEAN	Association of South-East Asian Nations
B-o-P	Balance of payments
CAP	Common Agricultural Policy
CER	Closer Economic Relations
CMS	Constant market share
CPI	Consumer price index
CVD	Countervailing duty
DAE	Dynamic Asian Economy
DCF	Domestic capital formation
DFI	Direct foreign investment
DRAM	Dynamic random access memory
EAEG	East Asian Economic Grouping
EC	European Community
EP	Export Promotion
EPR	Effective rates of protection
EPU	Economic Planning Unit
FIDA	Federal Industrial Development Authority
FRN	Floating rate note
FTA	Free Trade Area
FTZ	Free Trade Zone
GATT	General Agreement on Tariffs and Trade
GDP	Gross domestic product
GNP	Gross national product
GSP	Generalized System of Preferences
HICOM	Heavy Industries Corporation of Malaysia
IAPG	Inter-Agency Planning Group
IC	Integrated circuit
ICA	Industrial Co-ordination Act

ICU	Implementation and Co-ordination Unit
IMF	International Monetary Fund
IMP	Industrial Master Plan
ISIC	International Standard Industrial Classification
JAIC	Japan–ASEAN Investment Corporation
JETRO	Japan External Trade Organization
LDC	Less developed country
LIBOR	London inter-bank offer rate
LMW	Licensed manufacturing warehouse
LNG	Liquefied natural gas
MAMPU	Malaysian Administrative and Modernisation Planning Unit
MFA	Multifibre Arrangement
MFN	Most-favoured-nation
MIDA	Malaysian Industrial Development Authority
MNC	Multinational corporation
MOP	Margin of preferences
MTN	Multilateral trade negotiation
MVA	Manufacturing value-added
NDPC	National Development Planning Committee
NEER	Nominal effective exchange rate
NEP	New Economic Policy
NFP	Net factor payment
NFPE	Non-financial public enterprise
NIE	Newly industrializing economy
NPR	Nominal rates of protection
NTB	Non-tariff barrier
OBA	Off-budget agency
ODA	Overseas Development Assistance
OECD	Organization for Economic Cooperation and Development
OECF	Overseas Economic Cooperation Fund
OMA	Orderly marketing arrangement
PAFTAD	Pacific Area Free Trade and Development
PBEC	Pacific Basin Economic Council
PECC	Pacific Economic Cooperation Conference
PETRONAS	National Petroleum Corporation
PFI	Portfolio foreign investment
PLCC	Plastic leaded chip carrier
PORIM	Palm Oil Research Institute of Malaysia
PTA	Preferential Trading Arrangement
R & D	Research and development
RCA	Revealed comparative advantage
REER	Real effective exchange rate
RRIM	Rubber Research Institute of Malaysia
S & D	Special and differential
SDR	Special Drawing Right
SEPU	State Economic Planning Unit

SERU	Socio-Economic Research Unit
SITC	Standard International Trade Classification
SOIC	Small outline integrated circuit
SPARTECA	South Pacific Regional Trade and Economic Co-operation Agreement
TSUS	Tariff Schedule of the United States
UNCTAD	United Nations Conference on Trade and Development
UNIDO	United Nations Industrial Development Organization
US	United States
VER	Voluntary export restraint

1
Introduction

DISPLAYING many an attribute of a truly advanced developing economy, Malaysia (see Map 1.1) is marching into the 1990s and beyond with renewed confidence. It has gone a long way since achieving political independence in 1957. Dramatic transformation and changes have taken place in the structure and profile of the Malaysian economy over the last three decades. The Malaysian economy has always been, and continues to be, one of the most open economies of the Third World. Indeed, the economy has become increasingly internationalized, especially in recent years, integrating itself with the rest of the world mainly through trade flows. It has been estimated that the exports of goods and non-factor services accounted for as much as 77.7 per cent of the country's gross national product (GNP) in 1989, while the ratio of imports of goods and non-factor services to GNP stood at 73.2 per cent. These ratios are estimated to have risen further to 82.0 per cent and 80.0 per cent respectively, in 1990.[1]

The Malaysian economy is also one of the most dynamic in the world. In the 1970s, it grew rapidly at an annual rate of 7.8 per cent. Its impressive growth record was marred by a deep recession in the mid-1980s with the gross domestic product (GDP) registering a negative growth rate for the first time in 1985. But the economy has since recovered remarkably and smoothly, posting high real GDP growth rates of 5.4 per cent, 8.9 per cent, and 8.8 per cent in 1987, 1988, and 1989 respectively. In 1990, GDP growth exceeded 10 per cent.

Although the Malaysian economy is extremely vulnerable to externally induced fluctuations by virtue of the country's economic openness and trade dependence, the economy has remained relatively stable. To be sure, the volatility of the external sector does impact on the domestic sector, but to a much lesser extent than would appear at first sight, thanks to the resilience of the latter. The high degree of domestic resilience is reflected to a great extent in the remarkable stability of domestic price levels and the low rate of inflation, which in recent years has ranged from 0.4 per cent in 1985 to 2.8 per cent in 1989, very mild rates indeed by world standards.

Malaysia has not experienced chronic external imbalances, although there have been spurts of deficits in the current account in the balance of payments, which, however, have not been persistent or large enough

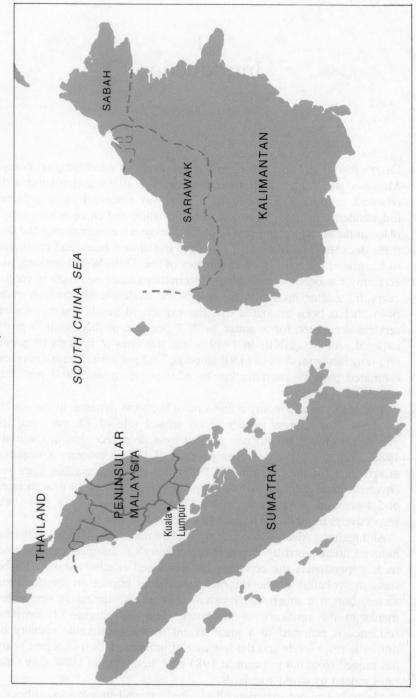

MAP 1.1
Malaysia

to cause too severe a strain on the country's external reserves. More often than not, the current account deficits have been offset by investment inflows in the capital account. It was only in the difficult years in the first half of the 1980s that Malaysia ran into prolonged current account deficits. In 1987 and 1988, Malaysia enjoyed sizeable surpluses in the current account. Data for 1989 show a small current account deficit. Malaysia's net external reserves have been growing steadily except during 1981–4. The external reserves are substantial relative to the country's foreign exchange requirements. In 1988, its reserves amounted to nearly 6 months of imports, a comfortable level by developing-country norms.

In short, there are only a few developing countries in the world that can match Malaysia's economic performance. Indeed, Malaysia is an object of envy for many developing countries that are beset with economic problems of sorts. All this, however, does not mean that all is well with the Malaysian economy. To begin with, there are problems associated with the exposure of the economy to the external vagaries. There are also thorny structural problems. Despite serious attempts at diversification, the economic base remains fragile, with a few primary commodities exerting a powerful influence on the economy. The manufacturing sector has grown impressively, but its narrow focus on electronics and textiles remains a source of grave concern. Malaysia has emerged as an important exporter of manufactures, but much of it is accounted for by the multinationals with very little local involvement. Although Malaysia is not a populous country, unemployment constitutes a major problem in some sectors, which ironically coincides with acute labour shortages elsewhere. The country's macroeconomic management has been fairly sound, but there are weaknesses in the system which were exposed during the recession of the mid-1980s. Its budget deficits have been large by Asian standards, while its external debt burden has become disproportionately heavy. The thorniest problem facing the country relates to socio-economic disparities among the various ethnic groups, which is an issue of considerable political sensitivity.[2]

Notwithstanding all this, Malaysia's medium-term economic outlook seems fairly bright, assuming that the country's politicians will continue to behave in a pragmatic and responsible fashion so that racial harmony and political stability are not jeopardized. Important structural changes are underway, with the manufacturing sector taking the lead and the primary sector upgrading itself through research and development (R & D). Malaysia's comparative advantage in primary production, especially in natural rubber and palm oil, is in no immediate danger, thanks mainly to its R & D efforts, although in the long run Malaysia may lose out to Indonesia where labour is much cheaper, barring any major technological breakthrough that would cause a factor-intensity reversal in primary production, rendering it capital-intensive. None the less, it is almost certain that Malaysia will figure less and less as an exporter of primary commodities and more and more as an exporter of manufactured goods, now that downstream value-added activities are being stepped up. Thus, Malaysia may gradually reduce resource-intensive exports in primary forms.

There is evidence of significant industrial restructuring taking place within the Malaysian manufacturing sector itself. For example, in the electronics industry, the country is moving away from the simple assembling of semiconductors towards the manufacturing of components and consumer electronics products. A shift from unskilled labour-intensive operation towards technology-intensive and human capital-intensive processes seems inevitable, given Malaysia's factor endowments. In the long run, the Malaysian manufacturing sector may entrench itself in resource-intensive industries which also happen to be capital-intensive, technology-intensive, and skill-intensive as well.

All indications are that Malaysia will become a newly industrializing economy (NIE) joining the ranks of Korea, Taiwan, Hong Kong, and Singapore before the end of the 1990s. Strange as it may seem, Malaysia apparently is not excited by this prospect and is not keen to be 'stigmatized' as an NIE for fear of attracting the attention of protectionist forces in developed-country markets and losing the special privileges it now enjoys. Nevertheless, the fact remains that movement towards NIE status has begun and is gathering momentum.

A key element in the whole process is what may be termed the 'Pacific factor'. The Pacific Basin (see Map 1.2) has emerged as the most dynamic region and there are signs that world economic activity is gravitating from the Atlantic to the Pacific. Malaysia has been contributing to, and is benefiting from, the dynamism of the Pacific through trade and investment networks.

The interface between trade flows and investment linkages has helped strengthen the Malaysia–Pacific nexus. Industrial development in Malaysia is closely related to structural changes and industrial adjustments taking place in the industrial countries and the NIEs, especially those in the Pacific region. Some activities which have been edged out or phased out in the process of industrial restructuring in these countries have migrated to Malaysia through direct foreign investment channels. Foreign investment activities, in turn, have helped open up additional conduits for trade flows between the home and host countries. As a result, the complementarity of the Malaysian economy to the rest of the Pacific has grown even stronger, as manifested by the increased intra-industry trade flows between Malaysia and its major sources of direct foreign investment in the Pacific Basin.

To put it in a nutshell, the Pacific has emerged as a crucial factor in the Malaysian economic calculus. The fortunes of the Malaysian economy are so inextricably wedded to those of the Pacific that Malaysia cannot afford not to pay serious attention to changes taking place in the Pacific region. In addition to the significant industrial restructuring and adjustments occurring in the individual countries of the Pacific, important constellations of regional forces are constantly at work reshaping the

MAP 1.2
The Pacific Basin

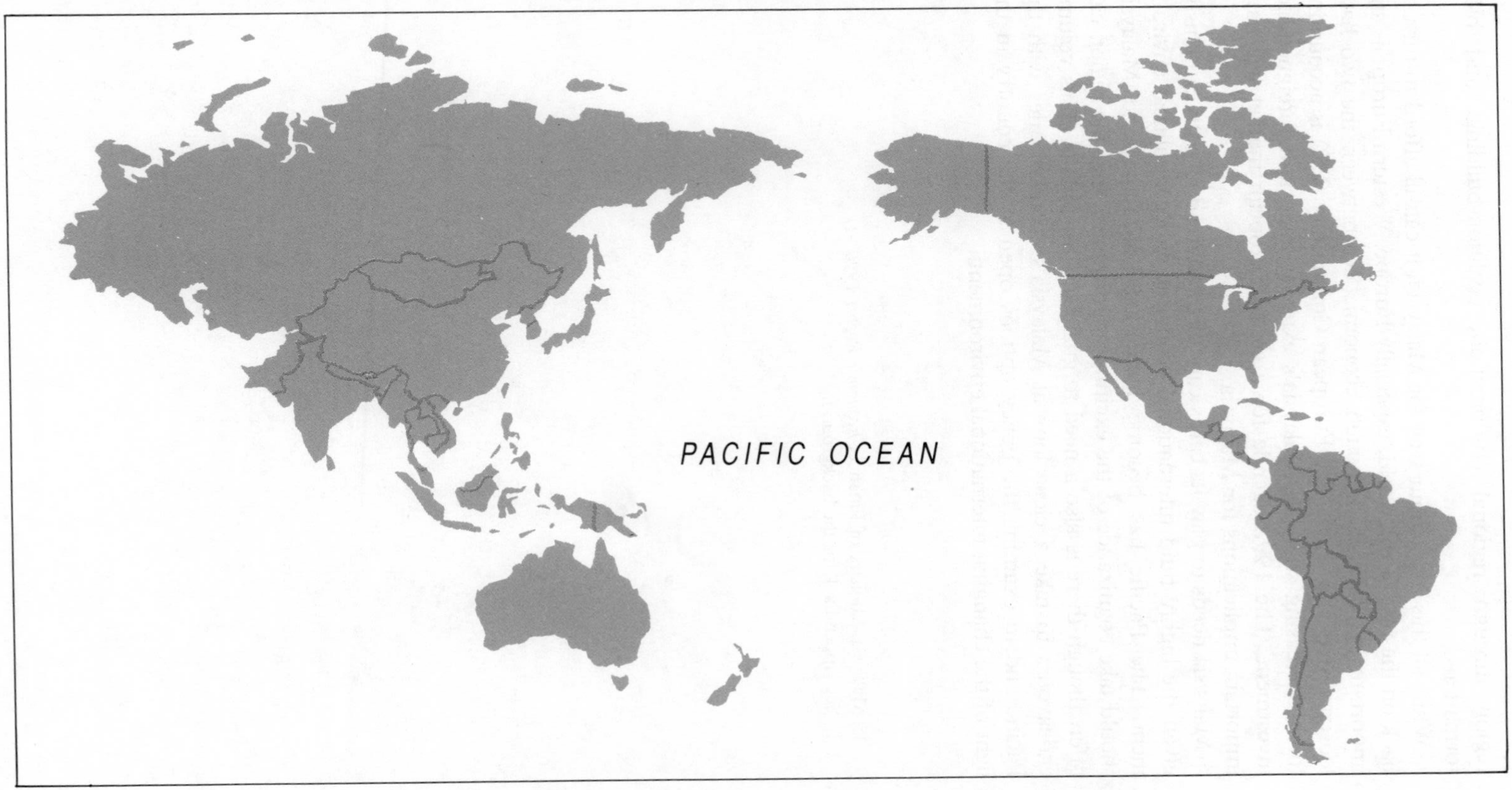

PACIFIC OCEAN

region through regional co-operation, coalition-building, and bloc formations.

While all this may augur well for Malaysia, it can ill afford to turn its back on the rest of the world, especially Europe. Western Europe is still important to Malaysia, although economic ties between the two have loosened over the years. The European Community (EC) is accounting for a decreasing share of Malaysia's external trade and foreign direct investment. The 1992 agenda for a single European market will have important implications for Malaysia.

Malaysia needs to play its cards carefully and tread its path cautiously, given the highly fluid international economic and geopolitical environment. The Pacific has become increasingly attractive and Malaysia should take cognizance of the exciting opportunities that the region can offer, though there is also a need to guard against pitfalls. This volume endeavours to take a close look at Malaysia's economic ties with the Pacific and to examine the policy options open to the country in the light of the changing international environment.

1. Malaysia, Ministry of Finance, *Economic Report 1990/91*.
2. See Appendix 1 for the background.

2
The Economy in Transition

THIS chapter attempts to paint a portrait of the Malaysian economy, using broad-brush strokes, so as to capture the many facets of the vibrant, modern economic entity. The chapter is designed not only to serve as a backdrop to the detailed analyses of Malaysia–Pacific economic relations presented in subsequent chapters, but also to trace, objectively, the progress the economy has undergone over the years. Significant structural changes have taken place in the economy; in the process, the economy has experienced tremendous stresses and strains. It appears that the Malaysian economy has once again arrived at a crossroads. There is a need to review past policies and to draw lessons from past experiences before the Malaysian economy changes gear and steers itself into the next century.

Structure and Profile

The profile of the Malaysian economy has changed radically, through three decades of transformation since Independence in 1957. It is no longer precariously dependent on a few primary commodities. Its production base has broadened, with manufacturing accounting for a growing share of national output and employment. The Malaysian economy has become more open and outward-oriented over the years. In fact, the economy has become increasingly internationalized in recent years, thanks mainly to deregulation and decontrol, now that the public sector has taken the back seat and the private sector has been allowed to steer the course.

Structural Change

The changing structure of the Malaysian economy is reflected in the changing composition of the country's gross domestic product. As shown in Table 2.1, the share of the agricultural sector in GDP has declined over the years from 30.8 per cent in 1970 to 20.4 per cent in 1989, while that of the manufacturing sector has grown rapidly from 13.4 per cent to 25.1 per cent over the same period. The share of the mining sector would have been much smaller, had it not been for the fortuitous discovery of oil. The construction sector exhibited consider-able ups and downs, as the property subsector is particularly vulnerable to speculative activities. However, the maturity of an economy is often mirrored in the contribution of the services sector to the GDP. In the Malaysian case, the tertiary sector has become increasingly important

TABLE 2.1

Malaysia: Composition of Gross Domestic Product, 1970–1989
(percentage)

	1970	1975	1980	1985	1989
Agriculture, livestock, forestry, and fishing	30.8	27.7	23.4	20.8	20.4
Mining and quarrying	6.5	4.6	5.0	10.5	10.2
Manufacturing	13.4	16.4	20.5	19.7	25.1
Construction	3.9	3.8	4.5	4.8	3.3
Electricity, gas, and water	1.9	2.1	2.2	1.7	1.9
Transport, storage, and communication	4.7	6.2	6.3	6.4	6.7
Wholesale and retail trade	13.3	12.8	12.4	12.1	10.7
Finance, insurance, real estate, and business services	8.4	8.5	7.8	8.9	9.4
Government services	11.1	12.8	12.5	12.2	11.3
Other services	2.5	2.8	2.6	2.3	2.1
GDP at constant prices (M$ million)	12,308	17,365[1]	25,650[1]	57,150[2]	72,134[2]

Source: Malaysia, Ministry of Finance, *Economic Report*, various issues.
[1] At 1970 constant prices.
[2] At 1978 constant prices.

TABLE 2.2

Malaysia: Employment by Sector, 1970–1989 (percentage)

	1970	1975	1980	1985	1989
Agriculture, forestry, and fishing	53.2	47.6	38.6	31.3	30.8
Mining and quarrying	2.6	2.2	1.8	0.8	0.6
Manufacturing	9.0	12.4	15.8	15.2	17.0
Construction	2.7	4.2	5.5	7.6	6.1
Finance, insurance, business services, and real estate	12.3	13.7	2.9	3.5	3.5
Transport, storage, and communication	4.0	4.7	4.1	4.3	4.2
Government services	11.9	13.6	14.6	14.6	13.3
Other services	4.3	4.9	5.7	22.6	24.4
Total (millions)	3.34	4.02	5.08	5.62	6.35

Source: Malaysia, Ministry of Finance, *Economic Report*, various issues.

over the years, although it is not totally immune to cyclical fluctuations.

Structural changes in the Malaysian economy are also reflected in the changing pattern of sectoral employment, as depicted in Table 2.2. Of particular interest is the rising proportion of the labour force in the manufacturing sector, while the share of government services in total employment declined between 1985 and 1989, due mainly to the privatization of some public-sector activities.

It is the manufacturing sector which exhibits most vividly the modernization of the Malaysian economy. As was seen above, the role of the manufacturing sector has become increasingly important over the years. Even more striking is the industrial restructuring taking place within the manufacturing sector. In particular, the shares of chemical products and of electrical machinery and appliances in total manufacturing value-added have increased significantly, as shown in Table 2.3.

TABLE 2.3

Malaysia: Manufacturing Value-added by Major Industry Group, 1973–1986 (percentage)

	1973	1981	1986
Processing of estate-type agricultural goods	n.a.	10.3	8.0
Food	15.7	8.8	8.9
Beverages	2.6	3.2	2.2
Tobacco products	5.6	2.9	4.3
Textiles	4.5	4.3	3.7
Made-up textiles and wearing apparel	1.5	2.4	2.5
Wood products	13.1	9.2	6.1
Furniture and fixtures	0.8	1.1	0.8
Printing and publishing	4.9	4.4	3.4
Paper and paper products	0.8	1.0	1.3
Leather and leather products	0.1	0.1	0.0
Rubber products	9.7	4.0	3.8
Chemical and chemical products	7.5	4.9	14.0
Products of petroleum and coal	2.2	5.7	3.9
Non-metallic mineral products	4.5	5.1	5.6
Basic metal industries	3.7	3.3	3.6
Metal products	4.9	4.1	2.8
Non-electrical machinery	3.7	3.5	2.1
Electrical machinery	8.1	13.0	15.3
Transport equipment	2.7	4.6	2.9
Miscellaneous	3.4		4.7
Total value-added (M$ million)	2,327	9,4	

Sources: Malaysia, Department of Statistics, Census of Manufacturin 1973; Malaysia, Department of Statistics, Census of Manufacturin 1981; and Malaysia, Department of Statistics, Industrial Survey, n.a. = Not available.

Industrialization

Serious attempts at industrialization were made only in the late 1950s. A World Bank study (1955), which formed the main basis of Malaysia's industrialization programme, had recommended import substitution under mild protection backed by investment incentives. The Pioneer Industries Ordinance 1958 offered specific incentives to stimulate investment in manufacturing. In the initial stage, the focus was primarily on the production of consumer goods, not only because the domestic market was then oriented towards such items but also because the cost disadvantage between domestically produced and imported goods was less for consumer goods than for intermediate or investment goods. However, the need to extend industrialization upstream, especially the manufacturing of intermediate goods, was stressed in the First Malaysia Plan 1966–1970.

A radical shift from an inward-looking, defensive industrialization strategy of import substitution to an outward-looking, aggressive strategy of export promotion took place after 1968, when it became obvious that import substitution could no longer provide a viable basis for sustained industrial expansion, given the small domestic market. However, export orientation of the Malaysian manufacturing sector did not mean an abandonment of import substitution. Indeed, export orientation and import substitution have been pursued in a somewhat parallel fashion, although stronger emphasis has apparently been placed on the former. Accordingly, investment incentives were restructured so as to offer a variety of export incentives under the Investment Incentives Act 1968, including export allowances and accelerated depreciation, in addition to tax holidays, investment tax credit, and other fiscal incentives which were aimed increasingly at export-oriented industries. Pre-shipment and post-shipment export credit refinancing facilities were also introduced.

A major measure taken by Malaysia to promote manufactured exports was the establishment of Free Trade Zones (FTZs) from 1971 onwards. There are twelve FTZs operating throughout Malaysia. These FTZs have acquired the character of foreign 'enclaves' with duty-free access to imported inputs and machinery while at the same time enjoying a wide range of investment and export incentives. Nearly three-quarters of the FTZ firms in Malaysia are foreign-owned, and they account for more than 90 per cent of the total direct employment within the FTZs (Ariff and Semudram, 1987).

Malaysia ventured into an ambitious heavy industrialization pro-gramme in the early 1980s with the establishment of the Heavy Industries Corporation of Malaysia (HICOM), which marked yet another manifestation of active government participation and interven-tion in the country's industrial development. The term 'heavy industry' has been used rather loosely in Malaysia, connoting projects with high capital intensity, long gestation periods, and substantial scale economies. In the Malaysian context, heavy industrialization has meant the setting up of iron and steel mills, petrochemical plants, and the manufacturing of motor vehicles. There are already six steel mills in operation in the country, with the HICOM–Perwaja steel mill having the largest capacity (615 000 tonnes per year). The production of the national car, Proton Saga, represents another 'milestone' in the development of heavy industries in Malaysia. The first batch of cars which rolled out in 1985 had 38 per cent domestic content. The local content of the national car is programmed to increase progressively.

The Malaysian heavy industries are in deep trouble, saddled with excess capacity, high production costs, market gluts, and heavy debts, but it appears they are here to stay—a clear case of politics overriding economics. Besides, exit will not be easy for these industries since a large amount of capital has been sunk into them. Under such circumstances, economic theory tells us, it would make sense for these firms to continue operation so long as the variable costs are covered. Reportedly, some of these projects are already making 'profits'. However, as is well known to economists, financial performance cannot be equated with economic performance, for the former is based on money costs and prices which may not reflect the real opportunity cost of resources, especially where they have been distorted by policy interventions. Thus, profits posted by heavy industries under protection provide no vindication for the heavy industrialization policy. The crucial test of efficiency lies in profits at world prices.

The Industrial Master Plan (IMP) expects the manufacturing sector to grow at 8.8 per cent per annum in real terms during the period 1986–95. The IMP also envisages the creation of 705,400 new jobs, bringing the total number of workers in the manufacturing sector to 1.5 million by 1995. The IMP singles out several industries for special focus. Resource-based industries have received considerable attention, including tyre manufacturing, downstream palm oil and palm-kernel oil based oleochemicals, food processing, and wood-based industries. The overall message of the IMP is that Malaysia must resort to large-scale manufactured exports in order to maintain rapid industrial growth.

It is possible to gain considerable insight into the nature and character of industrial restructuring by means of a shift-share analysis which decomposes the gross output growth into three components, namely domestic market expansion, import substitution, and export expansion.[1] It can be seen from Table 2.4 that import substitution has contributed negatively to the growth of manufacturing output as a whole during the period 1968–86. About 70 per cent of the increase in output is attributable to domestic market expansion, while nearly 41 per cent of it is due to export expansion. Of course, there are considerable inter-industry variations. Industries where import substitution has made significant contributions to output growth include paper and paper products, basic metal products, and transport equipment. Industries where export expansion has made a strong impact on the growth of output include textiles and wearing apparel, wood products, non-electrical machinery and, most important of all, electrical machinery and

TABLE 2.4

Malaysia: Sources of Gross Output Growth by Major Industries,
1968–1986 (percentage)

Sources of Growth	Domestic Market Expansion	Import Substitution	Export Expansion
Total manufacturing	70.12	−10.94	40.82
Food	52.06	12.26	35.67
Beverages	66.76	13.87	19.38
Tobacco	83.11	3.26	13.63
Textile	41.51	23.21	35.29
Made-up textile goods, wearing apparel, and footwear	−13.20	−29.23	142.43
Leather products	73.95	−31.28	57.33
Wood and cork products	26.58	−2.75	76.16
Furniture and fixtures	77.68	−2.61	24.93
Paper and paper products	50.20	36.37	13.43
Printing and publishing	86.75	7.74	5.51
Industrial and other chemical products	98.51	−21.12	22.61
Petroleum and petroleum products	125.08	−20.89	−4.19
Rubber products	94.44	0.57	4.99
Plastic products	89.61	−1.85	12.24
Non-metallic mineral products	82.81	11.31	5.88
Basic metal	49.71	36.19	14.09
Fabricated metal product	70.17	8.37	21.47
Non-electrical machinery	76.33	−29.14	52.81
Electrical machinery and appliances	29.98	−38.32	108.34
Transport equipment	53.94	32.76	13.30
Miscellaneous	33.39	−18.56	85.17

Source: K. F. Lee (1990).

appliances. In almost all cases, domestic market expansion has also made significantly positive contributions to the growth of gross output.

The External Sector

The pace at which the Malaysian economy can move is dictated mainly by the external demand for its products, while the vulnerability of the economy to external influences is exacerbated by the high degree of concentration in the commodity-mix. To be sure, exports have been diversified to some extent, but commodities which figure prominently as a result of the diversification drive, e.g. palm oil, are just as prone to price fluctuations as the traditional items like natural rubber and tin. Complementing the diversification efforts in the agricultural sector, new non-traditional export bases have been established, notably in electronics and textiles. These developments have enabled the Malaysian economy to maintain a high trade profile.

Malaysia is still essentially a primary producer and exporter. Primary exports accounted for as much as 54.1 per cent of the total exports even as late as 1988. In 1970, though, primary exports contributed 72.8 per cent of the total exports. The commodity concentration of primary exports has also decreased over the years. Thus, four items (rubber, sawlogs, crude palm oil, and tin) formed 95.6 per cent of the total in 1970, compared with 42.8 per cent in 1989 (Table 2.5). It is significant to note that no single commodity is dominant enough any longer to form even one-quarter of the total primary exports.

Although equally significant changes have taken place in the composition of the Malaysian manufactured exports, the picture is slightly different. For one thing, the commodity concentration of manufactured exports has increased conspicuously, with electrical and electronic products accounting for an increasingly dominant share of the total (56.7 per cent in 1989), as shown in Table 2.6. For another, the share of manufactures in total exports has increased from 11.9 per cent in 1970 to 54.0 per cent in 1989 (Table 2.7).

Table 2.7 shows that the relative importance of the traditional primary commodities, rubber and tin, in total exports has dwindled markedly, their joint share falling from 53.0 per cent in 1970 to just 7.5 per cent in 1989. By contrast, the proportion of manufactured exports has risen sharply from 11.9 per cent to 54.0 per cent over the same period. In addition, petroleum has emerged as the top export earner since 1976.

The structure of Malaysian imports has also undergone major changes as depicted in Table 2.8. The ratio of consumption goods to

TABLE 2.5
Malaysia: Composition of Primary Commodity Exports,
1970–1989 (percentage)

	1970	1975	1980	1985	1989
Crude petroleum	4.4	11.5	33.3	33.7	23.9
Crude palm oil	5.8	20.9	12.5	15.3	14.2
Rubber	45.9	32.0	22.9	11.1	11.9
Sawlogs	17.1	10.6	13.0	10.7	13.2
Tin	26.8	19.1	12.4	6.4	3.5
LNG	–	–	–	8.9	6.2
Cocoa beans	–	0.6	n.a.	1.6	1.6
Others	–	5.3	n.a.	12.3	25.5
Total (M$ million)[1]	3,759	6,329	20,177	25,832	33,049

Source: Malaysia, Ministry of Finance, Economic Report, various issues.
[1]SITC 0-4.
n.a. = Not available.

TABLE 2.6
Malaysia: Composition of Manufactured Exports, 1970–1989
(percentage)

	1970	1975	1980	1985	1989
Food, beverages, and tobacco	18.3	13.7	7.8	4.9	4.9
Textiles, clothing, and footwear	6.5	11.0	13.2	10.6	8.7
Wood products	14.4	10.4	7.7	3.0	3.2
Rubber products	2.8	2.2	1.4	1.1	3.1
Chemicals and petroleum products	31.8	9.4	5.9	11.7	7.3
Non-metallic mineral products	3.3	1.2	1.0	1.2	1.8
Iron and steel and metal manufactures	4.2	2.5	2.6	2.5	4.0
Electrical and electronic machinery and appliances	2.8	15.4	46.4	49.8	56.7
Other machinery and transport equipment	11.1	13.4	6.7	8.5	3.4
Other manufactures	4.4	20.8	7.3	6.9	6.7
Total manufactured exports (M$ million)	612	1,978	6,101	12,111	36,592

Source: Malaysia, Ministry of Finance, Economic Report, various issues.

TABLE 2.7
Malaysia: Structure of Exports, 1970–1989 (percentage)

	1970	1975	1980	1984	1987	1989
Rubber	33.4	21.9	16.4	9.6	8.7	5.8
Tin	19.6	13.1	8.9	3.0	1.9	1.7
Logs and timber	16.5	12.1	14.1	10.3	13.4	10.7
Palm oil	5.1	14.3	9.2	11.8	7.3	6.9
Petroleum	3.9	9.2	23.8	22.6	13.9	11.6
Manufactures	11.9	21.4	21.7	31.2	45.1	54.0
Others	9.6	8.0	5.9	11.5	9.7	9.3
Total	100.0	100.0	100.0	100.0	100.0	100.0

Sources: Malaysia, Bank Negara Malaysia, Quarterly Economic Bulletin, various issues; and Malaysia, Ministry of Finance, Economic Report 1990/91.

TABLE 2.8

Malaysia: Composition of Imports, 1970–1989 (percentage)

Category	1970	1975	1980	1985	1989
Consumption goods	28.5	22.2	18.4	21.5	21.8
Investment goods	25.2	31.7	30.0	31.1	34.4
Intermediate goods	35.3	41.3	49.8	46.5	42.7
Imports for re-export	11.0	4.8	1.7	0.9	1.1
Total (M$ million)	4,288	8,530	23,451	30,438	60,858

Source: Malaysia, Bank Negara Malaysia, *Quarterly Economic Bulletin*, September 1989 and September 1990.

total imports has fallen significantly, while investment goods and inter-mediate goods have been accounting for a growing proportion of the total imports. Imports for re-export have diminished in importance, indicating that entrepôt trade is definitely on the decline. The changing structure of imports reflects the industrialization process, which in itself is import-dependent with increased demand for machinery and inter-mediate inputs.

The directions of trade flows have not changed much in the sense that three countries, namely Japan, Singapore, and the United States, have continued to account for the bulk of both exports and imports of Malaysia. Underneath all this, however, one can see important shifts taking place in the direction of trade flows. The share of the European Community fell from 20.3 per cent in 1970 to 14.4 per cent in 1988 in terms of exports, and from 23.4 per cent to 13.3 per cent corres-pondingly in terms of imports (Table 2.9). By contrast, the share of the Asian NIEs in both exports and imports rose significantly during the same period. Two other strikingly important observations in Table 2.9 merit special mention. First, Malaysia trades increasingly with developed countries. Secondly, Malaysia's trade linkages in terms of both exports and imports with the Asia–Pacific countries have grown remarkably stronger.

In addition to trade, Malaysia is integrated with the rest of the world through investment linkages of sorts. Foreign investment in Malaysia consists of both direct and portfolio components. Obviously, external linkages established by direct investment are much stronger and more lasting. Joint ventures form the bulk of the direct foreign investments, although new forms of foreign investment, e.g. licensing and franchising arrangements and management contracts, are also growing in import-ance. Table 2.10 presents foreign investment approvals by country. It is evident that Singapore, Japan, the United Kingdom, and the United States are the most important sources of foreign investment for Malaysia; they jointly accounted for about one-half of the total invest-ment approved during the period 1978–86.

TABLE 2.9
Malaysia: Exports by Destination and Imports by Origin,
1970 and 1988 (percentage shares)

Export to/Imports from	Share of Malaysian Exports		Share of Malaysian Imports	
	1970	1988	1970	1988
Developed Countries				
Australia	2.2	2.4	5.7	4.2
Canada	1.9	0.7	1.1	1.2
Japan	18.3	19.9	17.5	23.0
New Zealand	0.5	0.2	0.9	0.8
United States	13.0	17.3	8.6	17.7
NIEs				
Hong Kong	1.2	3.4	2.2	2.3
Korea	2.6	4.8	0.3	2.6
Singapore	21.6	19.3	7.5	13.2
Taiwan	1.6	3.0	0.9	4.6
Other Developing Countries				
Brunei	0.6	0.3	6.5	0.0
Indonesia	0.6	1.3	4.8	1.7
Philippines	1.7	1.5	0.2	0.8
Thailand	0.9	2.0	3.6	3.0
China	1.3	2.0	5.3	2.9
Developed Countries	35.9	37.6	33.8	46.9
NIEs	27.0	30.5	10.9	22.7
ASEAN[1]	25.4	24.4	22.5	18.8
Asia–Pacific	68.1	75.1	65.1	78.0
EC	20.3	14.4	23.4	13.3
Malaysia's total exports/ imports (US$ million)	1,687	21,125	1,399	16,567

Sources: International Monetary Fund, *Direction of Trade Statistics*, 1970–6, and International Monetary Fund, *Yearbook 1989*.
[1]Brunei, Indonesia, the Philippines, Singapore, and Thailand.

Malaysia has, more often than not, enjoyed balance-of-payments surpluses. These surpluses, particularly in the late 1970s, were largely supported by favourable trade balances resulting from high commodity prices. Malaysia suffered trade deficits in 1981 and 1982, exacerbating the country's balance-of-payments difficulties. The current account was severely strained in the 1980s by the sharp decline in commodity prices and sizeable deficits in the services account. The current account ran into a deficit in 1980 and continued to remain in the red for seven consecutive years, until 1986. Despite continuing deficits in the services account, current account surpluses reappeared in 1987 and 1988,

TABLE 2.10
Malaysia: Foreign Investment Approvals by Country, 1978–1986

	1978		1982		1986		1978–1986	
	US$m.	Percentage Share	US$m.	Percentage Share	US$m.	Percentage Share	US$m.	Percentage Share
Australia	4.1	2.3	62.1	12.0	16.3	3.1	172.6	5.2
Germany FR	9.8	5.5	22.7	4.4	1.4	0.3	106.1	3.2
Hong Kong	9.7	5.5	4.9	0.9	27.5	5.2	181.3	5.4
Japan	25.2	14.2	136.9	26.4	58.1	11.1	660.6	19.8
Korea	0.2	0.1	0.3	0.1	1.6	0.3	112.0	3.4
Singapore	13.4	7.5	9.4	1.8	90.0	17.2	350.4	10.5
United Kingdom	19.9	11.2	80.2	15.5	19.1	3.6	373.9	11.2
United States	33.0	18.6	22.9	4.4	17.1	3.3	243.7	7.3
Others	62.5	35.2	179.6	34.6	293.4	55.9	1,137.0	34.0
Total	177.8	100	519.0	100	524.5	100	3,337.6	100

Source: Data Base, East–West Center, Honolulu.

TABLE 2.11
Malaysia: Balance of Payments, 1980–1989 (M$ million)

	1980	1985	1989
A. Merchandise Account			
Balance	+5,238	+8,883	+10,562
Exports	28,013	37,576	67,247
Imports	22,775	28,693	56,685
B. Services Account Balance	−5,813	−10,391	−11,243
Freight and insurance	−1,781	−1,852	−3,093
Other transportation	−56	+64	+25
Travel	−885	−1,332	−1,453
Investment income	−1,820	−5,434	−5,122
Government transactions	−7	−31	−270
Other services	−1,264	−1,806	−1,330
C. Balance on Goods and			
Services	−575	−1,508	−681
D. Transfers (net)	−45	−14	+208
E. Current Account Balance	−620	−1,522	−473
F. Balance on Long-term			
Capital	+2,213	+4,229	+2,366
Official long-term capital	+180	+2,504	−2,634
Corporate investment	+2,033	+1,725	+5,000
G. Basic Balance			
(G = E + F)	+1,593	+2,707	+1,893
H. Private Capital (net)	+902	+870	+815
I. Errors and Omissions	−1,493	−368	+624
J. Overall Balance	+1,002	+3,209	+3,332
K. Allocation of Special			
Drawing Rights (SDRs)	+76	0	0
L. IMF Resources	0	−382	0
M. Net Change in International			
Reserves	−1,078	−2,827	−3,332
N. Net International Reserves	10,304	12,457	21,660

Source: Malaysia, Ministry of Finance, Economic Report, various issues.

thanks to strong export expansion. However, in 1989 Malaysia again ran into a sizeable current account deficit, with a reduced trade surplus owing to imports growing faster than exports.

Malaysia has always had deficits in the services account. The two most important components which contribute to the deficits in the invisible account are (a) investment income payments, and (b) freight and insurance. The former represents the single largest item in the invisible account deficit. Its contribution reached 52.3 per cent of the services deficit in 1985, although it has fallen subsequently to 46.4 per cent in 1989 (Table 2.11). Net investment income payments, which have been fluctuating around M$5 billion a year since 1984, comprise mainly interest payments on foreign loans and repatriation of profits and dividends on foreign investments. Freight and insurance together are the second largest source of payments abroad, with freight accounting for about 90 per cent. Net payments from these sources increased from M$1.8 billion in 1980 to M$3.1 billion in 1989, thus accounting for 30.6 per cent and 27.5 per cent of the services deficit respectively.

Malaysia has not been very successful in its efforts to reduce the size of the services bill, as shown by the experience in shipping. Only about 15 per cent of Malaysian exports are transported by Malaysian vessels. It is the overseas importer who decides on the ships to be used, as goods are exported on an f.o.b. basis. Thus, it is not surprising that less than 4 per cent of the cargo in the Malaysia–Japan sea lane is handled by Malaysian vessels, while Malaysian ships have hardly any role in the country's trade with the United States and West Asia. However, Malaysian vessels account for about 18 per cent of the cargo on the Malaysia–Europe shipping route.[2]

Structure of Protection

Industrialization in Malaysia was facilitated to a considerable extent by the system of protection, although the protective measures were fairly mild by developing-country standards. Nominal rates of protection (NPR), which refer to protection given to the final products, influence consumer decisions, while effective rates of protection (EPR), which measure protection given to the production processes, affect investors' decisions and hence resource allocation. EPRs take into account not only tariffs on the final products, which give protection against foreign competition, but also tariffs on intermediate inputs, which raise production costs.

In the Malaysian case, the average EPRs have been significantly high, although NPRs have been rather low. This is due mainly to low tariffs on inputs. The structure of protection has undergone substantial changes in both nominal and effective terms. The nominal and effective rates, which averaged 13 per cent and 25 per cent respectively in 1965 (Power, 1971), rose to 18 per cent and 44 per cent respectively in 1970 (Ariff, 1975), The average EPR increased further to 55 per cent in 1973 (EPU, 1978). The NPR exhibited a general upward trend in the 1970s, the average NPR for all sectors increasing from 16 per cent in 1970 to 22 per cent in 1978 (K. H. Lee, 1986).

There have been major changes in the structure of effective protection. In 1965, about 39 per cent of manufacturing industries had negative EPRs, while only 8 per cent of them had EPRs of over 100 per cent. The proportion of industries with negative EPRs declined to 31 per cent in 1970 and to 14 per cent in 1978, while that of industries with EPRs of more than 100 per cent increased to 16 per cent in 1970 but subsequently dropped to 10 per cent in 1978. Both NPRs and EPRs have exhibited wide dispersions, the former showing no clear trend and the latter a downward trend.

There have been marked changes in EPRs for the major product categories. Effective protection for consumer durables rose sharply from −6 per cent in 1965 to 173 per cent in 1978, while non-durables ranked second in order of magnitude. Intermediate goods with a lower level of fabrication received much less protection than those with a higher level, with tariffs escalating with the degree of fabrication. Protection for beverages and tobacco, despite the high average NPR of 147 per cent in 1978, has been eroded by high tariffs on inputs.

Although the system of protection in Malaysia seems less severe than elsewhere, it has tended to pamper some firms and certain subsectors, sheltering inefficiency and penalizing export activities, not to mention the cost of tariffs to consumers and that of subsidies to taxpayers. The structure of protection has given rise to distortions in the manufacturing sector. The phenomenon of tariff escalation, in particular, has tended to discourage backward linkages and upstream activities. On the whole, the structure appears biased in favour of consumer goods industries at the expense of producer goods industries.

More recent estimates of EPRs are not readily available. However, as there was no major overhaul of tariff rates in the 1980s, apart from minor *ad hoc* adjustments through the annual Budgets, one may safely conjecture that the structure has remained basically unchanged for more than a decade now. Ironically, the protection structure, which was designed under the import substitution phase, is incompatible with the current strategy of export-oriented industrialization. This anomaly has been redressed to some extent by mitigating the implicit penalty on manufactured exports through countervailing subsidies in the form of export incentives, although the first-best solution would require the distortions to be removed at the source and not to be neutralized by compensatory measures.

Regulation and Intervention

Government intervention in general and regulation in particular are quite pervasive in the Malaysian economy, although there have been some efforts since 1985 to deregulate and decontrol the economy on an *ad hoc* or piecemeal basis. Much of the regulation and intervention revolves around the New Economic Policy (NEP), aimed at eradicating poverty and restructuring society, so that the pattern of employment, ownership, and control in the economy will reflect the racial composition of the country. The NEP, which was launched in 1970, was supposed to achieve these objectives by 1990 not through any disruptive redistribution of income and wealth but through sustained growth and active participation of all ethnic groups. To achieve the NEP goals, the government introduced legislation and guidelines and established a number of public enterprises which would hold in trust the 'Bumiputra share' of the equity.

The NEP objectives are indeed laudable. None the less, undeniably, the NEP has imposed additional constraints on business activities. These constraints, especially with respect to employment and ownership, might have inhibited economic activities in certain sectors. Foreign investors, in particular, have found it difficult to comply with the NEP guidelines, especially with regard to equity requirements. Admittedly, the NEP has resulted in huge economic rents accruing to the Bumiputra élite. In the same vein, it also appears that the benefits of the NEP have not been equitably distributed within the Bumiputra community. In retrospect, it is readily obvious that the targets were pitched at too high a level, considering the short time-frame of 20 years. It is now obvious that the NEP targets have not been achieved as planned and it is certain that the NEP will continue, one way or another, beyond 1990, probably under a new label. New strategies and a new time-frame will have to be set to achieve the NEP goals.

As mentioned, much of the regulation and intervention in the country revolves around the NEP. Consequently, the extent of direct government involvement in the economy has increased dramatically since 1970. Public sector expenditure, for instance, as a proportion of GNP increased from 22.1 per cent in 1970 to about 38.3 per cent at the peak in 1982, although it has subsequently fallen to about 25.6 per cent in 1988.

Public enterprises have been the main instruments of direct government involvement in the economy. Many of them have failed to perform and have incurred huge losses. With the worsening economic conditions and budgetary constraints in the mid-1980s, they have become unacceptably burdensome to the government. This has forced the government to rethink. The upshot of all this has been the privatization of several public enterprises.

Several legislative measures have been introduced with the implementation of the NEP. The most controversial among them is the Industrial Coordination Act of 1975 which empowers the Minister of Trade and Industry to impose any condition (including compliance with the 30 per cent Bumiputra share in line with the NEP) before a licence is issued or renewed. Similarly, the Companies Act 1965 was tightened by the Companies (Amendment) Bill 1984 containing 73 amendments, one of which provides for the establishment of a panel to administer, supervise, and control take-overs and mergers. These regulations were not designed to stifle private sector activities, but they have given rise to some cause for concern. The spate of legislation might not have created an environment of uncertainty, but it has caused the business environment to take on a highly regulated look.

There are signs that the government wants to be pragmatic about the NEP. It has relaxed some of the stringent NEP rules, especially those governing foreign equity. Thus, for instance, any company set up with foreign capital between October 1989 and December 1990 is exempted for good from the NEP equity restructuring requirement, provided (a) it exports[3] at least 50 per cent of its output, and (b) it employs at least 350 full-time Malaysian workers in proportions corresponding to the racial composition of the country.

It is argued by policy-makers that the NEP has never been a negative factor. The fact that the Malaysian economy continued to grow at creditable rates during the 1970s and 1980s is cited as evidence. Critics, however, claim that the Malaysian economy could have grown at a faster pace, had it not been for the NEP; the government's decision to downplay the NEP in the mid-1980s in the face of the recession seems to lend credence to this view. In any case, it is clear that the NEP could be implemented vigorously only under expansionary economic conditions.

The role of the government seems to be changing. It is increasingly seen as one of facilitating and promoting rather than competing with private sector activities. The 'new' government philosophy apparently favours no more than minimal government participation in business. However, there has been no serious attempt to deregulate the economy. Whilst it cannot be denied that some of the regulations have sound economic justification and some others have been rendered politically necessary, most of them bear little relation to the realities of the regulatory environment. Be that as it may, the main drawback of the regulatory system anywhere is that it creates incentives for corruption, especially where the government officials have substantial discretionary authority.

All this notwithstanding, the Malaysian government has always adopted a pro-private sector posture. In fact, it has taken various measures to create opportunities for the private sector, which has also benefited considerably from the various incentive schemes launched by the government. However, the very nature of government support has tainted the character of private sector development. In this regard, several worrisome trends may be highlighted. First, the private sector in general, and the Bumiputra subsector in particular, has grown so used to government support that it finds it difficult to operate independently of it. Secondly, local firms have become so inward-looking, presumably due to the anti-export bias created by the protection regime, that they have not been venturing out into international and regional markets. And, thirdly, small-scale enterprises which could contribute significantly to employment generation have not received much government attention, as the system of incentives has been biased in favour of large-scale enterprises.

Planning and Development

Although the Malaysian economy is essentially a market economy where the primacy of the private sector is duly recognized, and where market forces are given substantial freedom to determine resource allocation, the state has also been playing a responsible role, especially through economic planning. In fact, there has been considerable co-operation and collaboration between the government and the private sector, as embodied in the concept of 'Malaysia Incorporated' which gained currency in the mid-1980s.

The Malaysian planning machinery has been fairly liberal and flexible.

The various development plans have served as guideposts for the private sector. This indicative nature of economic planning has kept government intervention in the economic affairs of the country at a 'tolerable' level. None the less, the government has been actively influencing resource reallocation through its planning process.

The Planning Process

The Federal Cabinet of ministers represents the highest policy-making body in the country (see Appendix 2). Economic planning at the federal level is carried out by a number of institutions, including the Economic Planning Unit (EPU) and the Socio-Economic Research Unit (SERU) of the Prime Minister's Department, and the planning cells of the Treasury, the Central Bank, and various ministries. The responsibility and the authority for planning are vested in the Federal Cabinet, which is assisted by the National Development Planning Committee (NDPC), for which the EPU serves as a Secretariat. The Inter-Agency Planning Group (IAPG), in which the EPU, Treasury, Central Bank, and Department of Statistics are represented, is central to the planning process, providing inputs for policy formulation at the NDPC level (see Appendix 3). The co-ordination of the development plans at the inter-state and inter-departmental levels is handled by the Implementation and Co-ordination Unit in the Prime Minister's Department. At the state level, each state has its own State Economic Planning Unit (SEPU) whose role corresponds to that of the EPU at the federal level.

As mentioned, development planning in Malaysia is only indicative, showing directions in which the economy might move, with the private sector acting as the main locomotive. The principal planning agency, the EPU, is directly responsible to the Prime Minister. The EPU formulates the various five-year plans in consultation with both the private and the public sectors. Various government agencies and departments participate in the planning process in the form of proposals for expansion, development, and restructuring.

In the implementation of development plans and monitoring of progress, the government has adopted the 'Operations Room' technique,[4] keeping a vigil on the development efforts. The National Operations Room has access to information relating to the progress of development programmes at the state and district levels through its networks linking all the State and District Operations Rooms.

Five-year Plans

Development planning was not undertaken until after political independence, prior to which the so-called development plans of the colonial regime had amounted to no more than aggregations of various departmental expansion programmes and projections of annual budgets. Between political independence of Malaya in 1957 and the formation of Malaysia in 1963, there were two five-year plans in operation. The First

Malaya Plan (1956–60) was based largely on a comprehensive study of the Peninsular Malaysian economy undertaken by a World Bank mission. The First Malaya Plan tied about 60 per cent of its M$1.2 billion development expenditure with economic goals, and 30 per cent with social objectives, leaving the rest for a variety of other purposes.

The Second Malaya Plan (1961–5) was more sophisticated than the preceding one, with a well-defined and prioritized set of objectives. The Plan aimed at a better rural standard of living, greater employment opportunities, faster rate of growth, diversification of the export sector, and improved infrastructural facilities. The public sector was assigned a more important role than previously, with as much as 42.6 per cent of the planned expenditure of M$5.05 billion accruing to the public sector.

The First Malaysia Plan (1966–70) was essentially an extension of the Second Malaya Plan, especially in terms of policy objectives and planning technique. The public sector was allocated 36.7 per cent of the planned expenditure of M$9.73 billion. It is noteworthy that the private sector was assigned 63.3 per cent of the share of the estimated expenditure, compared to 57.4 per cent in the previous Plan.

The Second Malaysia Plan (1971–5) differed from the previous Plans in terms of both policy objectives and planning strategies. While the previous Plans had paid little attention to equity aspects, distributive considerations had strong underpinnings in the Second Malaysia Plan in response to the communal riots of May 1969 which exposed the dangers of extreme inter-ethnic economic imbalances in the multiracial Malaysian society. The civil disturbances of 1969 led to the formulation of the 20-year Outline Perspective Plan which provided the basis or framework for the New Economic Policy, which in turn became the basis of all subsequent development plans. The twin NEP objectives of poverty eradication and social restructuring were to be achieved over a 20-year period at the end of which Bumiputras would account for 30 per cent of equity, and the employment pattern would reflect the racial composition of the country.

It is important to reiterate that the NEP targets were to be achieved not through any disruptive redistribution but through active Bumiputra participation and contribution to the country's economic growth. The Second Malaysia Plan called for an investment of M$12 billion, 55.4 per cent being the share of the public sector. Thus, the public sector was assigned, for the first time, an active and dominant role in the economy.

The Third Malaysia Plan (1976–80) marked yet another significant step towards the NEP goals. The importance of the growth strategy was stressed even more forcefully. The Plan also laid greater emphasis on the contribution of the private sector to output growth than had the Second Malaysia Plan.

The Fourth Malaysia Plan (1981–5) was more ambitious than the previous ones, setting heroically high targets which were completely out of tune with the realities of the early 1980s. The Plan had anticipated soaring oil prices and generally high commodity prices, an expectation which turned out to be diametrically opposed to the subsequent happenings. The harsh realities of the 1980s, as will be seen below, were at variance with the scenario which the planners had in mind when they formulated the Fourth Malaysia Plan. The Plan was derailed by the worst recession in Malaysian history.

The Fifth Malaysia Plan (1986–90) was drafted in a relatively sombre tone in the light of the bitter experience of the early 1980s. It took a pragmatic turn and reversed the importance hitherto attached to the role of the public sector, recognizing the prowess of the private sector and the limitations of the public sector enterprises. The public sector then backpedalled, allowing the private sector to take the lead. During the course of the Plan, the total public sector expenditure was further reduced from the original ceiling of M$74 billion to M$47.7 billion.

The Score Board

Malaysia's track record in terms of economic development is quite impressive. Per capita income increased from M$1,170 in 1970 to M$6,638 in 1989. The overall incidence of poverty (percentage of poor households) in the country declined from 49.3 per cent in 1970 to 19.3 per cent in 1987. The incidence of poverty among the various ethnic groups has also been declining in the country, with the notable exception of Sabah, where a slight worsening of poverty, especially among Bumiputras, between 1984 and 1987 has been reported. Overall, the ratio of the Bumiputra mean household income to that of the non-Bumiputra has improved from 1 : 2.3 in 1970 to 1 : 1.6 in 1987. In terms of rural–urban disparity, the ratio of rural mean income has increased from 47 per cent in 1970 to 58 per cent in 1987.[5]

Although the inter-ethnic gap has narrowed considerably, it still remains wide. The real mean income of the Chinese in 1987 stood 65 per cent higher than that of the Bumiputras.[6] Intra-Bumiputra income distribution has become less skewed in recent years: the ratio of the mean income of the top 20 per cent to that of the bottom 40 per cent has decreased slightly from 7.82 in 1984 to 7.12 in 1987. Regional imbalance in income distribution remains, despite some improvements in the less developed states, including Kedah, Kelantan, and Perlis.

The ownership structure in the country has improved in favour of Bumiputras, but it has fallen far short of the 30 per cent target set up by the NEP. In 1988, the Bumiputra share in the corporate sector stood at 19.4 per cent, compared with 4.3 per cent in 1971. It is obvious that the NEP will have to be extended, in spirit if not in form, well beyond 1990 so that its objectives can be realized in an orderly fashion. There are indications that the post-1990 national economic policy will be designed in such a way as to create a Bumiputra community that can compete confidently with other communities, without being too dependent on the government. The new policy is expected to place emphasis on entrepreneurship, managerial expertise, and skill development within the Bumiputra community, rather than on a 30 per cent equity participation

TABLE 2.12
Malaysia: Selected Socio-economic Statistics, 1970–1989

	1970	1980	1985	1989
GNP per capita (M$)	1,170	3,673	4,594	6,638
Savings per capita (M$)	240	1,036	1,263	1,705
Crude birth rate (per 100)	3.24	3.09	3.19	2.98
Crude death rate (per 100)	0.67	0.53	0.50	0.40
Infant mortality rate (per 100)	3.94	2.39	1.65	1.39
Life expectancy (age in years)				
Male	61.6	66.4	67.7	68.8
Female	65.6	70.5	72.4	73.3
Television sets per 1,000				
population	22	90	n.a.	n.a.
Passenger motor cars per				
1,000 population	26	63	n.a.	n.a.
Population per doctor	4,302	3,568	3,175	2,656

Source: Malaysia, Ministry of Finance, Economic Report, various issues.
n.a. = Not available.

per se, so that the Bumiputras will be able to acquire and retain wealth with minimum government assistance.

The significant economic development strides Malaysia has made are amply reflected in the key socio-economic indicators presented in Table 2.12. For instance, the crude death rate and infant mortality rate have declined dramatically, while life expectancy has improved markedly. There have also been substantial improvements in terms of 'amenities' in relation to population size. Thus, for example, the number of passenger cars per 1,000 population has increased, while population per doctor has declined. Clearly, there are only a few developing countries in the world that can match Malaysia's track record.

Macroeconomic Performance and Management

The Malaysian economy has been performing reasonably well by developing-country standards, registering fairly rapid, albeit not stable, GDP growth. Its per capita income in nominal terms has risen from US$334 in 1970 to US$2,056 in 1989, which ranks second only to Singapore in the South and South-East Asian region, excluding of course Brunei, which has one of the highest per capita incomes in the world, thanks to its enormous oil wealth. As a matter of fact, Malaysia has now been included in the 'Dynamic Asian Economy' (DAE) group.

As mentioned in Chapter 1, Malaysia is essentially an open developing economy with exports and imports representing substantial proportions of the country's GNP. As a result, the economy is exposed to the vagaries of external influences. Accordingly, the country's macroeconomic performance is affected to a considerable extent by external factors over which Malaysia has absolutely no control, although the impact of external shocks has been ameliorated to some extent by appropriate domestic policy measures. In what follows, an effort is made to trace the movements and trends of the key macroeconomic indicators of Malaysia and to examine how the economy has been managed. The experiences of the 1970s and 1980s may have lessons for the 1990s.

The Growth Pattern

During the 1970s, Malaysia exhibited all the attributes of a small, open economy exposed to cyclical changes in world economic activity. Its ability to obtain foreign exchange earnings to finance development was circumscribed by external conditions, given the small domestic market and a comparative advantage primarily in primary exports, the prices of which have always been highly volatile. All this goes to show how dependent the Malaysian economy was on the fluctuating fortunes of its major trading partners, particularly the developed countries of the Organization for Economic Cooperation and Development (OECD).

The decade of the 1970s was marked by a high degree of correlation between the growth of exports and of GDP, exports rising sharply on three occasions at an annual growth rate of over 16 per cent and falling, on the downturn, by about 3 per cent (Figure 2.1). Such oscillations testify to the fact that the external sector was an important contributing factor to the cyclical economic instability experienced throughout the decade. However, the impact of external influences was cushioned to a considerable extent by counter-cyclical measures which helped reduce fluctuations in GDP.

The 1980s were different from the 1970s in that counter-cyclical stabilization policies and export booms and recessions apparently exerted a reduced influence on growth rates. At the turn of the decade, Malaysia entered a new phase marked by a sharp deterioration in the terms of trade and the emergence of sizeable deficits in the current account of the country's balance of payments. The terms of trade plunged by 24 percentage points during 1981–6 (1980 = 100), as shown in Table 2.13. It has been estimated that adverse external price movements during 1981–3 eroded Malaysia's national income by 4.5 per cent (World Bank, 1989a). The deteriorating terms of trade served to dampen private sector investment in the early 1980s, to which the government responded by compensating the shortfall through an accelerated public investment and expenditure programme. Government intervention thus protected the economy against the global recession of 1981–2 by sustaining real growth at an artificially high level, but only at the cost of soaring current account deficits in the balance of payments. Regardless of this, the government continued to prop up the economy in 1983 and 1984 so that real GDP could grow at 6.3 per cent and 7.8 per cent respectively, at the cost of twin deficits in the balance of payments and the budget. In 1984, the ratio of current account deficit to GNP stood at 5.2 per cent while that of overall public sector deficit

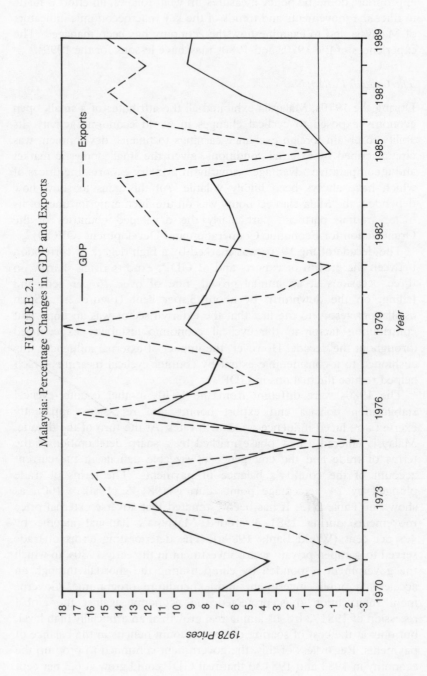

FIGURE 2.1
Malaysia: Percentage Changes in GDP and Exports

TABLE 2.13

Malaysia: Key Macroeconomic Developments, 1981–1989

	1981–1984	1985	1986	1987	1988	1989
Terms of trade index (1980 = 100)	80.4	79.2	76.0	79.3	n.a.	n.a.
Current account surplus (percentage of GNP)	–10.2	–2.1	–0.5	8.6	5.5	–0.5
Overall public sector deficit (percentage of GNP)	–17.6	–4.5	–9.8	–4.9	–2.0	–2.9
Real Growth:						
GDP	6.7	–1.1	1.2	5.4	8.9	8.8
Agriculture	2.9	2.5	4.2	7.0	5.4	5.8
Manufacturing	8.6	–3.8	7.5	13.4	17.6	12.0
Construction	8.1	–8.4	–14.0	–11.8	2.7	11.6
Government services	6.5	2.1	4.3	4.0	3.7	4.0

Sources: 1981–4: World Bank (1989a); 1985–9: Malaysia, Ministry of Finance, *Economic Report 1990/91*; Malaysia, Bank Negara Malaysia, *Quarterly Economic Bulletin*, September 1989.

amounted to 13.6 per cent. During 1981–4, government services and construction expanded while the rest of the economy grew weaker. All these resulted in a ballooning of public debts and an overhang of unsold properties.

The crunch came in 1985 with the collapse of the prices of all major export commodities. The government, already strained by its past policies, was unable to undertake anti-recessionary measures, and the Malaysian economy demonstrated its worst performance ever by posting a negative GDP growth in 1985 (–1.1 per cent). The unemployment rate rose from 5.8 per cent in 1984 to 6.9 per cent in 1985, while the rate of inflation moderated to 0.4 per cent from 3.6 per cent previously, presumably due to the recessionary influences.

The modest economic recovery in 1986, with 1.2 per cent real GDP growth, was attributable mainly to domestic demand expansion. In fact, the prices of most primary exports remained depressed, with total export earnings falling by 7.1 per cent in 1986. The real turnaround came about in the following year when the real GDP grew by 5.4 per cent, thanks mainly to better prices for Malaysia's primary exports and increased external demand for its manufactures. The latter grew by 31.9 per cent, while total export earnings rose by 28.0 per cent. Domestic demand expansion played only a small contributory role in the country's strong economic recovery in 1987. The last two years of the 1980s were even better for Malaysia, with GDP growing at an average rate of over 8 per cent per annum. The economy registered an impressive growth of 8.9 per cent in 1988 and 8.8 per cent in 1989. Domestic demand expansion played a key role in the strong income growth in 1988, as aggregate domestic expenditure expanded by 18.8 per cent, compared with the mere 1.9 per cent increase in 1987 and absolute contraction in 1985 and 1986.

Fiscal Management

Before the end of the 1970s, the Malaysian authorities pursued a prudent fiscal policy, accumulating surpluses in good years and incurring deficits in lean years, which helped insulate the economy to a considerable extent from external shocks. However, the government committed itself to an accelerated development programme in the wake of the commodity boom of the late 1970s and the substantial growth of oil exports after 1977. During 1979–83, fiscal policy was highly expansionary. The scale of fiscal expansion particularly in 1981 and 1982 was unprecedented. Development expenditure as a proportion of GNP nearly doubled from 14.3 per cent in 1976–80 to more than 27 per cent in both 1981 and 1982, as shown in Table 2.14. This sharp increase in public sector spending was a major factor boosting the economy in the face of the global recession.

Federal government current expenditures rose rapidly in the early 1980s, constituting 28 per cent of GNP in both 1981 and 1982 compared to 2.3 per cent in 1979. The bulk of the increase was accounted for by the provision of economic services in agricultural and rural development, commerce and industry, and general administration. The cost of the last-mentioned more than doubled between 1979 and 1987, as a result of an expansion of the civil service and wage adjustments. Debt servicing increased sharply from M$1.3 billion in 1979 to over M$2.7 billion in 1982.

Structural adjustment after 1982 was facilitated by (a) a steady increase in the operating surpluses of non-financial public enterprises (NFPEs), thanks to the coming on stream of liquefied natural gas (LNG) and the expansion in petroleum output, and (b) a cut-back in development expenditures which were trimmed down from M$11.5 billion in 1982 to M$7.1 billion in 1985. The NFPEs have been a major factor in the country's public finance. Although federal government development expenditure was reduced after 1982, the NFPE investment continued to grow until 1984, partly because such off-budget expenditures were not directly controlled by the Treasury. Thus, the NFPE investment grew by 39 per cent annually during 1982–4, and accounted for one-half of all public investment in 1984 as against a one-tenth share in 1979.

Government efforts to restructure public finances began to show results in 1985. For one thing, the federal government deficit narrowed. For another, the NFPEs for the first time in the 1980s brought their overall expenditure below their revenue. Fiscal austerity of the government in general, and cut-backs in development expenditure in

TABLE 2.14

Malaysia: Consolidated Government Accounts, 1976–1989 (percentage of GNP)

	1976–80 (average)	1981	1982	1983	1984	1985	1986	1987	1988	1989
Federal and State Governments										
Revenue	29.2	32.8	33.1	33.2	32.5	36.5	37.2	32.6	33.5	33.1
Current expenditure	26.1	30.9	30.5	30.6	29.5	30.8	34.7	31.0	29.3	28.0
Operating surplus	3.1	1.8	2.6	2.6	2.9	5.8	2.5	1.6	4.2	5.2
Operating surplus of non-financial public enterprises (NFPEs)	1.0	4.0	5.7	6.6	6.7	7.8	4.2	4.9	4.3	5.4
Consolidated public sector operating surplus	4.1	5.8	8.3	9.2	9.7	13.6	6.7	6.5	8.5	10.6
Development expenditure	14.3	27.6	27.2	26.2	22.9	18.1	16.5	11.4	10.5	13.5
Federal and state governments	12.0	23.4	20.5	16.8	12.4	9.5	10.8	7.2	6.5	8.6
NFPEs	2.3	4.2	6.7	9.4	10.5	8.6	5.8	4.2	4.0	4.9
Overall deficit	-10.2	-21.7	-18.9	-17.0	-13.2	-4.5	-9.8	-4.9	-2.0	-2.9

Sources: 1976–80 data from the World Bank (1989a); 1981–9 figures computed from Malaysia, Ministry of Finance, *Economic Report*, various issues.

particular, reduced the overall deficit to 4.5 per cent of GNP in 1985 from 18.9 per cent in 1982. However, the deficit widened to 9.8 per cent of GNP in 1986, due mainly to the declining tax buoyancy under the recessionary spell. Nevertheless, the strong turnaround in 1987 and sustained expansion in 1988 and 1989 increased government revenue markedly while the government continued to keep tabs on public expenditures. Consequently, the deficit–GNP ratio fell remarkably to 4.9 per cent in 1987 and 2.0 per cent in 1988. The ratio increased only slightly to 2.9 per cent in 1989. It can be argued that the fiscal austerity drive was a good thing, given the severe resource constraints. But, at the same time, it cannot be denied that it tended to have a deflationary effect by dampening aggregate demand at a time when the economy was already reeling under the impact of an externally induced recession. In particular, the significant reductions in development expenditures during 1983–6 had substantial effects on the components of aggregate demand. Public expenditures as a proportion of GNP fell from 38.2 per cent in 1982 to 32.1 per cent in 1985. For the period 1980–6, aggregate domestic expenditures continuously exceeded gross national income.

In retrospect, it appears that the negative growth in 1985 could have been avoided, had the government acted differently in 1979 and 1980 when times were good. Resources were then siphoned off into several ambitious programmes, of which the heavy industrialization scheme represents an outstanding example. The upshot of all these has been that the government had no means to ride out the recession which continued until the mid-1980s. Expansionary fiscal policies were ruled out, as they would have meant an increase in the debt burden which had already become heavy. Expansionary monetary policies were postponed, lest they exert inflationary pressures. The government thus had no choice but to tighten its belt. There was an uneasy sense of retreat in government responses. The public sector was assigned a low profile and the task of pulling the economy out of the recession was left to the private sector.

Monetary Policy

By and large, Malaysia has pursued a rather conservative monetary policy. Monetary policy has rarely been used as an instrument in a counter-cyclical fashion in Malaysia. The Central Bank seems more concerned with ensuring stable interest rates. Of course, there have been important exceptions to this under exceptional circumstances, as shown by the experience in the mid-1970s when money supply was squeezed and interest rates were tightened up in the face of double-digit inflation. The usual practice has been to use restrictive monetary policy to counterbalance expansionary fiscal policy so as to reduce the inflationary pressure emanating from the latter. Thus, during the 1979–84 period when fiscal policy was for the most part expansionary, monetary policy remained restrictive not only to contain deterioration in the current account of balance of payments but also to subdue the inflationary forces in the economy.

The Central Bank has kept down interest rates on loans and deposits in an attempt to stimulate investment. As a result, the loan–deposit ratio has increased sharply, with banks having to borrow from the interbank money market, the interest rates of which have consequently shot up to extremely high levels.[7] The Central Bank's attempts to keep interest rates low were negated by its interventions in the foreign exchange markets in support of the ringgit, which led to the ringgit being mopped up. Thus, there was a conflict between the interest rate and the exchange rate policies of the Central Bank.

It has been argued that the above policy mix was partly responsible for the recession of the mid-1980s (Gan, 1989): it applied tremendous pressures on the domestic interest rate and the exchange rate.

The deceleration of monetary growth in the first half of the 1980s was due not only to the decline in the net foreign exchange reserves, but also to the reduction in net lending to the public and private sectors, as can be seen in Table 2.15. It is of relevance to note that a slowdown in the growth rate of $M1$ (which consists of currency and demand deposits of the private sector) during 1983 and 1984 preceded the contraction of economic activity in 1985. Net lending to the public sector fell absolutely and abruptly in 1985, while the growth of credit to the private sector decelerated (Table 2.15).

The monetary contraction caused the nominal base lending rate to rise from 8.5 per cent in 1982 to 12.3 per cent in 1984. The real borrowing cost was higher, now that the monetary restraint had effectively reduced the rate of inflation from 5.7 per cent in 1982 to 3.6 per cent in 1984. The reductions in the base lending rate to 10.8 per cent in 1985 and 10 per cent in 1986 were largely offset by lower rates of inflation (0.4 per cent in 1985 and 0.6 per cent in 1986) so that the real cost of borrowing remained high. The real prime lending rate increased from 7.1 per cent in 1984 to 12.3 per cent in 1985 and 18.4 per cent in 1986 (Table 2.16). The tradable sector was thus hurt by the sharp increase in the real cost of credit, especially since most firms in Malaysia, as indeed in other developing countries, tend to rely heavily on bank credit for working capital. The tradable sector was also squeezed by the massive channelling of funds to the real estate and construction sector, whose share of total bank lending rose from 25 per cent in 1980 to 33 per cent in 1984, while that of agriculture and manufacturing shrank from 30 per cent to 24 per cent.

As a result, real private investment, which grew at 6 per cent and 10.5 per cent in 1983 and 1984 respectively, plunged dramatically by 19 per cent in 1985. It therefore appears on the basis of all this that the high nominal and real interest rates and the substantial transfer of resources from the tradable to the non-tradable sector were the crucial factors in the deep recession of 1985. It also appears that the high interest rate prevailing during 1984–5 was due mainly to excess demand for liquidity in the face of declining money supply, exacerbated by the expectation of depreciation of the ringgit in the foreign exchange market which provided an incentive for capital flight.

TABLE 2.15

Malaysia: Contributions to Monetary Base and Money Supply, 1979–1988 (M$ billion)

Year	Monetary Base (1)		Central Bank Foreign Assets (2)		Central Bank Net Lending to Central Government (3)		M1 (4)		Net Lending to Government (5)		Net Lending to Private Sector (6)		Net Foreign Exchange Reserves (7)		Other Influences (8)	
1979	5.5	(–)	9.2	(24.9)	−2.6	(–)	8.5	(17.2)	−0.7	(−173.0)	1.9	(14.4)	9.5	(42.7)	−2.2	(4.0)
1980	6.5	(18.1)	10.3	(11.5)	−0.7	(71.8)	9.8	(15.0)	0.5	(173.9)	3.0	(64.3)	9.4	(−1.8)	−3.2	(47.9)
1981	7.2	(10.3)	9.8	(−4.9)	−0.3	(61.1)	11.0	(12.8)	2.2	(317.5)	4.4	(43.2)	8.2	(−12.3)	−3.8	(20.5)
1982	8.4	(16.7)	9.3	(−4.8)	0.7	(332.4)	12.5	(13.2)	4.0	(73.7)	4.7	(8.8)	8.3	(1.2)	−4.5	(18.3)
1983	8.7	(4.2)	9.5	(1.3)	1.7	(154.7)	13.4	(7.7)	3.4	(13.8)	8.7	(82.4)	7.9	(−4.5)	−6.6	(44.8)
1984	9.0	(3.7)	9.7	(2.1)	2.5	(48.1)	13.4	(−0.6)	4.1	(20.8)	10.4	(20.6)	6.1	(−22.8)	−7.4	(11.7)
1985	9.7	(7.6)	12.5	(29.2)	1.8	(−30.6)	13.6	(1.7)	1.4	(−67.1)	14.0	(33.9)	9.1	(48.9)	−10.9	(48.1)
1986	10.1	(4.2)	16.4	(31.1)	1.5	(−17.5)	14.0	(2.8)	2.8	(105.4)	12.6	(10.2)	14.0	(53.9)	−15.4	(41.8)
1987	10.7	(5.2)	19.5	(19.3)	0.9	(−37.7)	15.8	(13.0)	4.9	(76.7)	11.7	(−7.1)	19.5	(38.7)	−20.3	(31.5)
1988	11.3	(6.3)	18.3	(−6.1)	0.7	(−21.2)	18.1	(14.6)	3.8	(−22.8)	15.6	(34.0)	20.9	(7.1)	−22.2	(9.5)

Source: Gan (1989).

Note: Figures in parentheses are percentage changes.

TABLE 2.16

The Malaysian Financial Sector: Nominal and Real Interest Rates, and Cost of Foreign Borrowing, 1979–1988

Year	Nominal 3-month Deposit Rate (1)	Nominal Savings Deposit Rate (2)	Nominal Base Lending Rate (3)	Real 3-month Deposit Rate (4)	Real Savings Deposit Rate (5)	Real Prime Lending Rate (6)	Domestic Foreign Deposit Interest Rate Differential Adjusted for Exchange Rate Changes[1] (7)	Real Private Cost of Foreign Borrowing[2] (8)
1979	5.82	5.88	7.38	-3.10	-3.04	-1.54	-0.89	8.82
1980	8.64	5.7	9.0	2.01	-0.94	2.36	-5.02	7.03
1981	10.92	7.0	12.0	9.94	6.02	11.02	-11.79	21.74
1982	9.31	6.5	8.5	5.98	3.18	5.18	-5.34	11.32
1983	8.77	6.0	10.75	3.93	1.15	5.90	-0.34	4.27
1984	10.92	7.5	12.25	5.76	2.34	7.09	-0.98	6.74
1985	7.45	6.0	10.75	8.96	7.51	12.26	-6.86	15.82
1986	6.40	6.0	10.0	14.81	14.42	18.42	-4.46	19.28
1987	2.50	3.50	7.50	1.71	2.71	8.94	-2.29	3.99
1988	3.25	3.50	7.00	0.72	0.98	6.54	-8.67	9.40

Source: Gan (1989).

[1] 3-month fixed deposit rate less 3-month London inter-bank offer rates on US dollar deposit less depreciation of the ringgit–US dollar exchange rate.

[2] 3-month LIBOR on US dollar deposit plus depreciation of ringgit–US dollar exchange rate less domestic rate of inflation.

The high interest rate situation began to ease towards the end of 1986. During the period January–October 1986, the Central Bank injected M$4.4 billion of liquidity into the financial system. In October 1986, the Central Bank lowered the statutory reserve requirement from 4 per cent to 3.5 per cent and the liquidity ratio from 18.5 per cent to 17.0 per cent. Since 1985, the Central Bank has let the ringgit slide in the foreign exchange market, as will be seen in the next subsection. As a result, money supply $M1$ (currency in circulation plus private sector demand deposits) increased by 13.0 per cent in 1987, 14.6 per cent in 1988, and 17.6 per cent in 1989, compared with a decline of 0.6 per cent in 1984. The easier money policy, coupled with the pragmatic exchange rate policy, seems to have facilitated the subsequent transfer of resources from the non-tradable to the tradable sector. The continuation of tight fiscal policy despite significant improvements in the external sector during the 1987–8 commodity boom helped prevent a temporary appreciation of the ringgit which would have delayed the adjustment process through resource transfers from the non-tradable to the tradable sector.

Exchange Rate Regime

Prior to Independence, the Malaysian currency, then known as the Malayan dollar, was tied absolutely to the sterling with a fixed exchange rate. After Independence until mid-1972, Malaysia was pegging the ringgit, using the sterling as the intervention currency with a margin of 0.3348 to 1.0 per cent on either side of-par. In June 1972, Malaysia adopted the US dollar as the intervention currency, with the floating of sterling and the dismantling of the sterling area, and widened the support margin to 2.25 per cent. The parity of the ringgit was set at M$2.81955. Following the 10 per cent devaluation of the US dollar in February 1973, the ringgit–dollar parity was changed from 2.81955 to 2.5376 and the support rates were set at 2.4805 and 2.5947. However, in June 1973, the ringgit was allowed to float upward *vis-à-vis* the US dollar, rendering the floor rate ineffective.

In September 1975, the Malaysian authorities opted for a new exchange rate regime which would determine the value of the ringgit in terms of a basket of representative currencies. This meant that the exchange rate of the ringgit was no longer determined in terms of the US dollar alone, although the US dollar continued to be the intervention currency. The composite basket is known only to the Central Bank, but it is believed to be weighted on the basis of the key currencies of settlement as well as those of the major trading partners of Malaysia.

That the external value of the ringgit has been 'tied' to a representative composite basket of currencies does not necessarily mean that it has been pegged strictly to the basket. In fact, the value of the ringgit has been fluctuating relative to the basket. For example, during the period 1981–4, the composite index deviated from the September 1975 base value of 100 to a range of 103.5–109.5, which amounted to an appreciation of the ringgit up to 5 per cent a year (Lin, 1989).

The appreciation of the ringgit during the recessionary years of 1980–4 was due partly to the massive inflows of official long-term capital to the tune of M$4.8 billion a year and partly to the periodic intervention of the Central Bank to prevent substantial ringgit depreciation against the US dollar which was riding high *vis-à-vis* other major currencies.

It was no secret that the Central Bank was *de facto* pegging the external value of the ringgit to the US dollar and the Singapore dollar up to the end of 1984. The policy up till then was to keep the ringgit relatively stable against the Singapore dollar, presumably for political reasons. The US dollar being the intervention currency, this also meant support for the ringgit against the greenback. During the period 1981–3, the premium of the Singapore dollar was checked at about 9 per cent and the depreciation of the ringgit against the US dollar was kept at 4.3 per cent. Another 'compelling' reason behind the Central Bank's stance against substantial depreciation of the ringgit during the period 1981–4 was its concern over the country's growing external debt burden: exchange depreciation would increase the value of external debts in ringgit terms. It was also feared that exchange rate depreciation would unleash inflationary pressures.

In August 1984, the composite index of the ringgit reached its peak at 110.7 against the basket, appreciating 67 per cent against the sterling, 34 per cent against the Deutschmark, and 14 per cent against the yen. It has been estimated that the ringgit had been overvalued to the tune of 20 per cent by the end of 1984 (Semudram, 1985), while the real effective exchange rate appreciated by 10 per cent from the first quarter of 1981 to the fourth quarter of 1984 (Ariff and Semudram, 1987).

There are several ways of estimating the effective exchange rate, both nominal (NEER) and real (REER), using different weights. In the case of the latter, different deflators may be used to arrive at the real rates. Table 2.17 presents both nominal effective rates and real effective rates using multilateral trading partner weights, and consumer price index (CPI) and GDP deflators. It can be seen that these multilateral indices started to rise (depicting a strong appreciation of the ringgit) from 1980, peaking in 1984. The dramatic decline in these rates from 1985 onwards show that the ringgit depreciated substantially in the second half of the 1980s. Since 1985, the ringgit has been depreciating against all major currencies except the US dollar, as the latter itself was depreciating *vis-à-vis* other major currencies. The progressive depreciation of the ringgit came to an end in March 1989. Since April 1989 the ringgit has been exhibiting considerable stability.

Two important observations merit special attention. First, the maintenance of the overvalued exchange rate of the ringgit during the period 1980–4 hurt the economy badly by (a) rendering Malaysian exports uncompetitive, (b) encouraging the transfer of resources from the

TABLE 2.17

Malaysia: Indices of Nominal and Real Effective Exchange Rates
of the Ringgit, 1970–1988 (1979–1981 = 100)

| | Multilateral Trading Partner Weights | | |
Year	Nominal Effective Exchange Rate (1)	Real Effective Exchange Rate (CPI) (2)	Real Effective Exchange Rate (GDP) (3)
1970	83.4	112.8	99.0
1971	83.8	109.1	95.0
1972	85.9	111.5	91.9
1973	92.7	122.1	106.9
1974	95.7	129.0	109.5
1975	95.9	119.2	95.4
1976	95.1	111.4	97.9
1977	97.1	109.8	99.0
1978	96.0	106.4	99.8
1979	99.6	104.7	103.3
1980	100.1	100.1	100.0
1981	105.3	104.8	97.5
1982	112.9	110.4	100.6
1983	120.0	115.8	106.5
1984	127.8	122.1	114.6
1985	125.1	115.2	106.1
1986	103.3	93.8	77.8
1987	97.1	86.8	n.a.
1988	89.2	78.3	n.a.

Source: Gan (1989).
n.a. = Not available.

tradable to the non-tradable sector, (c) providing incentives for capital flight, and (d) negating the Central Bank's attempts at keeping interest rates low. It cannot be denied that the overvaluation of the ringgit contributed to the severity of the recession. In the same vein, it is evident that the drastic depreciation of the ringgit since 1985 has helped the economy turn around dramatically and contributed enormously to the expansion of Malaysian manufactured exports.

Second, the external value of the ringgit is affected more by capital account than by current account transactions in the balance of payments. During the period 1981–4, the ringgit was appreciating despite the worsening of the current account balance; by the same token, it was depreciating in 1985 and 1987 despite the strengthening of the current account balance. The seemingly strange behaviour of the ringgit can be easily explained in terms of the happenings in the capital account during these two periods. Thus the 'strength' of the ringgit in the early 1980s stemmed mainly from the substantial inflow of official capital, while the 'weakness' of the ringgit in the late 1980s was associated largely with the sizeable repayment of external debts.

External Debt

External debt is used to fill the domestic resource gap. The resource gap widens if savings cannot keep pace with investment. The expansionary fiscal policy of the early 1980s led to a widening of the resource gap by stimulating aggregate demand at a rate which could not be financed by higher levels of savings. Thus, throughout the period 1981–5, the ratio of gross national savings to GNP was considerably less than that of gross capital formation to GNP. The situation, however, reversed during 1986–8 (Table 2.18). This explains why Malaysia's external debts increased sharply in the early 1980s and eased considerably in the later years of the decade.

Malaysia has been borrowing heavily from external sources to finance its development projects and industrial ventures. External borrowing comprises project loans and market loans. Project loans are obtained from multilateral lending institutions such as the World Bank and the Asian Development Bank, as well as from government-to-government bilateral sources at concessional rates of interest. Market loans are largely syndicated loans obtained in international markets at commercial rates of interest.

In the Malaysian case, market loans have grown relatively more important over time. The proportion of the federal government's market loans in total external debt increased from 45 per cent in 1980 to 68 per cent in 1989 (Table 2.19). In 1984, roughly three-quarters of market loans were denominated in US dollars while the rest were denominated in other currencies, including the yen, sterling, and the Deutschmark. However, as a result of the dramatic appreciation of the yen after the Plaza Accord (September 1985), the share of yen loans increased sharply. In 1986, it accounted for 20 per cent of the total, rising to 35 per cent (M$17.5 billion) by the end of 1987.

TABLE 2.18
Malaysia: Resource Imbalance, 1981–1988 (percentage of GNP)

	1981	1982	1983	1984	1985	1986	1987	1988
Gross national savings	26.1	25.0	28.0	30.7	27.5	28.1	33.7	33.5
Gross capital formation	36.3	39.1	40.4	36.0	29.7	27.9	24.9	27.6
Resource gap	−10.2	−14.1	−12.4	−5.3	−2.2	0.2	8.8	5.9

Source: Malaysia, Bank Negara Malaysia, *Quarterly Economic Bulletin*, 4(2), September 1989.

Table 2.19 provides only a partial picture of the country's external debt situation, as it does not present figures relating to the external debt of the off-budget agencies (OBAs) guaranteed by the government, and excludes the private sector external debt. An estimate for 1984 has put Malaysia's total national external debt at M$37.1 billion, consisting of government loans of M$20.8 billion, the OBAs' M$7.1 billion, and the private sector's M$9.2 billion.[8] Thus, in 1984, the private sector's external debt constituted only one-quarter of the total. Private sector external loans have declined from M$7.2 billion in 1985 to M$4.9 billion in 1989. Total public sector external loans increased from M$35.0 billion in 1985 to M$44.4 billion in 1987, falling thereafter to M$37.2 billion in 1989.[9]

Malaysia was the fifth largest borrower in the Asia–Pacific region in 1984. In that year, it signed 16 deals worth US$1.2 billion which, however, was 14 per cent less than the US$1.4 billion borrowed in 1983, when Malaysia was ranked fourth in the Asia–Pacific region. External debt increased by 7 per cent in 1985 compared to 18 per cent in 1984 and 31 per cent in 1983. However, external debts incurred by OBAs continued to increase sharply by about 21 per cent in 1985. Malaysia's external debt as a proportion of its GNP increased from a mere 10.8 per cent in 1970 to a hefty 74.3 per cent in 1987.[10]

Debt-servicing (interest and principal payments) in 1984 was equivalent to 22.5 per cent of export earnings. Debt-service increased from 2.0 per cent in 1970 to 14.3 per cent in 1987 as a proportion of GNP, and from 4.5 per cent in 1970 to 20.0 per cent in 1987 as a proportion of export earnings.[11] During the period 1981–5, debt-servicing increased at the rate of 28.5 per cent per year; interest payments alone grew at the rate of 30.2 per cent per year.[12] Interest payments on external debt increased from US$25 million in 1970 to US$1.46 billion in 1987.[13] By the end of 1986, the ratio had exceeded 20 per cent, due mainly to falling exports and exchange rate depreciation of the ringgit.

The growing debt-servicing burden was a source of major concern which led the government to seek refinancing in 1984 and 1985 on more favourable terms. Thus, the government refinanced US$2.6 billion syndicated loans through four refinancing exercises undertaken during the period 1984–5 which resulted in a saving of M$217 million. The government also resorted to a diversification of currencies, instruments, markets, and sources of external loans. Thus, for example, the government has been switching occasionally from conventional syndicated loans to instruments like floating rate notes (FRNs).

Another area of concern has been the adverse impact of the appreciation of the yen on the external debt of Malaysia. As mentioned, yen-denominated loans totalling M$17.5 billion constituted 35 per cent of the country's total external debt in 1987. The servicing of these loans became a painful affair, following the sharp appreciation of the yen. The ringgit grew weaker against the yen by 20 per cent in 1985, 26 per cent in 1986, 20 per cent in 1987, and 5.5 per cent in 1988. Exchange rate

TABLE 2.19

Malaysia: Federal Government Outstanding External Debts, 1975–1989 (M$ million)

	1975	1980	1985	1986	1987	1988	1989[1]
External Market Loans	1,348	2,184	16,299	20,310	18,940	17,265	16,375
USA	982	1,409	11,234	12,729	9,970	8,917	8,596
Japan	n.a.	n.a.	2,276	3,545	3,747	3,761	3,318
West Germany	70	131	1,376	1,875	2,437	2,358	2,487
Others	296	644	1,413	2,161	2,786	2,229	1,974
External Project Loans	1,077	2,663	5,683	6,988	7,692	7,925	7,253
USA	126	210	139	184	22	15	133
UK	105	173	123	114	116	105	85
Japan	341	845	2,448	3,318	4,047	3,996	3,022
World Bank	330	703	1,381	1,446	1,427	1,565	1,604
Asian Development Bank	91	512	982	1,103	1,112	1,234	1,227
West Germany	34	129	42	105	206	263	469
West Asia	–	34	214	251	255	261	242
Others	50	57	354	467	507	486	471
Suppliers Credit	–	–	825	1,012	997	732	554
IMF	–	–	263	–	–	–	–
Total	2,425	4,847	23,070	28,310	27,629	25,922	24,182

Source: Malaysia, Ministry of Finance, *Economic Report*, various issues.
[1]Preliminary.
n.a. = Not available.

changes alone added M$9.6 billion to the country's yen-denominated debt burden.

It has become increasingly difficult for Malaysia to obtain loans from international financial institutions and developed countries at concessional rates of interest, as the country is no longer regarded as poor. Besides, Malaysia's needs have also changed considerably with greater emphasis on industrial projects than on basic sectoral developments. As multilateral institutions do not cater to such purposes, Malaysia has been forced to look elsewhere for loans—hence the sharp increase in market loans, much of which is associated with greater government involvement through OBAs under the NEP. Outstanding market loans secured directly by the government increased sharply from M$1.35 billion in 1975 to M$15.46 billion in 1985, while those obtained with government guarantees increased from M$588 million to M$9.1 billion. However, most of the market loans obtained in 1985 were for refinancing old ones which carried higher interest rates. Thus, out of M$5.36 billion market loans secured in 1985, M$5.06 billion was used for repayment.

One must concede that Malaysia's debt management in the second half of the 1980s was commendable. Nevertheless, there are still some thorns in the flesh. Much of the country's external debt problem is closely linked with the OBAs. In 1985 alone, about 40 OBAs had borrowed M$2.015 billion from external sources. Unfortunately, many of them are in such bad shape that they are in no position to repay the loans guaranteed by the government. In addition, some of the programmes mounted by the government, especially the heavy industrialization projects, which were financed mainly with borrowed money, have turned out to be questionable investments. The government has learned bitter lessons from all this and seems to have grown wiser, keeping a close watch on external debt-based activities, especially those of the OBAs. However, it also seems to have developed a phobia against external debt to such an extent that it might not dare use external loans to fight economic downswings anymore.

The Pacific Factor

The preceding discussion has brought to light the main strengths and weaknesses of the small, open economy of Malaysia. The economic openness of Malaysia and the outward orientation of Malaysian development strategies are strongly reflected in the country's economic structure and profile, pattern of economic development, and macro-economic behaviour. External forces have exerted such a powerful influence on the economy that the Malaysian policy-makers have to be on the alert all the time. While the government can take credit if things go right and blame the rest of the world if things go wrong, managing an open economy like Malaysia's is by no means an easy task. The toughest thing to do is to factor in the external factor, for it is extremely difficult to put a handle to it.

This subsection will focus on the Pacific, which represents an important subset of the outside world with which the Malaysian economy continually interacts. The discussion will be necessarily brief, since detailed analysis is postponed to subsequent chapters; suffice it to highlight or underscore some of the salient features of the complex phenomenon called the Pacific factor.

Macro Influence

The Pacific is a vast ocean on which borders numerous countries. It is much easier to define the Pacific region in geographical than in geopolitical terms, as will be seen in Chapter 5. For the present purpose, from Malaysia's commercial standpoint, the Pacific factor can be simply reduced to those countries with which Malaysia has substantial economic intercourse: for it is through the channels of trade, investment, and finance that the Malaysian economy is influenced by external forces. The major trading partners of Malaysia in the Pacific are Japan, the United States, the East Asian NIEs, Australia, New Zealand, Canada, China, and the rest of ASEAN, all of which jointly accounted for 74 per cent of Malaysia's exports and 78 per cent of its imports in 1988. The major Pacific investors in Malaysia are Japan, the United States, the East Asian NIEs, Australia, and the rest of ASEAN, which jointly accounted for over 70 per cent of foreign investment in the country in 1988. The United States and Japan together provided 73 per cent of the external market loans to the federal government in 1986, while more than 50 per cent of external project loans was provided by Japan alone.

In view of the above, it will be useful to relate the changes in the key macroeconomic indicators of Malaysia to those of the major countries in the region. Of course, these countries are not of equal importance in so far as their impact on Malaysia is concerned. Some are obviously more important than others, depending not only on their extent of 'involvement' in the Malaysian economy but also on how significant they are in global terms. Seen in this perspective, the United States is the most important of all, not only to Malaysia but also to many other countries. It has often been remarked that when the United States sneezes, the rest of the world catches cold; and when the United States suffers from a cold, the rest of the world has pneumonia. Although this probably is an overstatement, it does serve to underline the importance of the US economy to countries like Malaysia. Japan has established itself as a major economic power whose economic outreach and spin-offs ought to be recognized and factored in as well. These two countries jointly accounted for 37 per cent of Malaysia's external trade and 27 per cent of direct foreign investment in Malaysia in 1988. Together, they contribute nearly one-half of the world output and almost one-third of the world trade.[14]

Among the other developed countries in the region, Australia means much more to Malaysia than Canada or New Zealand which are really marginal players in so far as the Malaysian economy is concerned. The East Asian NIEs have been moving towards the centre stage and have also emerged as an important source of imports and investments as well as an export market for Malaysia in recent years. Within ASEAN, Singapore is by far the most important in terms of both trade and investment, with Thailand trailing far behind, followed by Indonesia, Brunei, and the Philippines in descending order.

Figures 2.2–2.7 portray the movements of key macroeconomic indicators in Malaysia's major trading partners in the Pacific Basin. They all tend to move together, although not necessarily in tandem, exhibiting a fairly high degree of economic interdependence among the countries represented in these figures. Malaysia's real GDP growth dipped during 1974 and 1982 along with all other countries, caused apparently by negative growth rates in Japan and the United States (Figure 2.2). However, the drastic economic contraction Malaysia experienced in 1985 seems to have had little to do with the growth pattern in Japan or the United States. The severity of the 1985 recession in Malaysia, as noted earlier, was mainly due to the poor handling of the issue, especially the sudden withdrawal of funds by the public sector.

It is fascinating to observe the great extent to which export growth rates (Figure 2.3) and import growth rates (Figure 2.4) of the various countries overlap. All this reflects the high degree of economic integration among these Pacific countries through trade flows. However, the balance of payments of these countries behave differently (Figure 2.5), as it is a zero-sum game in the sense that not all countries can have surpluses or deficits at the same time.

In the case of inflation rates, the behavioural pattern is strikingly similar in most cases (Figure 2.6). Malaysia suffered double-digit inflation during 1973–5 along with all the other countries, particularly Japan and the United States. It appears that much of the inflationary pressure in Malaysia has been generated externally through imports. None the less, it is evident that the degree of price instability in Malaysia has been relatively low, which may be attributed mainly to the conservative monetary policy discussed earlier.

Unemployment rates in these countries tend to move in a much less synchronized fashion, with considerable divergence in the unemployment levels (Figure 2.7). The high level of unemployment in Malaysia is matched only by Australia, but neither of them is overpopulated by any means. The problem is structural rather than cyclical.

In Malaysia, the unemployment rate increased from 5.8 per cent in 1984 to a peak of 8.3 per cent in 1986. It fell marginally to 8.1 per cent in 1988. Severe labour shortages in some sectors coexist with labour gluts in some others. There seems to be a gross mismatch between demand and supply with respect to labour skills. High GDP growth rates in the late 1980s have not resulted in any substantial absorption of the surplus labour in the country. Output has been growing faster than employment, which suggests that the fastest growing sectors are not labour-intensive.

FIGURE 2.2
Growth of Real GDP

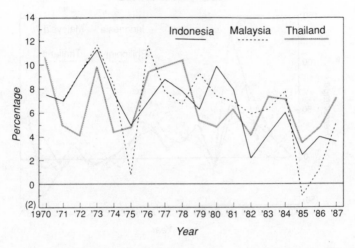

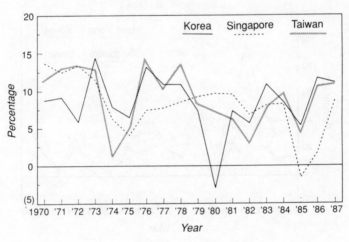

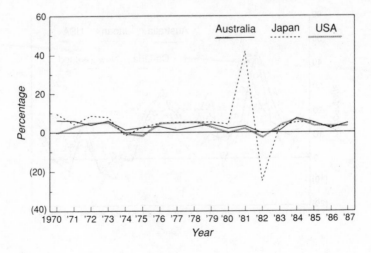

FIGURE 2.3
Export Growth Rates

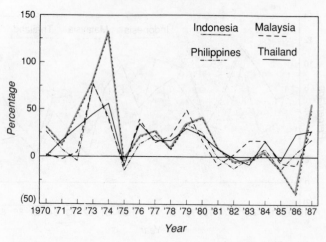

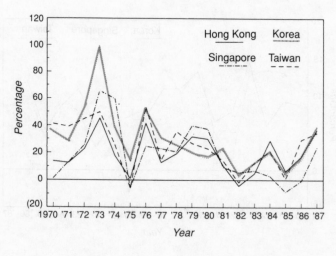

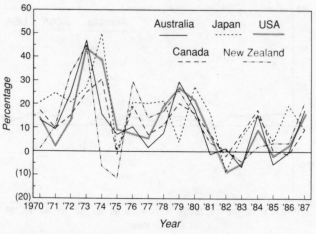

FIGURE 2.4
Import Growth Rates

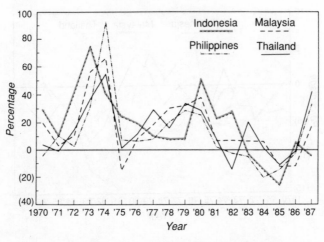

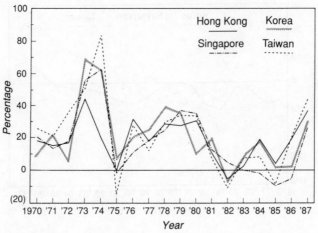

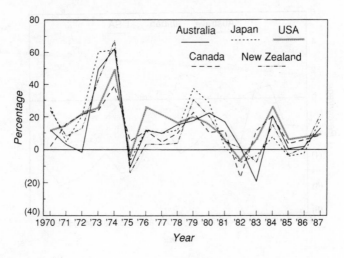

FIGURE 2.5
Current Account Balance (as a percentage of GDP)

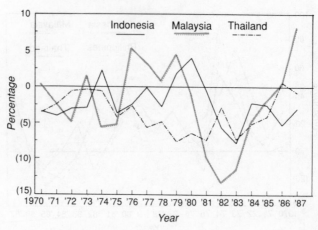

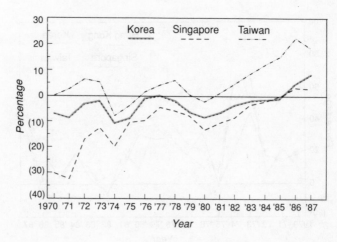

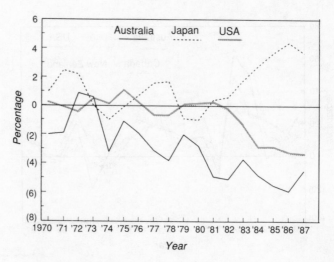

FIGURE 2.6
Inflation Rates (change over previous period)

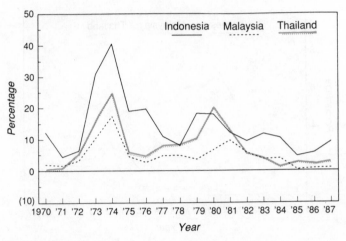

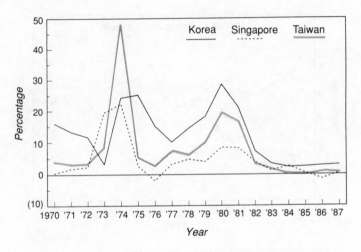

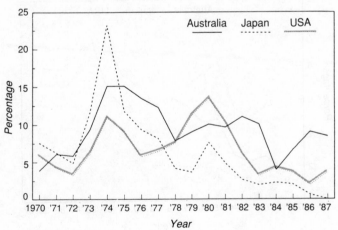

FIGURE 2.7
Unemployment Rates

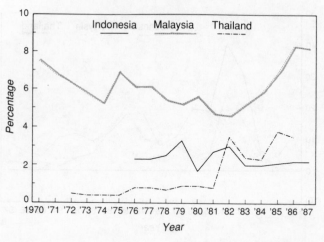

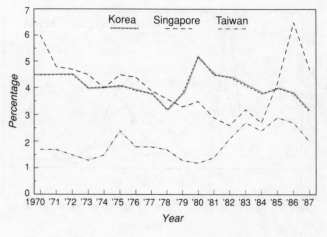

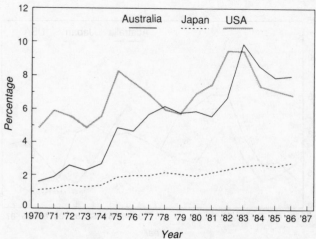

In the realm of exchange rate management, too, the Pacific weighs heavily. Although the currency composition of Malaysia's composite basket (around which the external value of the Malaysian ringgit revolves) remains a well-kept national secret, it is not hard to figure out roughly the role played by the major currencies of the Asia–Pacific region. Apparently, four currencies, namely the US dollar, the Singapore dollar, the Japanese yen, and the Australian dollar (presumably in that order of importance) constitute the bulk of the basket, with the European currencies, mainly the sterling and Deutschmark, accounting for the bulk of the balance.

The ways in which the exchange rates of these key currencies are managed in their own countries can have an impact on the management of the ringgit exchange rate in Malaysia. For instance, if the brunt of the adjustment in the US external imbalance is undertaken through the US exchange rate policy, the exchange rate of the ringgit will have to shift even more sharply. The prospect of the internationalization of the Japanese yen adds more weight to the Pacific dimension in the ringgit exchange rate regime and would make the design and conduct of Japan's macroeconomic policy all the more relevant to Malaysia.

The Malaysian economy is essentially demand-driven. Import demand abroad for Malaysian exports often sets the pace at which output and employment can expand at home. An insight into this relationship can be gained by looking at the propensities of the major export markets to import Malaysian products. Table 2.20 presents estimates of average and marginal import propensities.[15] Evidently, the marginal propensity tends to exceed the average propensity, meaning that a larger share of the foreign incremental income is spent on imports from Malaysia than that of total income. The average propensities are understandably small for Japan and the United States where imports from Malaysia constitute no more than a drop in the import bucket. The figures for Indonesia, however, are surprisingly small, the propensity being smaller at the margin than on the average.

TABLE 2.20
Propensity to Import Malaysian Products: Selected Countries, 1987

	Average Propensity	Marginal Propensity
Australia	0.0019	0.0050
Indonesia[1]	0.0007	0.0005
Japan	0.0020	0.0020
Korea	0.0095	0.0101
Singapore	0.2199	0.4837
Taiwan	0.0076	0.0097
Thailand	0.0118	0.0356
United States	0.0007	0.0037

Sources: Computed from International Monetary Fund, Direction of Trade Statistics, computer data tape; and International Monetary Fund, Yearbook 1989.
[1]Data for 1986.

Although Japan's average propensity exceeds that of the United States, the marginal propensity of the latter is significantly higher than that of the former, which means that a larger proportion of the US incremental income is spent on Malaysian products than is the case with Japan. In other words, for every US$100 increase in income, imports from Malaysia increase by US$0.27 in the United States and by US$0.20 in Japan.

Korea and Taiwan play a significant role, since they spend roughly 1 per cent of their incremental income on imports from Malaysia. Thailand features even more prominently in that about 3.6 per cent of its incremental income is used for importing Malaysian products. This can be easily explained in terms of geographical proximity and historical ties.

The case of Singapore is very different from the rest, for both its average and marginal propensities are very large. In a sense, this is to be expected since the economies of Singapore and Malaysia are closely integrated with the latter serving *de facto* as a hinterland for the former. Table 2.20 suggests that 22 per cent of Singapore's annual income is spent on imports from Malaysia and that for every US$100 increase in income, Singapore's imports from Malaysia rise by over US$48. These estimates, however, should be interpreted with the utmost caution for two related reasons: (a) Singapore is perhaps the only country in the world (Hong Kong, though experiencing a similar situation, is not a country) where exports exceed GNP by a substantial margin, and (b) a significant proportion of its imports from Malaysia are re-exported and not retained.

Demonstration Effect and Developmental Impact

Malaysia has benefited immensely from its strategic geographic location by taking advantage of opportunities arising from the dynamics of the Asia–Pacific region. It is no exaggeration to state that Malaysia has been 'inspired' by the remarkable success of the Asian NIEs. The spectacular growth of their labour-intensive manufactured exports in the 1960s was particularly instructive for Malaysia, as it effectively demolished the arguments of the 'export pessimism' school, prevalent in the 1950s and 1960s, led by Prebisch (1950) and Nurkse (1959). Structural changes taking place in the NIEs, with rising real wages and shifting comparative advantage towards capital-intensive and skill-intensive activities, stimulated Malaysia to look upon itself as belonging to the next generation of exporters of manufactures.

Major structural changes in the industrial countries of the Asia–Pacific region in the 1970s, especially Japan, in the face of rapidly rising energy and raw material prices and the successful export thrust of the NIEs, provided incentives for Malaysia to emulate them. Malaysia did not lose the opportunity to profit from the international migration of industries forced by 'product cycles'.[16] Direct foreign investment, especially from the Asia–Pacific countries, has facilitated the structural transformation of Malaysian industry, by injecting not only capital but also technology, as will be seen in Chapter 4. The significant demonstration effect of all this on the rest of the economy is discernible even though it is hard to quantify.

There are important spillover effects for Malaysia, particularly from the export-oriented industrialization of the NIEs. Malaysia seems well placed to enter export markets being vacated by the NIEs, especially for products which are resource-intensive rather than labour-intensive. Malaysia has an edge over other ASEAN countries on account of its excellent infrastructural facilities and technological absorptive capacity for capturing such overspills.

Already there are signs of a symbiotic relationship developing between ASEAN and the NIEs; the latter are beginning to serve as export markets for Malaysian-made intermediate products. There is evidence to show that intra-industry trade flows between Malaysia and the NIEs—and, for that matter, between Malaysia and the developed countries of the region—are increasing, as will be seen in Chapter 3, and that industrial linkages between Malaysia and the Pacific are growing strong, as will be seen in Chapter 4. It suffices to note here that the relationship between Malaysia and the rest of the Pacific, especially the developed countries and the NIEs, is largely one of complementarity rather than rivalry, given the differences in their resource endowments.

Malaysia's relationship with other ASEAN countries, excepting Brunei and Singapore, is, however, on a somewhat different footing. Although the resource endowments of Indonesia, Malaysia, the Philippines, and Thailand are similar, Malaysia differs from the other three on two important counts. First, Malaysia is not a labour-abundant economy. Malaysia's population of 17 million (density of 51 persons per square kilometre) pales in comparison with Indonesia's 176 million (density of 93), the Philippines' 59 million (density of 196), and Thailand's 55 million (density of 107) as of the end of 1988.[17] Secondly, Malaysia is already in the lead in terms of economic development. Malaysia's per capita income in 1988 stood at US$1,862, which compares very favourably with Indonesia's US$450, the Philippines' US$597, and Thailand's US$924. It is therefore unlikely that Malaysia will compete with these countries in the regional and international markets for labour-intensive manufactures. Malaysia's long-term comparative advantage, discussed in Chapter 5, seems to lie in resource-intensive and human capital-intensive activities, which would signify increased complementarity with its immediate neighbours.

1. Chenery (1960) classified the sources of industrial growth into (a) import substitution, (b) expansion of final demand and export demand, and (c) expansion of intermediate demand. The classification used here is based on Hoffmann and Tan (1971). For a detailed analytical framework, see Ariff (1976), Appendix to Chapter 3.

2. See Ariff and Semudram (1987), p. 15.

3. Sales to FTZ firms or licensed manufacturing warehouses (LMWs) are also considered as 'exports'.

4. This technique was used as a military strategy to combat communist insurgency during the Emergency years of 1948–60.

5. See Malaysia (1989), Table 3.7, p. 55.

6. Ibid., p. 40.

7. Three-month interbank rate rose to 15.434 per cent on 22 October 1984 from 8.457 per cent on 29 February 1984.

8. See Ariff and Semudram (1987), p. 34.

9. Malaysia, Ministry of Finance, *Economic Report 1990/91*, Statistical Table 4.9.

10. World Bank (1989b), Table 23.

11. Ibid.

12. Ibid.

13. Ibid.

14. In 1987, the combined share of the United States and Japan in world output was 45.4 per cent and their joint contribution to world trade (exports + imports) was 32.1 per cent.

15. The average propensity of country j to import Malaysian products is defined as M_{ij}/Y_j, and the marginal propensity of country j to import Malaysian products as $\Delta M_{ij}/\Delta Y_j$

where M_{ij} = import of j from Malaysia

Y_j = real GNP of country j.

16. The product cycle theory was developed by Vernon (1979). A variant of this theory is what is referred to as the 'flying geese pattern' in Japanese international economics literature.

17. See Malaysia, Ministry of Finance, *Economic Report 1989/90*, Statistical Table 1.2.

3
Trade Flows

MALAYSIA'S trade linkages with the Asia–Pacific countries are rather extensive. They not only account for the bulk of Malaysia's exports and imports but also contribute most significantly to the growth and expansion of its external trade. This chapter will attempt to examine the Asia–Pacific trade flows of Malaysia in greater detail through decomposing Malaysia's exports and imports by country and product, using several standard methodologies in the international economics literature. It is hoped that this approach will enable us to gain further insights into factors that play an important role in Malaysia–Pacific trade relations.

Malaysia has a very open and outward-looking economy. The share of international trade in the country's GNP is relatively high by developing-country standards. Malaysia's trade regime is fairly liberal, with protection levels that pale in comparison with most developing countries. Although the Malaysian economy remains highly regulated, there has been very little government intervention in the realm of trade. Thus, market forces have been given a relatively free hand in shaping the structure and pattern of Malaysia's external trade. The growing Pacific orientation in Malaysia's trade relations may therefore be seen essentially as a market phenomenon and not as a product of deliberate policy distortions.

The above observation, however, does not imply that policies are irrelevant in the present context. Far from it. Liberal trade policies, export-oriented industrialization, and export diversification, for example, have helped the Malaysian economy to become what it is today. What all this amounts to is that government policies have apparently worked with, rather than against, the market forces, thereby expediting progress towards the internationalization of the Malaysian economy.

The preceding remarks are meant to pave the way for the analysis that is to follow. For, the approach adopted in this chapter implies that changes in trade trends, shifts in the country's comparative advantage, and movements in its resource allocation cannot be considered in isolation without relating them to external factors. Thus, a change in the structure of Malaysian exports, for instance, may have to be related to industrial restructuring taking place elsewhere.

The Trade Pattern and Structure

The pattern and structure of Malaysia's external trade have evolved over time, with important shifts taking place during the 1970s and 1980s. Although the ratio of exports and imports to GNP has not increased significantly over the years, the composition and direction of trade have changed remarkably, with manufactures occupying an increasingly important position in the country's export basket, intermediate goods growing in importance in the country's import mix, and the Pacific countries emerging as the major trading partners in the trade matrix. It is convenient to begin the analysis by looking closely at changes in the direction of exports and imports.

Direction

In the discussion of the pattern of exports and imports that follows, benchmark years are compared. The reader must be warned that trade statistics often show large year-to-year aberrations from the trend. However, this does not pose a serious problem, as the benchmark years were not particularly abnormal in the present context.

Developed countries have traditionally dominated as trading partners in Malaysia's external trade matrix. The European Community, Japan,

TABLE 3.1
Malaysia's Exports by Destination, 1970–1988
(percentage of total exports to the world)

Country/Region	1970	1975	1980	1985	1988
World (US$m.)	1,687	3,806	12,960	15,408	21,125
United States	13.0	16.1	16.3	12.8	17.3
Japan	18.3	14.4	22.8	24.6	16.9
Canada	1.9	1.0	0.5	0.7	0.7
Australia	2.2	1.9	1.4	1.7	2.4
New Zealand	0.5	0.4	0.4	0.1	0.2
NIEs[1]	5.4	4.2	6.9	10.6	11.2
ASEAN[2]	24.8	24.2	22.4	25.6	24.1
China	1.3	1.4	1.7	1.0	2.0
Total Asia–Pacific[3]	67.4	63.6	72.4	77.2	74.8
EC	20.3	24.4	17.6	14.4	14.4
Rest of the world	14.5	13.8	11.4	10.0	14.1

Sources: International Monetary Fund, *Direction of Trade Statistics*, computer data tape 1987, and International Monetary Fund, *Yearbook*, 1988 and 1989.
[1] Hong Kong, Korea, and Taiwan.
[2] Indonesia, the Philippines, Singapore, and Thailand.
[3] Includes all of the countries above.

and the United States have been the most important destinations for Malaysia's exports and the most important sources of Malaysia's imports as well. While the EC is still a major trading partner, its relative importance has declined over the years, as shown in Tables 3.1 and 3.2. By contrast, the Pacific countries have become increasingly important as the markets for Malaysia's exports and sources of its imports. The share of the Asia–Pacific region in Malaysia's exports has increased, albeit with considerable year-to-year fluctuations, while its share in Malaysia's imports has risen rather steadily. The Asia–Pacific region now accounts for about three-quarters of Malaysia's exports and imports.

The United States, in particular, has become increasingly important as a trading partner of Malaysia in terms of both exports and imports. While Japan continues to be a major trading partner, it features more prominently as a source of imports than as a market for Malaysian exports. The US share in Malaysia's exports rose from 13.0 per cent in 1970 to 17.3 per cent in 1988, while that of Japan fell slightly from 18.3 per cent to 16.9 per cent correspondingly, mainly due to the oil price decline (Table 3.1). The US share of Malaysia's imports rose from 8.6 per cent to 17.7 per cent and that of Japan increased from 17.5 per cent to 23.0 per cent between 1970 and 1988 (Table 3.2).

The ASEAN region accounts for about one-quarter of Malaysia's

TABLE 3.2
Malaysia's Imports by Source, 1970–1988
(percentage of total imports from the world)

Country/Region	1970	1975	1980	1985	1988
World (US$m.)	1,399	3,526	10,821	12,301	16,567
United States	8.6	10.7	15.1	15.3	17.7
Japan	17.5	20.1	22.8	23.0	23.0
Canada	1.1	1.0	1.1	1.2	1.2
Australia	5.7	7.9	5.5	4.1	4.2
New Zealand	0.9	1.1	1.0	0.7	0.8
NIEs[1]	3.4	3.6	5.0	6.6	9.5
ASEAN[2]	16.0	15.2	16.4	22.4	18.8
China	5.3	4.2	2.3	2.0	2.9
Total Asia–Pacific[3]	58.6	63.7	69.2	75.3	78.1
EC	23.4	20.6	15.8	14.4	13.3
Rest of the world	23.5	23.4	20.5	14.1	12.6

Sources: International Monetary Fund, *Direction of Trade Statistics*, computer data tape 1987, and International Monetary Fund, *Yearbook*, 1988 and 1989.
[1] Hong Kong, Korea, and Taiwan.
[2] Indonesia, the Philippines, Singapore, and Thailand.
[3] Includes all of the countries above.

exports and one-fifth of its imports. More strikingly, the East Asian NIEs have emerged as major trading partners of Malaysia, with their share of Malaysia's exports doubling and that of imports trebling between 1970 and 1980 (Tables 3.1 and 3.2). By contrast, Australia, Canada, and New Zealand have kept a low profile in the Malaysian trade network. Their combined share in Malaysia's exports fell from 4.6 per cent in 1970 to 3.3 per cent in 1988, and their stake in the country's imports shrank from 7.7 per cent to 6.1 per cent over the same period. Malaysia's trade with China has been punctuated with aberrations as it is affected by discontinuities in China's trade policies. However, it is evident that China plays only a somewhat peripheral role in Malaysia's external trade relations.

Malaysia has enjoyed prolonged bilateral trade surplus with the United States and this surplus has been growing rapidly in recent years. More often than not, Malaysia has had bilateral trade surpluses with Japan, but in recent years sizeable bilateral deficits have appeared instead. Australia, Canada, China, and New Zealand are countries with which Malaysia has had persistent bilateral trade deficits. By contrast, trade with other ASEAN countries and the East Asian NIEs has yielded increasingly substantial surpluses. Overall, the Asia–Pacific region has been contributing significantly to Malaysia's multilateral trade surplus—to the tune of about 58.2 per cent of the total in 1988, as shown in Table 3.3.

TABLE 3.3
Malaysia's Trade Balance by Country/Region, 1970–1988
(US$ million)

Country/Region	1970	1975	1980	1985	1988
United States	+99	+234	+478	+90	+722
Japan	+64	−160	+488	+961	−240
Canada	+17	+3	−54	−40	−43
Australia	−43	−206	−414	−242	−172
New Zealand	−4	−23	−56	−71	−90
NIEs[1]	+44	+33	+353	+821	+560
ASEAN[2]	+195	+385	+1,128	+1,189	+1,976
China	−52	−95	−29	−92	−58
Total Asia–Pacific[3]	+317	+175	+1,895	+2,632	+2,651
Rest of the world	−29	+105	+ 244	+475	+1,907
Global	+288	+280	+2,139	+3,107	+4,558

Sources: International Monetary Fund, Direction of Trade Statistics, computer data tape 1987, and International Monetary Fund, Yearbook, 1988 and 1989.
[1] Hong Kong, Korea, and Taiwan.
[2] Indonesia, the Philippines, Singapore, and Thailand.
[3] Includes all of the countries above.

TRADE FLOWS 59

Composition

Primary commodities (SITC 0–4 plus 67–68) have always accounted for the bulk of Malaysia's exports, although their share in the total declined from 92.8 per cent in 1970 to 61.3 per cent in 1987. The US accounts for only a small proportion of Malaysia's primary exports (4.3 per cent in 1987), while Japan represents the biggest single importer of Malaysia's primary products (28.4 per cent in 1987). The ASEAN share is substantial, but much of it is not retained within the region, reflecting the entrepôt character of the intra-regional trade in primary commodities. It is also worth noting that the East Asian NIEs have emerged as important importers of Malaysian primary products, mainly as inputs into their manufacturing output. All in all, the Asia–Pacific region absorbs about three-quarters of Malaysia's primary exports (Table 3.4).

The story is quite different with respect to manufactures; and there are again variations among the Pacific destinations. The share of manufactures (SITC 5–8 minus 67–68) in total exports increased from 6.3 per cent in 1970 to 38.3 per cent in 1987. The United States has always been the largest single importer of Malaysian manufactures with a growing share, while Japan has become relatively less important as a

TABLE 3.4
Malaysia: Direction of Primary Exports,[1] 1970–1987
(percentage of total primary exports to the world)

Destination	1970	1975	1980	1985	1987
World (US$m)	1,566	3,163	10,492	11,416	10,999
United States	13.1	14.0	12.8	3.1	4.3
Japan	19.3	16.0	26.8	30.1	28.4
Canada	2.0	0.9	0.4	0.5	0.5
Australia	2.2	1.3	1.1	1.4	2.3
New Zealand	0.5	0.3	0.3	0.1	0.1
NIEs[2]	5.2	4.4	5.2	11.1	12.2
ASEAN[3]	23.0	22.9	22.5	27.0	23.9
China	1.4	1.7	2.1	1.4	2.3
Total Asia–Pacific[4]	66.6	61.5	71.1	74.8	74.0
EC	20.9	25.6	16.7	13.5	12.4
Rest of the world	12.5	12.8	12.2	11.7	13.6

Sources: United Nations, Commodity Trade Statistics, various issues.
[1]SITC (0+1+2+3+4+67+68).
[2]Hong Kong, Korea, and Taiwan.
[3]Indonesia, the Philippines, Singapore, and Thailand.
[4]Includes all of the countries above.

market for Malaysia's manufactured exports. The picture, however, is likely to change significantly, as Japan is increasing its manufactured imports following the appreciation of the yen. Interestingly, the East Asian NIEs and ASEAN have become increasingly important as destinations for Malaysian manufactures. Once again, the Asia–Pacific region figures conspicuously as a market for Malaysian manufactures, accounting for about three-quarters of the total (Table 3.5).

The percentage shares of individual Pacific countries in the major export product categories, both primary and manufactured, are shown in Table 3.6. It can be gathered from all this how important the Asia–Pacific region is to Malaysia's exports.

Malaysian imports, too, exhibit similar trends. The share of primary products in the total declined from 46.2 per cent in 1970 to 27.4 per cent in 1987, but the share of the Asia–Pacific in Malaysia's primary imports rose from 61.1 per cent to 76.1 per cent. The ASEAN region, in particular, has become an increasingly important source of imports of primary products, its share in the total rising from 26.9 per cent to 33.0 per cent between 1970 and 1987 (Table 3.7). Developed countries have traditionally been relatively unimportant as sources of primary imports, with the notable exception of Australia whose share of Malaysia's primary imports increased from 8.5 per cent in 1970 to 12.2 per cent in 1987.

TABLE 3.5

Malaysia: Direction of Manufactured Exports,[1] 1970–1987
(percentage of total manufactured exports to the world)

Destination	1970	1975	1980	1985	1987
World (US$m.)	106	658	2,410	4,193	6,877
United States	12.7	26.7	31.7	39.8	36.2
Japan	6.0	7.6	5.7	6.7	5.4
Canada	0.9	1.5	0.8	1.2	1.3
Australia	1.7	4.4	2.7	2.4	2.0
New Zealand	0.4	0.7	1.0	0.2	0.3
NIEs[2]	4.7	3.3	7.6	5.4	8.8
ASEAN[3]	48.4	30.6	22.0	22.6	23.3
China	0.0	0.0	0.1	0.1	0.4
Total Asia–Pacific[4]	74.7	74.7	71.4	78.4	77.7
EC	12.3	18.2	21.7	17.5	17.2
Rest of the world	13.0	7.0	6.9	4.1	5.1

Source: United Nations, Commodity Trade Statistics, various issues.
[1]SITC (5+6+7+8−67−68).
[2]Hong Kong, Korea, and Taiwan.
[3]Indonesia, the Philippines, Singapore, and Thailand.
[4]Includes all of the countries above.

TABLE 3.6
Malaysia: Exports by Product and Country of Destination, 1970–1987
(percentage share in total)

	1970	1975	1980	1983	1987
Primary Products					
Rubber					
China	–	–	5.9	6.3	8.8
Korea	–	–	–	5.8	9.6
Singapore	25.3	25.7	25.9	18.6	11.0
USA	11.6	11.2	7.6	11.1	9.0
Wood and Cork					
Australia	4.3	–	–	–	1.5
China	45.1	40.9	46.8	44.7	2.3
Hong Kong	13.6	10.3	7.9	10.5	1.3
Japan	–	10.2	7.3	8.5	48.7
Korea	12.8	13.2	7.3	6.5	10.4
Taiwan	–	–	9.3	10.4	11.5
Petroleum and Petroleum Products					
Australia	16.0	–	–	–	4.0
Japan	–	36.2	41.6	22.3	25.3
Philippines	18.8	12.4	4.1	2.5	6.8
Singapore	46.3	29.3	23.3	45.8	30.1
Thailand	7.1	11.1	3.1	13.1	12.0
USA	–	–	26.9	–	2.9
Korea	–	–	–	8.3	13.6
Tin					
Canada	3.3	–	–	–	0.1
Japan	26.9	13.6	26.2	30.3	29.3
USA	36.8	–	15.2	–	6.9
Singapore	0.2	0.6	1.5	0.4	12.5
Palm Oil (Crude)					
Japan	–	–	12.7	7.4	–
Singapore	30.6	–	–	–	4.3
USA	5.3	26.8	–	–	–
Indonesia	–	–	–	–	41.6
Pepper (Black and White)					
Hong Kong	–	–	0.8	–	–
Japan	–	–	0.7	13.5	22.3
Singapore	82.2	73.1	73.1	68.0	44.9
USA	–	–	–	–	11.0

(continued)

TABLE 3.6 (*continued*)

	1970	1975	1980	1983	1987
Cocoa (Raw or Roasted)					
Australia	–	–	7.2	–	3.6
Singapore	47.7	17.8	35.2	52.6	32.0
USA	–	5.3	6.2	7.7	11.6
Manufactures					
Cork and Wood Products					
Australia	–	7.0	–	–	7.9
Hong Kong	–	–	5.7	4.7	5.7
Japan	20.0	18.0	7.3	7.3	10.2
Singapore	7.5	16.8	33.0	39.1	26.4
USA	29.1	14.2	13.2	10.9	10.6
Textile, Yarn, and Fabrics					
Australia	–	12.6	8.8	7.5	9.2
Canada	–	–	–	5.5	4.2
Hong Kong	–	–	11.6	13.0	8.2
Japan	–	–	9.4	7.6	12.4
New Zealand	4.0	8.9	–	–	2.4
Philippines	7.7	–	–	–	1.7
Singapore	27.4	17.4	7.1	9.2	12.0
USA	15.0	11.0	–	–	18.2
Non-ferrous Metals					
Canada	3.3	–	–	–	0.1
Japan	26.8	13.5	25.9	29.6	26.2
USA	36.7	29.4	15.0	4.0	6.1
Singapore	0.4	0.8	2.2	2.0	18.5
Electrical Machinery					
Hong Kong	–	3.5	7.1	5.5	8.6
Indonesia	5.8	–	–	–	0.1
Japan	–	6.6	4.8	6.6	5.7
Singapore	34.8	18.9	14.5	10.5	12.6
Thailand	9.3	–	–	–	1.5
USA	–	54.6	53.2	58.2	50.6
Articles of Apparel					
Australia	–	7.6	–	–	0.5
Canada	8.3	–	–	–	4.5
Philippines	6.9	–	–	–	–
Singapore	7.5	–	–	4.3	3.1
USA	64.2	12.7	20.2	45.7	52.5

Source: Malaysia, Department of Statistics, *External Trade Statistics of Malaysia*, various issues.

TABLE 3.7
Malaysia: Direction of Primary Imports,[1] 1970–1987
(percentage of total primary imports)

Source	1970	1975	1980	1985	1987
World (US$m.)	646	1,499	4,145	4,079	3,478
United States	3.9	3.4	4.6	4.3	5.3
Japan	8.2	11.3	12.0	10.7	10.9
Canada	1.0	0.8	1.1	0.9	1.5
Australia	8.5	15.0	11.7	10.3	12.2
New Zealand	1.7	2.3	1.4	1.8	2.4
NIEs[2]	3.8	2.4	3.3	4.0	4.3
ASEAN[3]	26.9	24.9	28.4	38.4	33.0
China	7.1	6.8	3.1	3.6	6.5
Total Asia–Pacific[4]	61.1	66.9	65.4	74.1	76.1
EC	8.1	6.3	5.4	5.8	7.3
Rest of the world	30.8	26.7	29.2	20.1	16.6

Source: United Nations, *Commodity Trade Statistics,* various issues.
[1]SITC (0+1+2+3+4+67+68).
[2]Hong Kong, Korea, and Taiwan.
[3]Indonesia, the Philippines, Singapore, and Thailand.
[4]Includes all of the countries above.

The share of manufactures in total imports of Malaysia rose marginally from 52.5 per cent to 54.8 per cent between 1970 and 1987, and the share of the Asia–Pacific in Malaysia's manufactured imports increased sharply from 57.4 per cent to 79.8 per cent. In particular, the United States, the East Asian NIEs, and ASEAN have become increasingly important as sources of Malaysia's imports of manufactured goods. However, it is Japan which represents the single largest source and whose share of the total has remained relatively stable. A striking observation is that the European Community has been eclipsed by the Asia–Pacific countries as sources of Malaysia's manufactured imports, as its share of the total dwindled from 36.9 per cent in 1970 to 15.6 per cent in 1987 (Table 3.8).

Trade Intensities

The trade intensity index, developed by Brown (1949) and Kojima (1964) and synthesized by Drysdale and Garnaut (1982), provides a useful analytical tool for gauging the relative importance of the bilateral trading relationship of Malaysia with other Asia–Pacific countries. The index measures the share of one country's trade with another country (or region) as a proportion of the latter's share of world trade.

TABLE 3.8

Malaysia: Direction of Manufactured Imports,[1] 1970–1987
(percentage of total manufactured imports)

Source	1970	1975	1980	1985	1987
World (US$m.)	734	2,000	6,528	8,394	9,073
United States	12.7	16.2	21.6	20.5	24.0
Japan	26.0	26.9	30.1	29.3	26.0
Canada	1.3	1.2	1.1	1.3	0.8
Australia	3.3	2.5	0.9	1.1	0.8
New Zealand	0.2	0.2	0.8	0.2	0.1
NIEs[2]	4.7	5.6	6.8	7.9	10.3
ASEAN[3]	5.4	7.7	8.8	14.6	15.8
China	3.9	2.3	1.9	1.3	1.7
Total Asia–Pacific[4]	57.4	62.4	72.5	76.2	79.8
EC	36.9	31.1	22.2	18.1	15.6
Rest of the world	5.7	6.5	5.3	5.7	4.6

Source: United Nations, Commodity Trade Statistics, various issues.
[1]SITC (5+6+7+8–67–68).
[2]Hong Kong, Korea, and Taiwan.
[3]Indonesia, the Philippines, Singapore, and Thailand.
[4]Includes all of the countries above.

By adjusting for shares in world trade, the intensity indices show that outside the ASEAN region, Malaysia trades most intensively with Japan as far as its exports are concerned (Table 3.9). Trade with other ASEAN countries exhibits high export trade intensities, which is explained in part by their small share in international trade. However, export trade intensity with respect to Malaysia's trade within the ASEAN subregion has been declining. The intensity indices of Malaysian exports[1] exhibit some volatility, particularly in its trade with the United States and the East Asian NIEs. However, Malaysia's export trade intensity indices with respect to the Asia–Pacific region as a whole have been relatively stable.

Malaysia's import trade intensity indices[2] also suggest that it trades most intensively with other ASEAN countries (Table 3.10). However, not all of its imports from the region are retained for domestic consumption, since a significant proportion of its primary imports from its neighbours is re-exported. Outside the ASEAN region, it is Australia with which Malaysia trades most intensively in so far as imports are concerned. Malaysia's import trade intensity vis-à-vis Japan is also large, while the indices with regards to the United States and the East Asian NIEs are significantly above unity. The Asia–Pacific region as a whole appears to be a region from which Malaysia imports intensively.

TABLE 3.9
Intensity Indices of Malaysian Exports by Destination, 1970–1988

Category/Region	1970	1975	1980	1985	1988
United States	0.90	1.25	1.23	0.66	1.05
Japan	2.86	2.04	3.13	3.53	2.51
Canada	0.37	0.24	0.15	0.16	0.19
Australia	1.33	1.43	1.24	1.24	1.88
New Zealand	1.14	1.04	1.42	0.47	0.59
NIEs[1]	2.50	1.73	2.08	2.47	1.71
ASEAN[2]	12.28	10.05	8.27	9.42	8.13
China	2.01	1.72	1.66	0.46	0.99
Total Asia–Pacific[3]	2.05	2.01	2.24	1.86	1.86
EC	0.48	0.61	0.44	0.41	0.37
Rest of the world	0.48	0.41	0.35	0.35	0.54

Sources: International Monetary Fund, Direction of Trade Statistics, computer data tape 1987, and International Monetary Fund, Yearbook, 1988 and 1989.
[1] Hong Kong, Korea, and Taiwan.
[2] Indonesia, the Philippines, Singapore, and Thailand.
[3] Includes all of the countries above.

TABLE 3.10
Intensity Indices of Malaysian Imports by Source, 1970–1988

Country/Region	1970	1975	1980	1985	1988
United States	0.56	0.79	1.29	1.29	1.48
Japan	2.54	2.89	3.30	2.33	2.34
Canada	0.19	0.24	0.30	0.23	0.29
Australia	3.35	5.29	4.69	3.22	3.40
New Zealand	2.05	4.03	3.41	2.35	2.53
NIEs[1]	2.00	1.76	1.64	1.30	1.38
ASEAN[2]	7.39	5.87	4.64	5.86	4.90
China	n.a.	5.84	2.43	1.34	1.64
Total Asia–Pacific[3]	1.71	2.00	2.21	1.94	1.94
EC	0.56	0.53	0.43	0.40	0.34
Rest of the world	0.72	0.52	0.46	0.40	0.41

Sources: International Monetary Fund, Direction of Trade Statistics, computer data tape 1987, and International Monetary Fund, Yearbook, 1988 and 1989.
[1] Hong Kong, Korea, and Taiwan.
[2] Indonesia, the Philippines, Singapore, and Thailand.
[3] Includes all of the countries above, except China in 1970.
n.a. = Not available.

The intensity of Malaysia's exports to and imports from the EC has been not only small but also steadily declining. It may be surmised in the light of all of this that Malaysia's trading relationship has been gravitating towards the Pacific Basin.

The high trade intensities observed in some cases may be explained by (a) the 'match' between the export commodity composition and the corresponding commodity composition of the importing country, and (b) the 'special country bias', i.e. the trade intensities for the particular commodities traded (Drysdale and Garnaut, 1982). The so-called 'bias' relates to such factors as relative proximity, the importance of historical trade linkages, and ease of communication and commercial contact. Thus, the high trade intensities of Malaysia in terms of both exports and imports in its trade with other ASEAN countries may be attributed largely to what has been termed 'special country bias'. The complementarity of resources and factor endowments probably is less important than is often assumed, as the 'match' factor is tarnished by the effects of protectionism and other official resistance to trade (K. Anderson, 1983).

Intra-industry Trade

Prior to export-oriented industrialization in the early 1970s, Malaysia's exports consisted almost entirely of primary products, while imports comprised mostly manufactures. Such exchanges of goods are termed in the literature as 'inter-industry' trade flows. The increasing share of manufactures in the total exports of Malaysia during the 1970s and 1980s has led to a growing volume of what are termed 'intra-industry' trade flows. While inter-industry trade refers to trade in 'different' products, intra-industry trade entails exchange of 'differentiated' or 'similar' products. Intra-industry trade may be defined as the value of exports of an 'industry' which is matched by imports of similar products.

The importance of Malaysia's intra-industry trade flows can be measured by the value of an intra-industry trade index which has been developed by Grubel and Lloyd (1975). This index is derived by subtracting the total trade of a given country from net imports or exports of that industry and then dividing the term by the total trade of the industry.[3] This measure would vary from 0 to 100 when expressed in percentage terms. It would be zero if there is only inter-industry trade (i.e. only export or import of product X, but not both); by the same token, it would be 100 where there is only intra-industry trade (i.e. exports of product X exactly equal imports of product X).

The intra-industry trade indices for each of Malaysia's major trading partners in the Asia–Pacific region (calculated at the three-digit SITC level) for manufactures are given in Table 3.11. It is remarkable that Malaysia's intra-industry trade with all of its major trading partners in the Asia–Pacific region has increased significantly during the period 1970–87, as shown by the increasing indices. Intra-industry trade is of the greatest importance for Malaysia in its trade especially with the United States, the East Asian NIEs, and the ASEAN partners. It is surprisingly small in the case of Japan, although there is evidence of sub-

TABLE 3.11
Malaysia: Intra-industry Trade Indices—Manuf

Trading Partner	1970	1975	1980		
United States	3.8	43.0	12.2		
Japan	1.6	10.5	9.7		
Canada	4.7	12.9	50.2		
Australia	10.2	24.4	32.0		
New Zealand	19.2	13.4	17.9		_٦.٥
NIEs[1]	12.5	25.5	27.2	3_.۱	43.1
ASEAN[2]	45.8	51.9	72.7	70.7	70.0

Source: International Economic Data Bank, Australian National University, Canberra.
[1]Hong Kong, Korea, and Taiwan.
[2]Indonesia, the Philippines, Singapore, and Thailand.

stantial improvement in the late 1980s. With the appreciation of the yen, Japan has stepped up its imports of manufactured items from Malaysia, while Japanese companies operating in Malaysia have increased their exports to Japan in recent times.

Care should, of course, be taken in interpreting the intra-industry trade indices even at the three-digit level, since large indices are not inconsistent with small trade volumes. But what matters is the general direction of the trends, about which the figures presented in Table 3.11 bear no ambiguities. The uptrend in intra-industry trade is not at all surprising, given Malaysia's export-oriented industrialization in which direct foreign investment, especially in the FTZs, plays a critical role. The high indices in the case of the trade between Malaysia and the rest of ASEAN may be explained largely in terms of the fact that it shares a common border with all ASEAN countries except the Philippines. Often, transport costs give rise to border trade in these countries where geographic regions are more closely integrated with other countries than with other regions within their own country. The high indices in the case of the trade with the United States may be attributed mainly to the internationalization of industries, especially electronics, with vertical intra-industry specialization which has generated bilateral trade in inputs, intermediate goods, and final products within the same industry. The rising intra-industry trade indices with respect to Japan and the East Asian NIEs seem to reflect the competitive dynamics which operate through product cycles and international subcontracting arrangements.

Trade Performance

The importance of trade to the open economy of Malaysia is obvious and requires no further elaboration. In particular, the success of its export-oriented industrialization hinges critically on how well it sells its manufactures abroad. Besides, its capacity to import in the final analysis is circumscribed by its ability to export and the terms of trade. The

trade performance may be evaluated by examining the growth,
penetration, and competitiveness of both exports and imports.

Growth

Average annual growth rates of Malaysian exports by trading partner for
various periods are provided in Table 3.12. Clearly, export growth has
decelerated over the years, growing more slowly in the late 1980s compared with the rapid expansion of the early 1970s. None the less, the
rate of export growth even in the 1980s has exceeded the world average.
To be sure, Malaysia's exports to the Asia–Pacific region expanded at a
slightly slower pace than its total exports during 1985–8. There are,
however, interesting inter-country variations. Exports to the United
States grew twice as fast as the exports to the region as a whole during
this period. Exports to Australia increased even faster. By contrast,
exports to Japan registered a negative average annual growth rate.

The picture looks quite different in the case of manufactured exports.
The performance of manufactured exports in the second half of the
1980s seems more impressive than that in the first half of the decade.
Manufactured exports to the Asia–Pacific region grew at a higher rate
than manufactured exports to the world as a whole during the period
1980–8 (Table 3.13). Exports of manufactures to the United States and

TABLE 3.12
Malaysia: Average Annual Growth of Exports by Trading Partner,
1970–1988 (percentage)

Country/Region	1970–1974	1975–1979	1980–1984	1985–1988
World	24.1	23.0	8.9	7.5
United States	23.6	27.0	5.4	14.4
Japan	22.4	36.6	9.1	−1.0
Canada	18.3	9.8	15.1	6.2
Australia	23.3	20.8	6.6	20.1
New Zealand	18.1	39.2	−12.9	6.6
NIEs[1]	24.3	32.3	17.6	10.6
ASEAN[2]	22.4	19.3	14.5	7.1
China	37.3	34.0	6.5	29.7
Total Asia–Pacific[3]	22.0	25.9	9.8	7.0
EC	30.5	17.7	1.5	9.9
Rest of the world	29.7	17.0	13.4	11.1

Sources: International Monetary Fund, *Direction of Trade Statistics*, computer data tape
1987, and International Monetary Fund, *Yearbook*, 1988 and 1989.
[1]Hong Kong, Korea, and Taiwan.
[2]Indonesia, the Philippines, Singapore, and Thailand.
[3]Includes all of the countries above.

TABLE 3.13
Malaysia: Average Annual Growth of Manufactured Exports,[1]
1970–1988 (percentage)

Destination	1970–1974	1975–1979	1980–1984	1985–1988
World	46.0	29.7	18.4	17.7
United States	63.0	39.4	23.4	12.7
Japan	71.6	27.8	18.8	13.5
Canada	93.2	5.6	28.9	19.3
Australia	76.2	24.4	4.6	21.5
New Zealand	87.1	53.3	−11.5	26.5
NIEs[2]	53.1	44.3	15.5	39.8
ASEAN[3]	31.4	19.5	17.4	21.9
China	–	–	54.7	118.8
Total Asia–Pacific[4]	45.0	29.2	19.2	17.8
EC	69.9	35.3	16.7	16.9
Rest of the world	33.4	23.5	16.3	23.0

Source: United Nations, Commodity Trade Statistics, various issues.
[1]SITC (5+6+7+8–67–68)
[2]Hong Kong, Korea, and Taiwan.
[3]Indonesia, the Philippines, Singapore, and Thailand.
[4]Includes all of the countries above, except manufactured exports to China in 1970–4 and 1975–9.
– = Data reflect inconsistencies in government policy.

Japan have continued to grow at double-digit rates. The growth rates in the case of manufactured exports to China were surprisingly high, but they are presumably due to small base values. Of greater interest are the high growth rates posted in the manufactured exports to the East Asian NIEs, ASEAN, Australia, and New Zealand during the period 1985–8. It may also be mentioned in passing that Malaysian manufactured exports to the European Community also grew rapidly during this period, although the exports to the Asia–Pacific region as a whole outpaced the exports to the European Community.

As in the case of exports, imports have also decelerated over the years. The average annual growth rate of 5.8 per cent during 1985–8 pales in comparison with the 31.2 per cent growth experienced during 1970–4. Imports sourced from the Asia–Pacific region have been growing at faster rates than total imports. It is also noteworthy that imports from the East Asian NIEs, in particular, have registered the highest growth rate in recent years (1985–8). The growth of imports from Japan has slowed down considerably from an average of 16.6 per cent in the first half of the 1980s to 4.4 per cent in the second half (Table 3.14), apparently due to the appreciation of the yen and despite the upsurge in Japanese direct investment in the country.

TABLE 3.14
Malaysia: Average Annual Growth of Imports by Trading Partner,
1970–1988 (percentage)

Country/Region	1970–1974	1975–1979	1980–1984	1985–1988
World	31.2	15.0	13.0	5.8
United States	45.7	25.7	15.4	7.5
Japan	39.3	16.0	16.6	4.4
Canada	41.2	17.0	8.7	14.6
Australia	34.0	11.2	4.3	6.3
New Zealand	32.6	12.9	14.0	9.3
NIEs[1]	33.9	22.0	19.9	17.1
ASEAN[2]	25.4	15.0	20.4	4.1
China	26.6	5.8	5.2	15.5
Total Asia–Pacific[3]	33.1	16.4	15.8	6.4
EC	29.5	11.5	7.6	4.6
Rest of the world	29.3	12.9	5.8	3.9

Sources: International Monetary Fund, *Direction of Trade Statistics*, computer data tape
1987, and International Monetary Fund, *Yearbook*, 1988 and 1989.
[1]Hong Kong, Korea, and Taiwan.
[2]Indonesia, the Philippines, Singapore, and Thailand.
[3]Includes all of the countries above.

Market Penetration

How successful a country has been in penetrating a foreign market may
be gauged by what is termed 'import penetration ratio'. The ratio refers
to the share of imports from a particular country (region) as a percentage of the importing country's (region's) consumption, which in turn
may be defined as production plus imports minus exports. An increase
in the ratio indicates an improvement in the export thrust, while a fall
indicates a deterioration.

For the purpose of this exercise, the Standard International Trade
Classification (SITC) data were first converted into the International
Standard Industrial Classification (ISIC) so that both the numerator and
the denominator have the same classification. The results of the computations by product and country are reported in Tables 3.15 and 3.16.

Malaysia's market penetration in the United States, Australia, the East
Asian NIEs, and ASEAN has risen sharply for its manufactures. By
contrast, considerable deterioration is detected in the Japanese market,
and a marginal decline is seen in the Canadian case (Table 3.15). Some
interesting inter-country and inter-commodity comparisons may also be
made. Between 1970 and 1986, Malaysia's export thrust in the US
market was particularly impressive in the cases of textiles and wearing
apparel (ISIC 32) and fabricated metal products, machinery, and equipment (ISIC 38). In the case of the Japanese market, Malaysian market

TABLE 3.15

Malaysian Manufactured Exports: Market Penetration Ratio in Asia–Pacific Countries by Product

Exports to ISIC Product Category	USA		Japan		Canada		Australia		NIEs		ASEAN	
	1970	1986	1980	1986	1970	1986	1970	1986	1975	1984	1975	1985
3 Manufacturing	0.02	0.08	0.07	0.04	0.05	0.04	0.08	0.19	0.18	0.27	0.07	2.98
31 Food, beverages, and tobacco	0.01	0.05	0.10	0.05	0.09	0.03	0.05	0.28	0.31	0.31	0.02	1.99
32 Textile, wearing apparel, and leather	0.01	0.21	0.05	0.03	0.01	0.22	0.01	0.31	0.13	0.17	0.05	3.46
33 Wood and wood products	0.08	0.07	0.20	0.16	0.05	0.07	0.18	1.20	0.42	1.97	0.08	7.89
34 Paper, paper products, and printing	0.00	0.01	0.00	0.00	0.00	0.00	0.01	0.02	0.04	0.04	0.02	0.86
35 Chemicals and chemical products	0.00	0.01	0.01	0.04	0.01	0.01	0.07	0.17	0.10	0.14	0.10	2.86
36 Non-metal mineral products	0.00	0.01	0.00	0.00	0.00	0.01	0.00	0.03	0.03	0.02	0.04	1.31
37 Basic metal industries	0.25	0.03	0.38	0.09	0.59	0.00	0.02	0.07	0.56	0.21	0.16	1.03
38 Fabricated metal products, machinery, and equipment	0.00	0.15	0.22	0.02	0.00	0.04	0.00	0.07	0.17	0.37	0.07	4.44
39 Other manufacturing industries	0.00	0.02	0.06	0.01	0.00	0.01	0.00	0.20	0:07	0.16	0.03	2.47

Source: International Economic Data Bank, Australian National University, Canberra.

TABLE 3.16

Malaysian Manufactured Imports: Market Penetration Ratio by Country and Product

Imports from	USA		Japan		Canada		Australia		NIEs		ASEAN	
ISIC Product Category	1970	1984	1970	1984	1970	1984	1970	1984	1970	1984	1970	1984
3 Manufacturing	5.25	9.50	11.86	16.28	0.57	0.50	2.64	1.63	2.45	3.76	6.12	10.35
31 Food, beverages, and tobacco	1.15	1.29	0.51	0.76	0.08	0.19	3.57	4.95	1.52	0.89	7.39	7.02
32 Textile, wearing apparel, and leather	0.81	3.40	24.40	13.66	0.02	0.69	0.76	0.80	9.40	30.52	5.33	8.94
33 Wood and wood products	0.43	1.29	2.43	3.13	0.01	0.14	0.38	0.17	1.38	1.33	1.67	5.60
34 Paper, paper products, and printing	3.71	5.58	7.86	7.70	4.33	3.27	3.06	0.99	2.72	3.27	5.46	3.66
35 Chemicals and chemical products	2.86	4.81	4.93	5.26	0.19	0.44	1.06	0.96	0.81	1.66	6.41	15.96
36 Non-metal mineral products	1.28	2.19	4.95	9.71	0.05	0.01	1.05	0.45	2.02	5.20	3.92	7.60
37 Basic metal industries	-1.59	1.90	-23.50	26.73	-0.02	1.39	-2.27	3.47	-2.66	5.76	-3.05	2.35
38 Fabricated metal products, machinery, and equipment	12.32	20.72	18.99	32.51	0.71	0.26	2.38	0.43	1.60	4.29	2.46	10.74
39 Other manufacturing industries	2.82	3.64	13.55	17.90	0.26	0.26	0.61	1.03	9.61	11.72	5.27	8.03

Source: International Economic Data Bank, Australian National University, Canberra.

penetration weakened for nearly all commodity groups between 1980 and 1986. Although there has been a decline in Malaysia's market penetration for its manufactures as a whole in the Canadian market, significant improvements have occurred in some product groups, especially textiles and wearing apparel (ISIC 32), wood and wood products (ISIC 33), and fabricated metal products, machinery, and equipment (ISIC 38). It is remarkable that Malaysia's penetration into the Australian market has improved significantly for *all* manufacturing categories at the two-digit ISIC level. Interestingly, too, Malaysia has either increased or maintained its export thrust in the markets of the East Asian NIEs except in the case of non-metal products (ISIC 36) and basic metal products (ISIC 37). However, the most impressive advances in Malaysia's export thrust are seen in the ASEAN markets for *all* product groups.

Let us now look at the reverse side of the coin and examine how the major countries in the Asia–Pacific region have fared in the Malaysian market. It is unfortunate that we cannot go beyond the year 1984, since more recent ISIC production data for Malaysia are not readily available. Nevertheless, the import penetration ratios given in Table 3.16 do provide useful insights into the export performance of the major Asia–Pacific countries in the Malaysian market for manufactures. It appears that Australia and Canada performed dismally, while the United States, Japan, the East Asian NIEs and ASEAN registered significant improvements in their penetration of the Malaysian market between 1970 and 1984. It is Japan which has scored the highest ratio as well as the biggest increase in the ratio. The performances of ASEAN and the United States in the Malaysian market are fairly impressive and are almost at par.

That the US penetration ratios in the Malaysian market increased for *all* manufacturing categories, notably fabricated metal products, machinery, and equipment (ISIC 38), is significant. While Japan registered significant increases in its penetration ratios in the Malaysian market for most product groups, it suffered a set-back in textiles and wearing apparel (ISIC 32). The import penetration ratios for Australia and Canada declined for most product categories with some exceptions including food, beverages, and tobacco (ISIC 31) and basic metal industries (ISIC 37). Impressive gains in terms of market penetration were made by the East Asian NIEs, especially in wood and wood products (ISIC 33) and fabricated metal products, machinery, and equipment (ISIC 38), notwithstanding losses in other product categories. Quite like the United States, ASEAN gained new ground in the Malaysian market for manufactures in *all* two-digit ISIC manufacturing categories, although in the ASEAN case the gains are more evenly spread across the various product groups.

The import penetration ratios clearly show that the Malaysia–Pacific trade ties have grown stronger over the years. They reflect the growing interdependence between Malaysia and the Pacific economy. The market penetration analysis has produced results which are quite consistent

with the intra-industry trade indices and trade intensity indices presented earlier.

Constant Market Share Analysis

Malaysian trade performance may be evaluated further by resorting to
the constant market share (CMS) analysis.[4] According to this measure,
the proportionate increase in exports over time comprises a number of
effects: (a) standard growth effect, (b) commodity composition effect,
(c) market distribution effect, and (d) a residual effect which may be
termed 'competitiveness' (see Appendix 4). In other words, the increase
in exports can be 'explained' in terms of four factors: the general growth
of world exports to the focus destination; the commodity mix of exports
and differential growth in import demand; the extent to which the particular market represents growing centres of demand; and finally a
residual term which captures the net gain or loss in the market shares
presumably due to changes in the relative price and/or quality of the
product, not to mention the marketing effort and skills of the exporters.

Before turning to the results of the CMS analysis in the Malaysian
context, it is necessary to say a little more about the way in which the
estimates are computed and to emphasize the need to exercise some
caution in interpreting the results. The estimates of each of the above-
mentioned effects depend on the 'standard' against which the focus
country's exports to the focus destination is to be matched. This study
has used the world standard, assuming that the commodity composition
of world exports bears a reasonably good relationship to that of the
focus exporter.

A positive commodity composition term would indicate that the focus
exporter's commodity composition consists mainly of those goods for
which import growth has been particularly strong in the focus destination. Likewise, a positive market distribution term would suggest that the
focus exporter's market distribution in the focus destination concentrates mainly on the most rapidly growing centres. The market distribution effect, however, is relevant only where the focus destination refers
to a region or a group of countries, like the East Asian NIEs or ASEAN.
These two effects depend on the composition/distribution of the focus
exports in the base year, which means that subsequent changes during
the interval of investigation are not taken into account. To minimize this
problem, the period 1970–87 has been divided into four sub-periods,
for the shorter the interval of investigation, the smaller the distortion
caused by the base-year pattern.

A positive residual term may be interpreted as a net gain in the focus
exporter's market share in the focus destination after all other effects
have been accounted for. It is assumed that a net gain or loss can only
be caused by changes in the relative prices of the focus exporter's product. Thus, a positive residual term is taken as a sign of competitive
strength, while a negative one is taken to indicate weakness. This interpretation is not entirely satisfactory, especially since trade values and not

volumes are used in the computation and no allowance is made for changes in discriminatory non-price trade policy. In other words, it would be incorrect to attribute the 'residual' to changes in relative prices *per se*, especially if the elasticity of substitution between the focus country's exports and those of its competitors is below unity. While the reader is thus urged to interpret the results with some caution, there is little doubt that the residual term does serve as a useful general index of export performance.

Table 3.17 presents the results of the CMS analysis for selected export markets. As noted earlier, the market distribution effect does not apply to single-country markets. It can be seen from the table that export growth, which has been decelerating over the years, is largely explained in terms of either the trend factor (standard growth) or

TABLE 3.17

CMS Analysis of Malaysian Manufactured Exports to
Selected Asia–Pacific Countries, 1970–1987

Exports to	Export Growth	Standard Growth	Commodity Composition	Competitiveness (Residual)
USA				
1970–5	11.39	0.94	−0.14	10.59
1975–80	3.35	1.49	0.81	1.05
1980–5	1.16	0.96	0.04	0.15
1985–7	0.50	0.36	0.16	−0.01
Japan				
1970–5	6.41	1.14	1.20	4.08
1975–80	1.74	1.70	−0.10	0.15
1980–5	1.06	0.32	−0.02	0.76
1985–7	0.33	0.69	−0.04	−0.32
Canada				
1970–5	8.47	1.46	0.97	6.04
1975–80	0.87	0.52	−.08	0.43
1980–5	1.58	0.52	−.09	1.15
1985–7	0.82	0.34	0.02	0.46
Australia				
1970–5	10.03	1.24	2.94	5.85
1975–80	1.17	1.00	−0.08	0.26
1980–5	0.48	0.35	−0.08	0.21
1985–7	0.39	0.14	0.10	0.15
New Zealand				
1970–5	7.28	1.47	9.40	−3.59
1975–80	3.82	0.52	−0.17	3.48
1980–5	−0.55	0.16	0.02	−0.73
1985–7	0.72	0.29	−0.04	0.48

Source: International Economic Data Bank, Australia National University, Canberra.

increased competitiveness. Commodity composition does not seem to have any major bearing on the results. The competitive strength of the Malaysian manufactured exports, especially in the markets of the United States, Japan, Canada, and Australia, is reflected in the positive values of the residual term. It, however, appears that Malaysian manufactured exports have become increasingly less competitive over the years, especially in the US and Australian markets.

The results of the CMS analysis on the markets of the East Asian NIEs and ASEAN are presented in Table 3.18. As was seen earlier, the market distribution effect does apply in regional markets. However, market distribution seems to have exerted a small, frequently negative, effect in the East Asian NIEs. This suggests that the Malaysian manufactured exports to these countries are not particularly concentrated in the fastest-growing market among the NIEs. In the ASEAN market, however, the reverse seems to be the case with positive, albeit weak, market distribution effects. The standard growth effect accounts for about one-half of export growth in the market of the East Asian NIEs and the bulk of the export expansion in that of the ASEAN. It should also be noted that the commodity composition effect is of some importance. The residual term is very revealing: the Malaysian manufactured exports to the NIE destinations appear to be competitive except in the first half of the 1980s, while competitiveness accounts for a significant proportion of Malaysia's export expansion in the ASEAN market in the 1980s.

The CMS analysis, when applied to the imports of Malaysia from the major Asia–Pacific sources, yields interesting results which are reported in Table 3.19. The imports from the United States are not competitive in the Malaysian market as shown by the negative residual term after

TABLE 3.18

CMS Analysis of Malaysian Manufactured Exports to the East Asian NIEs and ASEAN, 1970–1987

Exports to	Export Growth	Standard Growth	Commodity Composition	Market Distribution	Competitiveness (Residual)
NIEs[1]					
1970–5	2.93	1.68	0.23	−0.22	1.24
1975–80	6.97	2.13	0.51	0.23	4.10
1980–5	0.25	0.38	0.22	−0.04	−0.32
1985–7	1.66	0.78	0.04	−0.07	0.91
ASEAN[2]					
1970–5	2.54	2.28	0.23	0.04	−0.00
1975–80	1.58	1.68	0.19	0.13	−0.42
1980–5	0.79	−0.02	0.23	0.03	0.55
1985–7	0.73	0.36	−0.04	0.14	0.26

Source: International Economic Data Bank, Australian National University, Canberra.
[1]Hong Kong, Korea, and Taiwan.
[2]Indonesia, the Philippines, Singapore, and Thailand.

1975. The growth of imports from the United States is largely explained
by the standard growth and commodity composition factors. In the case
of imports from Japan, neither commodity composition nor competitiveness seems important. The CMS analysis has produced negative values

TABLE 3.19
CMS Analysis of Asia–Pacific Manufactured Exports to Malaysia,
1970–1987

Imports from	Export Growth	Standard Growth	Commodity Composition	Competitiveness (Residual)
USA				
1970–5	5.78	1.96	0.36	3.46
1975–80	2.62	5.45	−0.33	−2.51
1980–5	0.18	0.13	0.17	−0.12
1985–7	0.31	0.17	0.33	−0.20
Japan				
1980–5	0.07	0.13	−0.11	0.05
1985–7	−0.02	0.17	−0.09	−0.11
Canada				
1970–5	0.82	1.96	−0.12	−1.02
1975–80	1.74	5.45	1.86	−5.58
1980–5	2.04	0.13	−0.00	1.91
1985–7	−0.52	0.17	−0.36	−0.34
Australia				
1970–5	1.02	1.96	0.14	−1.08
1975–80	1.03	5.45	1.35	−5.78
1980–5	0.26	0.13	0.24	−0.11
1985–7	−0.37	0.17	−0.34	−0.21
New Zealand				
1970–5	1.52	1.96	−0.05	−0.38
1975–80	8.57	5.45	0.32	2.80
1980–5	−0.36	0.13	0.04	−0.53
1985–7	−0.12	0.17	0.05	−0.34
NIEs[1]				
1970–5	6.93	1.96	−0.73	5.70
1975–80	3.94	5.45	0.25	−1.77
1980–5	0.68	0.13	−0.12	0.67
1985–7	0.21	0.17	−0.36	0.39
ASEAN[2]				
1970–5	11.77	1.96	−0.08	9.89
1975–80	180.38	5.45	0.42	174.51
1980–5	0.23	0.13	0.07	0.03
1985–7	0.35	0.17	0.04	0.14

Source: International Economic Data Bank, Australian National University, Canberra.
[1]Hong Kong, Korea, and Taiwan.
[2]Indonesia, the Philippines, Singapore, and Thailand.

for the residual term in all four sub-periods for Australia, which suggests that the Australian products are uncompetitive in the Malaysian market. The imports from the East Asian NIEs have been highly competitive in the early 1970s and in the 1980s, as the residual term accounts for the bulk of their growth. The imports from ASEAN partners also appear to be fairly competitive. Commodity composition has had a negative impact on the imports from the East Asian NIEs, meaning that their products represent items for which demand was not rising rapidly. In the case of the imports from ASEAN, commodity composition seems to have had little effect, which suggests that the imports do not represent products which are in particularly great demand.

The CMS results provide general confirmation of the creditable export performance of Malaysia in the Asia–Pacific markets. The limitations of the CMS methodology notwithstanding, increased competitiveness of Malaysian exports seems manifest, although its importance as a major explanatory factor appears to have dwindled in later years. In contrast, the imports from the Asia–Pacific region do not appear to be competitive in the Malaysian market except for those from the East Asian NIEs and ASEAN.

Revealed Comparative Advantage

According to traditional trade theory, a country is better off if it specializes in the production of goods which it can produce relatively cheaply given its factor endowments, and trades with the rest of the world rather than going it alone and remaining an autarky. Although the theory is wanting in many respects, it has not lost its intellectual appeal. The principle of comparative advantage makes considerable sense to those concerned with allocative efficiency, although what constitutes comparative advantage and what contributes to it are subject to debate. None the less, the factor endowment hypothesis exhibits considerable robustness with respect to both inter-industry and intra-industry trade (Ethier, 1982).

It is now widely recognized that the comparative advantage of a country is by no means static in a dynamic world. It is subject to changes in response to such changes as shifts in resource and factor endowments, technology, and demand. Experience has shown that it is not unusual for a country to lose its comparative advantage in certain lines of production over time or to develop competitive advantage in an entirely new set of products (Porter, 1989). In industrial countries, several industries have exhibited distinct product cycles which have resulted in the international relocation of the labour-intensive and standardized production phases.[5] Malaysia has benefited from such industrial restructuring in the developed countries of the Pacific and the East Asian NIEs to the extent that its factor and resource endowments match the factor intensities of the migrating industries.

Needless to say, international shifts in comparative advantage constitute so complex a phenomenon that no single explanation is adequate.

There are so many forces at work that no simple two-factor model would suffice. These include the role of factor movements, human capital, natural resources, infrastructures, technology transfers and reversals, and research and development. In this section, an attempt is made to detect shifts in the comparative advantage of Malaysian manufactures, using standard methodologies.

In theory, comparative advantage is essentially related to pre-trade relative prices, whereas in empirical research one has to improvise with post-trade data. This difficulty was largely responsible for the emergence of the concept of 'revealed comparative advantage' (RCA) in empirical research (Balassa, 1965), which assumes that relative costs as well as differences in non-price factors are reflected in the observed pattern of commodity trade. To be sure, no single satisfactory measure of RCA is readily available, although several indicators of RCA are found in the current literature. In what follows, three RCA indicators are used to capture changes in the comparative advantage of Malaysian manufactures. These are (a) the ratio of net exports to total trade, (b) the export performance ratio, and (c) the export specialization ratio. The computations are based on Malaysia's world exports and world imports and no attempt is made to separate out exports to and imports from the Asia–Pacific, for no meaningful insights about the country's comparative advantage in manufactures can be gleaned from a partial picture. Besides, the exclusion of non-Pacific export destinations and import sources would not make much difference to the analysis, as commodity composition is basically the same regardless of destination or source.

The Net Export Ratio

Changes in the ratio of net exports (exports minus imports) to total trade (exports plus imports) at a fairly disaggregated level can provide rough insights into a country's shifting pattern of comparative advantage. This measure (nx_{ij}) expresses net exports of product j as a percentage of total trade in product j for country i.[6] This measure yields negative figures in the case of net imports, and the ratios can theoretically range between −100 (where a product is imported but not exported) to +100 (where a product is exported but not imported). Although the positive sign does not necessarily indicate revealed comparative advantage (nor the negative sign, for that matter, revealed comparative disadvantage), an increase in the ratio may be taken as a likely indication of some strengthening of comparative advantage.

Malaysia's net manufactured export ratios for the period 1970–86 are presented in Table 3.20 at the two-digit ISIC level. The main conclusion is that the country's RCA in manufacturing has improved significantly, especially in the 1980s. Malaysia is nearly a net exporter of manufactures. Of greater importance are the changes in the ratio for various commodity groups. Textiles and wearing apparel (ISIC 32) exhibit a strong turnaround from −76.3 per cent in 1970 to +20.0 per cent in 1986. Similarly, fabricated metal products, machinery, and

TABLE 3.20

Malaysia: Net Manufactured Exports as Percentage of
Total Trade, 1970–1986

ISIC	Product Category	1970	1975	1980	1984	1985	1986
3	Manufacturing	−19.6	−12.8	−19.1	−17.0	−14.2	−8.9
31	Food, beverages, and tobacco	−18.1	24.8	32.9	48.7	45.7	39.5
32	Textiles, wearing apparel, and leather	−76.3	−30.1	0.5	2.6	14.4	20.0
33	Wood and wood products	87.1	87.9	88.8	83.2	84.7	89.5
34	Paper, paper products, and printing	−81.2	−87.4	−88.8	−84.3	−85.1	−81.8
35	Chemicals and chemical products	−34.9	−34.6	−72.0	−47.2	−52.0	−48.8
36	Non-metal mineral products	−55.1	−71.4	−71.9	−63.0	−55.7	−27.6
37	Basic metal industries	58.7	38.0	16.1	−25.6	−2.1	−22.7
38	Fabricated metal products, machinery, and equipment	−84.7	−63.0	−47.6	−36.0	−31.1	−17.4
39	Other manufactures	−76.2	−61.6	−28.2	−43.7	−19.4	−16.6

Source: International Economic Data Bank, Australian National University, Canberra.

equipment (ISIC 38) display a significant improvement with the ratios
falling consistently from −84.7 per cent to −17.4 per cent between 1970
and 1986. The ratios are large and positive for wood and wood products
(ISIC 33), showing a strengthening of the RCA, especially in the later
years. It appears that Malaysia has developed an RCA in food, beverages, and tobacco (ISIC 31), although the comparative advantage seems
to have weakened a little since 1985. The product groups with
conspicuous revealed comparative disadvantage are paper and paper
products and printing (ISIC 34) and chemicals and chemical products
(ISIC 35).

These results are reasonably consistent with those of the earlier computations in the preceding analysis and may well be explained in terms
of the country's resource and factor endowments: Malaysia's comparative advantage apparently lies in resource-intensive and labour-
intensive manufactures. A word of caution, however, is in order in
interpreting the net export ratios. The ratios are affected by the level of
aggregation. Even at the two-digit level, the ratios can conceal a lot of
interesting variations and deviations. In addition, the ability of this
measure to 'reveal' the shifts in the country's comparative advantage
pattern is affected by the structure of protection in the export markets
(which distorts exports) and that at home (which distorts imports).

These caveats notwithstanding, the net export ratios do serve as a useful tool of analysis, especially when used in conjunction with other RCA indicators.

Export Performance Ratio

Another RCA measure found in the literature is what has been termed the 'export performance ratio'. This measure (ep_{ij}) expresses the share of country i's export of product j in total world exports of product j, as a ratio to the share of country i's total exports of manufactures in the world total exports of manufactures.[7] An export performance ratio of unity would imply 'normal' export performance of product j relative to the size of country i as an exporter, while a ratio of 2 would suggest that the product j's share in country i's exports is twice the corresponding world share, and so on. Although the ratio in theory can range from zero to infinity, large numbers beyond two digits are uncommon for obvious reasons.

As this measure does not require import data, unlike the net export ratio, the results are less distorted by policy interventions. An export performance ratio of more than unity is usually taken as an indication of comparative advantage, while an increase in the ratio supposedly suggests a strengthening of the comparative advantage so revealed.

Export performance ratios for Malaysia are presented in Table 3.21. As the data reported are at the three-digit SITC level and in view of the large number of categories within manufacturing, the table contains only the more significant results. In interpreting the data, one must bear in mind that the ratio, in effect, standardizes for a country's share of world manufactures. Thus, low figures are not attributable to the country's small aggregate manufactured exports, but rather to the export performance of the particular product world-wide.

It will be useful to focus attention on those commodities which are of importance in Malaysia's export drive. Resource-based and labour-intensive manufactures account for most product groups with an export performance ratio of more than unity. Rubber materials (SITC 621), wood products (SITC 631 and 632), and pig iron and iron and steel shapes (SITC 671 and 673) are the outstanding ones among the resource-based manufactures. In the labour-intensive category, textiles (SITC 65) are an important group. The more capital-intensive stage of textile production, i.e. yarn and thread (SITC 651), has recorded a lower ratio, while the more labour-intensive process, i.e. woven cotton fabric (SITC 652), has a much larger ratio. Non-fur clothing (SITC 841) also has a significantly large export performance ratio. The very large increase in the ratio for electrical machinery (SITC 729) exports reflects the importance of labour-intensive operations within the FTZs. Toys and sporting goods (SITC 894) have also assumed greater importance in recent years. Among what may be labelled technology-intensive, electrical power machinery (SITC 722) and telecommunications equipment (SITC 724) have quite large export performance ratios.

TABLE 3.21
Malaysian Manufactures: Export Performance Ratio, 1970–1987

SITC	Commodity	1970	1975	1980	1985	1987
553	Perfume, cosmetics, etc.	1.7	1.9	0.7	0.8	0.6
554	Soaps, cleaning preparations	7.8	2.2	1.1	0.9	1.1
561	Fertilizers	0.6	0.2	0.1	0.1	0.9
599	Chemicals n.e.s.	0.5	0.6	0.6	0.7	0.8
621	Materials of rubber	14.4	5.2	5.2	4.1	4.2
629	Rubber articles n.e.s.	2.2	1.7	0.7	0.6	0.8
631	Veneers, plywood, etc.	33.4	23.0	14.8	7.1	9.7
632	Wood manufactures n.e.s.	14.1	5.4	3.9	2.3	1.8
642	Articles of paper, etc.	2.4	0.7	0.4	0.5	0.7
651	Textile, yarn, and thread	0.4	0.6	0.8	0.6	0.5
652	Cotton fabrics, woven	2.5	3.7	2.6	1.7	1.4
653	Woven articles, non-cotton	0.3	0.3	2.1	1.3	0.9
661	Cement, etc., building products	11.8	1.2	0.5	0.9	1.4
664	Glass	0.2	0.6	0.5	0.4	0.7
665	Glassware	0.8	0.7	0.7	1.0	0.7
666	Pottery	0.5	0.2	0.3	1.1	1.0
671	Pig iron, etc.	0.0	0.0	0.1	1.8	2.8
673	Iron and steel shapes	0.2	0.1	0.0	0.2	1 2
692	Metal tanks, boxes, etc.	4.3	2.4	1.6	1.2	0.9
722	Electrical power machinery, etc.	0.4	5.9	1.6	1.4	1.4
724	Telecommunications equipment	0.3	1.1	1.4	2.8	3.5
725	Domestic electrical equipment	0.2	0.4	0.3	0.6	0.8
729	Electrical machinery n.e.s.	0.6	0.8	11.7	9.6	7.9
735	Ships and boats	0.0	0.1	0.0	1.8	2.3
841	Clothing not of fur	1.4	2.0	1.8	2.0	1.9
851	Footwear	1.2	2.1	1.5	0.4	0.4
861	Instruments, apparatus	0.4	10.7	0.5	0.7	0.6
864	Watches and clocks	0.1	0.7	2.3	0.5	0.7
891	Sound recorders, etc.	0.6	0.6	0.4	0.4	0.6
893	Articles of plastic n.e.s.	0.5	1.2	1.2	0.7	0.7

TABLE 3.21 (*continued*)

SITC	Commodity	1970	1975	1980	1985	1987
894	Toys, sporting goods, etc.	0.2	0.2	0.2	1.2	1.1
895	Office supplies n.e.s.	1.2	1.2	0.5	0.5	1.3
897	Gold, silverware, jewellery	1.1	1.1	0.9	0.6	1.4

Source: International Economic Data Bank, Australian National University, Canberra.
n.e.s. = Not elsewhere specified.

Products with very weak revealed comparative advantage are numerous and are not reported here. However, Malaysia appears to be losing its comparative advantage in several products including metal tanks and boxes (SITC 692) and footwear (SITC 851), as shown by the declining export performance ratios in Table 3.21.

Export Specialization Ratio

A more commonly used measure of RCA is the export specialization ratio which was introduced by Balassa (1965). This measure (es_{ij}) is based on the ratio of the share of a commodity in the total merchandise exports of a country to the commodity's share in world merchandise exports.[8] In effect, the formula is simply a rearrangement of the terms used in the case of the export performance ratio.[9] In other words, the present measure yields ratios with respect to total merchandise exports rather than to manufactured exports, although the results do not differ substantially.

To be sure, the export specialization ratio, like the export performance ratio, must be used cautiously as an RCA measure (Bowen, 1983). Nevertheless, its intuitive appeal as an RCA index is clear, especially since it obviates the need for import data, as in the case of the export performance ratio. An index exceeding unity, or one which is increasing, is taken as an indication of revealed comparative advantage.

The results are given in Table 3.22 using the same three-digit SITC commodity groups as in Table 3.21. The findings are in conformity with the earlier conclusions based on the previous table, showing generally strong and growing specialization in resource-based and labour-intensive manufactures. This may be seen as evidence of the inherent comparative advantage based on resource and factor endowments, or as a reflection of the effects of policy interventions to facilitate the export of those goods with large RCA indices.

It will be useful to classify manufactures formally into meaningful groups based on resource and factor intensity and then compute the RCA indices for these commodity groups. Industrial classification, however, presents problems. One such classification widely used in empirical

TABLE 3.22
Malaysian Manufactures: Export Specialization Ratio, 1970–1987

SITC	Commodity	1970	1975	1980	1985	1987
553	Perfume, cosmetics, etc.	0.2	0.6	0.2	0.3	0.3
554	Soaps, cleaning preparations	0.9	0.7	0.4	0.4	0.6
561	Fertilizers	0.1	0.1	0.0	0.0	0.5
599	Chemicals n.e.s.	0.1	0.2	0.2	0.3	0.4
621	Materials of rubber	1.7	1.6	1.7	1.7	2.3
629	Rubber articles n.e.s.	0.1	0.5	0.2	0.2	0.4
631	Veneers, plywood, etc.	4.0	7.0	5.0	3.0	5.3
632	Wood manufactures n.e.s.	1.7	1.6	1.3	1.0	1.0
642	Articles of paper, etc.	0.3	0.2	0.2	0.2	0.4
651	Textile, yarn, and thread	0.1	0.2	0.3	0.3	0.3
652	Cotton fabrics, woven	0.3	1.1	0.9	0.7	0.8
653	Woven articles, non-cotton	0.0	0.1	0.7	0.6	0.5
661	Cement, etc., building products	1.4	0.4	0.2	0.4	0.7
664	Glass	0.0	0.2	0.2	0.2	0.4
665	Glassware	0.1	0.2	0.2	0.4	0.4
666	Pottery	0.1	0.1	0.1	0.5	0.6
671	Pig iron, etc.	0.0	0.0	0.0	0.8	1.5
673	Iron and steel shapes	0.0	0.0	0.0	0.1	0.7
692	Metal tanks, boxes, etc.	0.5	0.8	0.6	0.5	0.5
722	Electrical power machinery, etc.	0.0	1.8	0.5	0.6	0.7
724	Telecommunications equipment	0.0	0.3	0.5	1.2	1.9
725	Domestic electrical equipment	0.0	0.1	0.1	0.3	0.4
729	Electrical machinery n.e.s.	0.1	0.2	4.0	4.1	4.3
735	Ships and boats	0.0	0.0	0.0	0.8	1.2
841	Clothing not of fur	0.2	0.6	0.6	0.8	1.0
851	Footwear	0.1	0.6	0.5	0.2	0.2
861	Instruments, apparatus	0.0	3.2	0.2	0.3	0.3
864	Watches and clocks	0.0	0.2	0.8	0.2	0.4
891	Sound recorders, etc.	0.1	0.2	0.1	0.2	0.3
893	Articles of plastic n.e.s	0.1	0.4	0.4	0.3	0.4.

TABLE 3.22 (*continued*)

SITC	Commodity	1970	1975	1980	1985	1987
894	Toys, sporting goods, etc.	0.0	0.1	0.1	0.5	0.6
895	Office supplies n.e.s.	0.1	0.4	0.2	0.2	0.7
897	Gold, silverware, jewellery	0.1	0.3	0.3	0.3	0.8

Source: International Economic Data Bank, Australian National University, Canberra.
n.e.s. = Not elsewhere specified.

studies is a ranking based on the United States per capita value-added in manufacturing, first developed systematically by Lary (1968). A major limitation of this classification for the present purpose is that it fails to identify resource-based goods which are of importance in the Malaysian case. Another classification developed subsequently by Krause (1982) is essentially a modification of the Lary-type classification, categorizing commodities into four broad groups according to the dominant factor input: natural resource, unskilled labour, technology, and human capital. In the Krause classification, labour intensity is measured on the basis of the US data relating to per capita value-added, while technology intensity is gauged using the US research and development expenditure data. A further modification by Tyers and Phillips (1984) splits resource goods into agriculture and mineral resource-intensive goods. In the analysis below, a five-tier commodity classification following Tyers and Phillips has been adopted.

Before examining the results of the factor intensity RCA analysis, it is appropriate to say a little more about the logic behind the manner in which manufactures are classified within the framework described above. No separate classification for physical capital-intensive goods is made on the grounds that internationally mobile physical capital is no longer an important determinant of a country's comparative advantage, especially where liberal foreign investment policies are pursued, as in the case of Malaysia. One may argue that resources and technology are also internationally mobile and that their production is not location-specific. But, then, many primary products require processing on-site as such processing often yields substantial economies. In the case of technology-intensive goods, the international relocation of production is often impeded by a lack of basic technical competence in the host country and the absence of adequate intellectual property protection.

Although the classification is generally transferable across countries, there are some activities whose production characteristics differ sharply between countries. Such differences are marked especially between developed and developing countries, exacerbated by the phenomenon of

TABLE 3.23

Malaysia: Export Specialization Ratio (RCA) by Commodity
Group According to Factor Intensity, 1970–1987

Commodity Classification	1970	1975	1980	1985	1987
Agricultural resource-intensive	16.06	9.73	6.22	2.87	3.57
Mineral resource-intensive	1.69	0.35	0.20	0.63	0.77
Unskilled labour-intensive	1.09	0.96	2.52	2.49	2.18
Technology-intensive	0.47	1.34	0.40	0.44	0.41
Human capital-intensive	0.77	0.40	0.36	0.45	0.59

Source: International Economic Data Bank, Australian National University, Canberra.

factor intensity reversals. Thus, what is classified as an unskilled labour-intensive activity in one country may well be technology-intensive in another. There is, therefore, a need to devise a country-specific classification. In this study, export products are grouped under various resource/factor intensity categories as shown in Appendix 5.[10]

The results, reported in Table 3.23, confirm our earlier notions regarding the revealed comparative advantage of the Malaysian manufactured exports. It appears that Malaysia has an overwhelmingly high RCA in agricultural resource-intensive and unskilled labour-intensive manufactures. It is interesting to observe some improvements in human capital- and mineral resource-intensive manufactures in the 1980s, which is not surprising in view of Malaysia's new-found oil and gas related manufacturing activities and the recent policy emphasis on the upgrading of labour skills. Another pertinent observation is that the RCA index for unskilled labour-intensive products has been declining.

Obviously, these results are affected by the ways in which various manufactures are grouped. The picture would not have been the same, had the manufactures been allocated differently under the various headings. This is indeed the case if one compares the RCA indices produced here with the figures presented in Chapter 5, where some international comparisons are made. To facilitate international comparisons, a standard classification has to be used for all countries. The RCA figures in question are based on the Krause classification. Since electrical/electronic manufactures are considered technology-intensive in the Krause framework, and as unskilled labour-intensive (since the bulk of it is really assembly operation) in the preceding computations, Figure 5.4 tends to understate Malaysia's RCA in unskilled labour-intensive manufactures, while Figure 5.5 tends to overstate Malaysia's RCA of technology-intensive goods. All this only serves to drive home the point that inter-country and inter-commodity comparisons are not easy.

Critical Issues

Trade is the life-blood of the Malaysian economy. The fortunes of
Malaysia are closely tied to that of the global economy through trade,
since Malaysia owes its prosperity in no small measure to its thriving
trade transactions with the rest of the world. While trade is thus a bless-
ing to Malaysia, it has not been without a price. A high ratio of trade to
GNP has meant a high degree of exposure to external influences. The
Malaysian economy has been very vulnerable to external fluctuations.
The accent placed on international trade has also led to a high level of
export specialization consistent with the principle of dynamic comparative advantage. This has not only meant that the country has had to
shoulder greater risks but has also warranted rapid structural changes
and adjustments at home in the face of the changing international
environment. In addition, Malaysia has to cope with protectionism in
developed-country markets and to deal with bilateral trade issues and
friction *vis-à-vis* its major trading partners. In what follows, an effort is
made to discuss these and other related issues in the Pacific context.

External Instability and Export Specialization

In the 1950s and 1960s, the Malaysian economy was extremely prone to
externally induced fluctuations, caused by highly volatile prices of primary commodity exports (Ariff, 1972). *Ceteris paribus,* the more specialized the external sector, the greater the risks associated with export
instability. As was seen in Chapter 2, the profile of the Malaysian economy has changed dramatically, especially in the 1970s and 1980s, and
in the process the economy has become diversified to a considerable
extent so that it is no longer precariously dependent on a few primary
commodities. However, the Malaysian experience has shown that while
diversification can help stabilize export earnings to the extent that commodity prices move in a neutralizing fashion, it does not guarantee stability in export proceeds as prices sometimes do move in an additive
manner, as was indeed the case in 1985 when the prices of almost all
commodities tumbled together, causing an absolute reduction in
Malaysia's GDP.

None the less, it does appear that the Malaysian economy is relatively
less susceptible to external fluctuations now than it was in the 1950s or
1960s, mainly owing to the emergence of a fairly resilient domestic
sector. As was observed in Chapter 2, the strong recovery of the
Malaysian economy in 1987 and 1988 was due in no small measure to
an expansion of the domestic sector.

The macroeconomic analysis in Chapter 2 has shown that the
Malaysian macroeconomic indicators tend to move with those of its
major trading partners. The issue is not whether such a macroeconomic
behavioural pattern is good or bad, but rather, whether it is a price
worth paying. Of course, it is harder to manage an economy that is
heavily influenced by exogenous factors than one which is completely
closed. The welfare implications of the two economies are obviously

very different. The fact, however, remains that Malaysia has opted for an open economy, and, having chosen this option, has tried to minimize the adverse effects of external variables on the domestic economy. Through the process of learning by doing, the Malaysian policy-makers and technocrats seem to have developed certain skills that can help ameliorate externally induced cyclical movements.

The adverse effects of export instability on the domestic economy are often exaggerated. Even in the 1950s and 1960s when the Malaysian economy was heavily dependent on a narrow range of primary commodities, the domestic economy remained relatively stable, thanks mainly to substantial external reserves which absorbed many of the external shocks (Ariff, 1972). The present situation is, however, different: on the one hand, the export sector is now relatively broad-based with manufactured exports accounting for a growing share of the total, and on the other hand, the size of external reserves in relation to imports has shrunk significantly.[11] This means that shocks felt in the export sector are now more readily transmitted to the rest of the economy, but the amplitude of fluctuations itself is moderated to some extent by the broad base.

It is incorrect to place the blame for the deep recession which Malaysia experienced in the mid-1980s on external factors alone. It appears, in retrospect, that the mismanagement of the economy in general, and the financial sector in particular, was partly responsible for the painful contraction the Malaysian economy went through. Had resources not been locked up in heavy industries and dissipated in non-viable projects undertaken by public enterprises, one might indeed argue, the recession of the mid-1980s would have been much milder and less painful. The recession nevertheless served a useful purpose in that it provided valuable lessons for policy-makers.

The fact that the Malaysian economy is integrating itself increasingly with the Pacific economy implies that the Malaysian policy-makers must attach more weight to the Pacific variables by factoring them into their policy formulations. Many of the problems discussed here can be better resolved through consultation and exchange of information with the trading partners.

Malaysia's new-found comparative advantage in manufactured exports presents problems of a different sort. It was thought that specialization in manufactures would render the economy more stable, since manufactures, unlike primary commodities, are thought not to be prone to price fluctuations. However, the Malaysian experience in the mid-1980s shows that manufactures are by no means immune to ups and downs. A case in point was the electronics subsector which resorted to severe cut-backs in production and massive retrenchment of workers in the wake of a slack in international demand for semiconductors.

Another source of concern is the narrow range of manufactured products exported, with a heavy concentration on electrical and electronic goods, and textiles, clothing, and footwear. The combined share of these products in total manufactured exports had risen from 59.6 per cent in

1980 to 62.7 per cent in 1988. The share of electrical and electronic goods alone increased from 46.4 per cent to 51.8 per cent between 1980 and 1988 (see Table 2.6). However, it is encouraging to note that the share of 'other manufactures' increased from 7.3 per cent in 1980 to 10.4 per cent in 1988, which suggests that some diversification has been taking place at least in the periphery.

International Competitiveness

The RCA analysis above has suggested that Malaysia's comparative advantage really lies not in labour-intensive manufactures but in natural resource-intensive manufacturing activities, while the CMS analysis casts doubts about Malaysia's competitiveness in several products. The production of primary exports is also subject to intense competition from rival producers and from substitutes. Thus, Malaysia has lost its leading position in tin to Brazil, and may lose its lead in natural rubber to Indonesia. Likewise, Malaysia's stake in palm oil is threatened by increased palm-oil production in the neighbouring countries and by substitutes such as soyabean oil.

Malaysian primary commodities being very labour-intensive, rising labour costs have blunted their competitive edge *vis-à-vis* rivals in the region. Malaysia has responded to this situation by allowing immigrant workers—mostly illegal—to work in rubber and oil-palm plantations at low wages in an attempt to maintain its competitiveness in the international market. While this might make some sense as a short-term or stop-gap measure, its implications have not been fully understood. One might seriously question the economic wisdom of such a move, although it is of great benefit to immigrant workers. For one thing, it is no more than an archaic solution in the sense that it amounts to a re-enactment of the British 'cheap labour' policy of the colonial days. For another, it impedes structural adjustments and labour-saving technological innovations which would otherwise have taken place.

As regards manufactured exports, available evidence clearly suggests that Malaysia does not really have a comparative advantage in labour-intensive activities. Malaysia has a relatively small population base with a fairly high standard of living in the region, with wages apparently pegged to the living standard. In recent years, real wages have been rising faster than labour productivity in Malaysia, especially in the manufacturing industry (Figure 3.1).

It is not the real wage *per se*, but the relationship between the real wage and labour productivity that is relevant as a determinant of competitiveness. Seen in these terms, Figure 3.1 reflects a loss of competitiveness for Malaysian manufactures. Of course, wages have been rising faster than productivity in other countries in the Western Pacific, too, but they have been able to hold down unit labour costs in terms of US dollars through aggressive devaluations, whereas in Malaysia, the rise in unit labour cost was aggravated by exchange rate policy until

FIGURE 3.1
Malaysia: Real Wage and Labour Productivity
(1980 = 100)

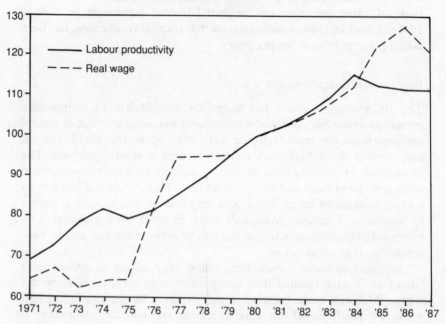

Manufacturing Industry (1980 = 100)

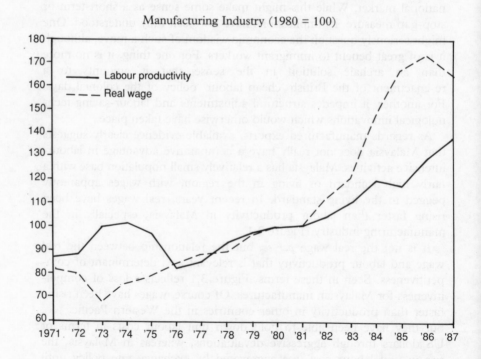

Source: World Bank (1989a).

FIGURE 3.2
International Competitiveness of Malaysia and Korea
Unit Labour Cost in Domestic Currency
(1980 = 100)

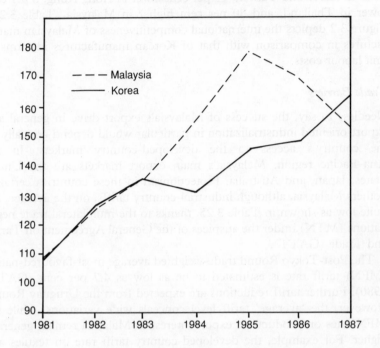

Unit Labour Cost in US$ (1980 = 100)

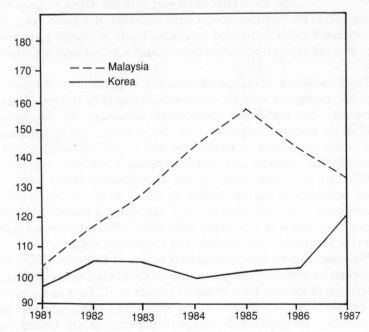

Source: World Bank (1989a).

recently, when the ringgit was allowed to depreciate sharply. A recent World Bank study (1989a) has shown that unit labour costs in manufacturing in US dollar terms were roughly level with their 1980 values in 1985 in Korea and Taiwan, 15 per cent lower in Hong Kong, 8 per cent lower in Thailand, and 50 per cent higher in Malaysia (Table 3.24). Figure 3.2 depicts the international competitiveness of Malaysian manufactures in comparison with that of Korean manufactures in terms of unit labour costs.

Trade Barriers

Needless to say, the success of Malaysia's export drive in general and export-oriented industrialization in particular would depend critically on the country's access to the developed-country markets. In the Asia–Pacific region, Malaysia's main export markets are the United States, Japan, and Australia. Protectionism in these countries certainly bothers Malaysia, although industrial-country tariffs, on the average, are quite low as shown in Table 3.25, thanks to the multilateral trade negotiations (MTN) under the auspices of the General Agreement on Tariffs and Trade (GATT).

The Post-Tokyo Round trade-weighted average most-favoured-nation (MFN) tariff rate is estimated to be as low as 4.7 per cent (GATT, 1980). Further tariff reductions are expected from the Uruguay Round. However, the 'average' tariff level conceals wide variations, while the MFN rates on products of export interest to Malaysia remain generally higher. For example, the developed-country tariff rate on textiles and clothing is nearly three times higher than that on manufactured goods as a whole. Worse still, tariff rates often vary with the degree of processing, giving rise to the phenomenon of tariff escalation that penalizes exports of processed and value-added products. Tariff escalation gives rise to high effective rates of protection even though nominal rates are relatively low.

Tariff escalation in industrial countries is particularly damaging to agro-processing and resource-based industrialization, in which Malaysia apparently has significant comparative advantage. In the Japanese market, for example, imports of logs are duty-free, while sawn timber and veneer are subject to 10 per cent and 15 per cent tariffs (after the quotas are fully utilized) and plywood imports are subject to 20 per cent tariff. Even more frustrating are the discriminatory tariffs imposed in some countries favouring similar products from developed-country counterparts. Thus, for example, in Japan, tropical hardwood plywood imports face tariffs of 17–20 per cent, while softwood plywood (mostly from the temperate zone) is subject to 15 per cent tariff.

Malaysian exports encounter greater non-tariff barriers (NTBs) in the European Community and Japan than in the United States. In fact, the proportion of imports from Malaysia subject to NTBs is in the order of 39 per cent and 26 per cent in the European Community and Japan respectively, compared with that of 6 per cent in the United States (Table 3.26).

TABLE 3.24

Manufacturing Unit Labour Costs in East and South-East Asia, 1981–1987 (1980 = 100)

		1981	1982	1984	1985	1986	1987
(A)	*Unit Labour Cost in Domestic Currency*						
	Korea	108.1	126.2	131.2	145.4	147.8	163.0
	Taiwan	113.9	121.9	132.7	128.5	126.4	124.8
	Singapore	111.9	131.9	140.0	151.0	134.1	n.a.
	Hong Kong	108.8	130.7	116.0	132.0	127.4	n.a.
	Malaysia	109.7	125.3	154.8	178.3	169.9	153.9
	Thailand	110.8	109.9	114.9	121.4	n.a.	n.a.
(B)	*Exchange Rate (LC/US$)*						
	Korea	112.1	120.4	132.7	143.2	145.1	135.4
	Taiwan	102.3	108.6	109.9	110.6	105.0	88.4
	Singapore	98.7	99.9	99.6	102.8	101.7	n.a.
	Hong Kong	112.5	122.0	157.1	156.6	156.8	n.a.
	Malaysia	105.8	107.3	107.7	114.1	118.6	115.8
	Thailand	106.6	112.3	115.4	132.6	n.a.	n.a.
(C)	*Unit Labour Cost in US$ (A/B)*						
	Korea	96.4	104.8	98.9	101.5	101.9	120.4
	Taiwan	111.3	112.2	120.7	116.2	120.4	141.2
	Singapore	113.4	132.0	140.6	146.9	131.9	n.a.
	Hong Kong	96.8	107.1	73.8	84.3	81.3	n.a.
	Malaysia	103.6	116.8	143.8	156.3	143.3	132.9
	Thailand	104.0	97.9	99.6	91.6	n.a.	n.a.

Source: World Bank (1989a).

n.a. = Not available.

TABLE 3.25

Actual Level of Tariffs Faced by Malaysian Exports

SITC	Commodities	Japan			USA			EC		
		Pre-Tokyo	Post-Tokyo	Reduction (%)	Pre-Tokyo	Post-Tokyo	Reduction (%)	Pre-Tokyo	Post-Tokyo	Reduction (%)
851	Footwear	10.0	10.0	–	23.1	23.1	–	11.0	11.0	–
653	Woven textiles	5.0	5.0	–	21.0	20.6	1.9	15.7	10.8	31.2
841	Clothing	8.9	7.8	12.4	19.7	9.8	50.3	1.8	1.3	27.8
651	Textile, yarn, and thread	6.9	5.7	17.4	16.3	12.0	26.4	10.8	8.8	18.5
652	Cotton fabrics, woven	3.0	3.0	–	11.0	7.9	28.2	0.1	0.1	–
729	Electrical machinery, n.e.s	4.5	1.6	64.4	5.8	4.0	31.0	0.4	0.4	–
621	Materials of rubber	–	–	–	4.6	–	100.0	–	–	–
51/55	Fresh and preserved fruits and vegetables	19.7	16.8	14.7	2.9	1.0	65.5	14.7	14.7	–
631	Veneers, plywood, etc.	0.6	0.6	–	2.7	2.6	3.7	12.4	9.6	22.6
722	Electric power machine, switchgear	5.4	2.6	51.9	0.8	0.8	–	–	–	–
632	Wood manufactures	10.0	5.7	43.0	0.1	–	100.0	3.9	2.3	41.0
821	Furniture	10.1	4.8	52.5	0.1	0.1	–	–	–	–
741	Other machinery	–	–	–	–	–	–	13.7	11.7	14.6
241/243	Wood and cork	0.1	0.1	–	–	–	–	0.1	0.1	–
725	Domestic electrical equipment	–	–	–	–	0.1	–	–	–	–

Source: World Bank.

n.e.s. = Not elsewhere specified.

TABLE 3.26
Developed-Country Non-tariff Barriers against Imports from
Malaysia, 1984
(percentage share of imports subject to NTBs)

NTBs	Japan	USA	EC
Fiscal measures	1.6	0.1	20.8
Volume control measures	3.0	0.0	3.0
Import authorization	1.2	0.0	6.5
Control of price level	0.0	5.7	0.4
Technical barriers	23.5	0.0	0.0
All NTBs	26.2	5.8	38.7
Imports subject to NTBs			
(US$ million)	371.1	156.2	827.6
Total imports (US$ million)	1,414.0	2,682.1	2,139.8

Source: UNCTAD, Data Base on Trade Measures.

NTBs are far more formidable than tariffs, as they involve administrative discretion rather than open rules of protection. The most notori-
ous hardcore NTBs are quantitative import restrictions, voluntary
export restraints (VERs), and orderly marketing arrangements (OMAs).
Among the other infamous NTBs are tariff quotas and anti-dumping
and countervailing duties. Appendix 6 presents an illustrative list of
NTBs. Imports of steel and steel products have been subject to VERs in
the United States, as are motor vehicles imported into Canada and the
United States; and consumer electronics have increasingly succumbed to
VERs in these markets. In the Pacific region, Australia and the United
States often resort to anti-dumping measures.

Malaysia has not been a major target of hardcore non-tariff measures,
quite unlike the East Asian NIEs, primarily because Malaysia is a small
exporter of manufactures to developed countries. However, it is highly
unlikely that Malaysia will be spared, should it emerge as a major
exporter of manufactured goods in the future. Already, there are signs
that Malaysia has caught the attention of protectionist forces in industrial countries. Malaysia has entered into Multifibre Arrangements
(MFAs) with several developed countries including Canada and the
United States. MFAs have, of course, imposed limits on Malaysia's
textile and clothing exports. It, however, appears that export losses
through MFA restrictions have been more or less offset by quota rents.
Perhaps, the Malaysian textile industry would not have developed the
way it has, in the face of increasing labour costs and outmoded technology, had it not been for the MFAs. Malaysia seems to have
'benefited' from MFAs which have become more restrictive towards the
'dominant' exporters, some of whom have relocated their bases to
Malaysia to take advantage of its unfilled quotas. Malaysian exporters
would probably have found it difficult to compete with the more
efficient producers in the absence of prior allocation of quotas.

There are other considerations which strongly weigh against the MFA. The MFA has become increasingly pervasive in terms of coverage. Thus, the bilateral agreements under the current MFA IV (August 1986–July 1991) are detailed down to 7-digit SITC categories to such an extent that the exporters would find it extremely difficult to diversify their products. Besides, the annual quota expansion of 1 to 2 per cent provided for in the MFA agreements is low compared with the average annual rate of growth of the Malaysian textiles exports. The industry's exports are estimated to have more than doubled from M$711 million in 1981 to M$1.53 billion in 1990 and are projected to rise to M$2.99 billion by 1995.[12] The MFA restrictions may render such targets untenable.

The most damaging aspect of the MFA lies in its adverse long-term effects. It has given rise to rent-seeking among the established firms in the industry, while trade cartelization tends to prevent new entry. While it appears that the MFA has encouraged foreign investment in countries with unfilled quotas, it really impedes the process of dynamic comparative advantage by allowing high-wage Hong Kong, Korea, and Taiwan to maintain their position as major exporters of textiles and clothing, thanks to handsome rent revenues, in the absence of which they would have lost their competitiveness sooner to low-wage countries. But Malaysia is not a low-wage country, and herein lies the dilemma for Malaysia: it might lose out if the textile trade were to be liberalized and placed under the GATT rules.

Countervailing duty (CVD) represents a hardcore NTB with adverse implications for Malaysia. CVD actions against exporters have increased in recent years, taking advantage of the GATT provision which permits countervailing duty against manufacturing subsidies if they cause or threaten injury to the importing country. The US record in this respect is particularly distressing on two counts: (a) the number of US CVD initiations against developing countries was almost double that brought upon industrial countries during 1980–7, and (b) the average CVD rate imposed by the United States was substantially higher on developing-country exports compared with industrial-country exports during the same period (Hufbauer, 1989).

In 1988, the United States imposed a CVD of 17.7 per cent on Malaysia's steel wire rods, while several other products, including thermoplugs and welded carbon steel pipes and tubes, have been under CVD investigation. In 1985, Malaysian textile exports were threatened in the United States by countervailing duties which are imposed whenever the exporting country's subsidy on textiles and apparel exceeds the trigger point of 0.5 per cent. However, investigations by the US Department of Commerce showed that Malaysia's export subsidy was only of the order of 0.22 per cent for textiles and 0.27 per cent for apparel.[13] Without a doubt, CVD investigations are bothersome. The fact that many CVD investigations have yielded negative results warrants more discipline in initiating investigations which have only a nuisance value.

What is particularly disturbing is the manner in which the United

States has been taking unilateral action in recent times. A special case in point is the so-called Super-301 hit list which has identified 34 countries as 'unfair traders'. Malaysia is included in the list, presumably because it has been registering substantial bilateral trade surpluses with the United States year after year. The US authorities seem to think that the bilateral trade gap would have been narrower in the absence of 'unfair trade practices'. The American grouses include Malaysia's import licences, quantitative restrictions, copyright violations, and barriers to investments and services trade. Malaysia was, however, taken off the Super-301 blacklist in April 1991 in appreciation of its efforts to provide protection for intellectual property rights.

While Malaysia has reason to cry foul on all these, it has benefited from special and differential (S & D) treatment from developed countries through the generalized system of preferences (GSP). Malaysia's GSP exports amounted to over M\$2 billion a year during the period 1980–5.[14] This amounted, on the average, to 8.1 per cent of Malaysia's total annual exports. In the Pacific region, Japan and the United States are the two most important preference-giving countries. The latter accounts for about one-fifth of Malaysia's total GSP exports. In 1986, Malaysian exports to the United States totalled US\$188 million, placing Malaysia among the top fifteen beneficiaries of the scheme. However, Malaysia's GSP exports to Japan have been declining. During the period 1980–4, about one-tenth of Malaysia's exports to Japan came under the GSP scheme. The ratio declined sharply from 9.2 per cent in 1984 to only 3.8 per cent in 1985.

About 60 per cent of Malaysia's GSP exports belong to the agricultural category.[15] Palm oil accounted for about 40 per cent of Malaysia's GSP exports to Japan in 1984, with a preferential duty of 3 per cent which was subsequently abolished. The US scheme excludes palm oil but provides duty-free preferential treatment to palm-kernel oil. Malaysian manufactured exports have benefited less from the GSP than primary commodities. The former include electronic items, wood products, rubber products, cocoa products, and textiles and garments. However, not all of these products have enjoyed duty-free treatment. Thus, for example, sawn timber faces a 5 per cent GSP tariff rate in Japan, while plywood exports attract a GSP tariff rate of 9 per cent in the United States. Electronic components, which account for about 20 per cent of Malaysia's exports under the GSP, enjoy duty-free treatment in the United States (since these products are the exports of its own multinationals) under 807.00 and 806.30 of the Tariff Schedule of the United States (TSUS).[16]

The GSP stimulus appears to have dwindled as a result of the low quota ceilings and the stringent rules governing GSP exports. Japan has slammed both overall and individual ceilings on the use of GSP for many products, while the United States limits its GSP imports by applying the 'competitive need' rule.[17] Meanwhile, preferential margins have been eroded by MFN tariff cuts under the various GATT rounds of multilateral trade negotiations.

Malaysia has discovered that the GSP facility is not without cost. For instance, the US GSP scheme has been blurred by the inclusion of restrictive elements such as conditionality, reciprocity, and linkage of non-trade issues with GSP offers, all of which impose undue encumbrances on the beneficiary. It is clear that Malaysia cannot depend on the GSP for its export expansion. There is the danger of Malaysia being graduated out of the scheme altogether. It, however, appears that Malaysia can gain more through MFN tariff cuts than from the GSP facility in the long run, if its products are internationally competitive. A case in point is provided by the exports of palm oil and oil-palm products which have increased at a much faster pace outside the GSP scheme than those under the scheme.[18]

Reference may also be made to the dangers from within. Malaysia's exports have been hurt not only by protectionist forces in the major export markets but also by its own protectionist structure and exchange rate policies. As was seen in Chapter 2, Malaysia's system of protection has given rise to anti-export bias which, however, has been offset to a large extent by export incentives of sorts. It would make considerable sense if Malaysia removed the anti-export bias at the source by reducing or eliminating tariffs instead of introducing another set of distortions through export incentives. The structure of protection which was instituted during the import-substitution phase of industrialization seems irrelevant to the present phase of export orientation.

Malaysian exports were also adversely affected by the past exchange rate policy of pegging the external value of the ringgit to a basket of currencies known only to the Central Bank. The resulting overvaluation of the ringgit only served to render Malaysian manufacturers less competitive in the international market until the Central Bank decided in 1985 to let the ringgit depreciate and find its own level based on supply and demand. It appears in retrospect that the impressive performance of Malaysian manufactured exports in recent years was due in no small measure to the exchange rate corrections through the depreciation of the ringgit.

1. The intensity index of Malaysian exports to country (I^{x}_{ij}) is defined as:
$$I^{x}_{ij} = (X_{ij}/X_i)/[M_j/(M_w - M_i)]$$
   where X_{ij} =   Malaysia's exports to country j,
   X_i =   Malaysia's total exports to the world,
   M_j =   Country j's total imports from the world,
   M_w =   Total world imports,
   M_i =   Malaysia's total imports from the world.

2. The intensity index of Malaysian imports from country j (I^{M}_{ij}) is defined as:
$$I^{M}_{ij} = (M_{ij}/M_i)/[X_j/(X_w - X_i)]$$
   where M_{ij} =   Malaysia's imports from country j,
   M_i =   Malaysia's total imports from the world,
   X_j =   Country j's total exports to the world,
   X_w =   Total world exports,
   X_i =   Malaysia's total exports to the world.

3. Formally: $\dfrac{R-S}{R}$

where $R = \sum\limits_{k} (X^k_{ij} + M^k_{ij})$

$S = \sum\limits_{k} (X^k_{ij} - M^k_{ij})$

and X^k_{ij} = exports of industry i to country j of industry k.

M^k_{ij} = imports of industry i from country j of industry k.

4. The CMS analysis employed in this section is based on the methodology of Tyers and Phillips (1984), as adapted from Leamer and Stern (1970) and Richardson (1971).

5. See Vernon (1979) for an exposition of the product cycle theory.

6. UNIDO (1982) provides an empirical application of the measure. The ratio is defined formally as:

$$nx_{ij} = [(X_{ij} - M_{ij})/(X_{ij} + M_{ij})] \cdot 100$$

where X_{ij} = country i's exports of product j

M_{ij} = country i's imports of product j.

7. The ratio is expressed in formal terms as:

$$ep_{ij} = \dfrac{X_{ij}}{X_{wj}} \bigg/ \dfrac{X_{im}}{X_{wm}}$$

where X_{ij} = country i's export of product j

X_{wj} = world exports of product j

X_{im} = country i's total manufactured exports

X_{wm} = world total manufactured exports.

8. It is defined as:

$$es_{ij} = \dfrac{X_{ij}}{X_i} \bigg/ \dfrac{X_{wj}}{X_w}$$

where X_{ij} = country i's export of product j

X_i = country i's total merchandise exports

X_{wj} = world exports of product j

X_w = world total merchandise exports.

9. By equating X_1 and X_w in es_{ij} with X_{im} and X_{wm} in ep_{ij} (the differences occur only in respect of commodity coverage) and rearranging the terms in the two equations, the identity is clearly evident.

10. Another study by Ariff and Hill (1985) has used the same methodology.

11. In 1988, net external reserves were equivalent to 5.8 months of imports, whereas in 1970 the net reserves were sufficient to finance 7.2 months of imports.

12. Salih et al. (1988), Table III-2, p. 78.

13. See Ariff (1988), p. 20.

14. Salih et al. (1988), Table III-3, p. 81.

15. Ibid., Table III-4, p. 83.

16. TSUS 807.00 and 806.30 provide for duty-free re-entry into the United States of domestically produced components after they have been assembled abroad.

17. This means that a beneficiary will lose its GSP facility for a particular product if its exports to the United States exceed a certain arbitrarily fixed amount.

18. See Salih et al. (1988), p. 84.

4
Investment Links

MALAYSIA has always had a favourable disposition towards foreign investment. Indeed, an important feature of the open Malaysian economy has been the large extent of foreign involvement, especially in the modern sectors of the economy. The role of Pacific countries in this respect has been particularly conspicuous.

There appears to exist a close link between trade in manufactures and foreign investment activities in the economy. This seems to be the case especially with regards to intra-industry trade flows, for intra-firm sales apparently constitute the bulk of such flows. Thus, an important explanation of Malaysia's trade phenomenon lies in the pattern of foreign investment in the country.

 Foreign investment in Malaysia comprises both direct and portfolio components. Direct foreign investment (DFI) may be further categorized into (a) joint ventures,[1] (b) wholly foreign-owned projects,[2] and (c) turnkey operations.[3] Joint ventures form the bulk of DFI, although the number of wholly foreign-owned enterprises grew sharply in the late 1980s. There are only a few turnkey projects. Portfolio foreign investment (PFI) has also been playing an increasingly significant role in the Malaysian economy. However, due to severe data constraints, only passing references will be made to the latter in this chapter. Moreover, it is the direct investment component that is apparently far more important and interesting in terms of not only volume but also impact. In any case, external linkages established by direct investment are much stronger and more lasting. Hence the focus on direct foreign investments.

An Overview of Foreign Investment in Malaysia

Foreign investment in Malaysia has a fairly long history. As early as the 1920s, there was already substantial British investment in the country. This British investment was heavily concentrated in the plantation and mining sectors which together accounted for over 90 per cent of the total. British investment in the country increased from £33 million sterling in 1913 to £108 million sterling by 1930.[4] In the post-Independence era, the structure of foreign investment in the country underwent dramatic changes in terms of both sources and uses of foreign capital. By 1970, foreign equity accounted for over 60 per cent of the total share capital in Malaysia. Foreign capital was particularly predominant in agriculture (75.4 per cent), mining (72.5 per cent), trade (63.6 per cent), and manufacturing (59.6 per cent) in 1970.[5] By 1980, though, foreign ownership of the Malaysian corporate sector had declined to 47.5 per cent[6] in response to the NEP. In absolute terms, however, foreign investment in the country has continued to grow.

Policy Measures

Malaysia has been towing a fairly liberal policy towards foreign investment. This is hardly surprising, given the economic openness of the country, the pro-private sector economic development philosophy of the government, and the export-oriented industrialization strategy of its development plans. Malaysia's policy towards foreign investment has been tied to the overall objective of diversification and modernization of the economy. Accordingly, Malaysia has been offering generous fiscal and other incentives to entice foreign investors in competition with neighbouring countries.

Import-substituting industrialization in the late 1950s provided an opportunity for foreigners to set up manufacturing plants in Malaysia. Their main objective was apparently to preserve their market share that would otherwise have been lost. It would, of course, have been more economical for them to export their products than to produce them locally, but the cost differential was largely absorbed by the implicit subsidy provided through tariff protection and investment incentives.

The Pioneer Industries Ordinance of 1958 played a pivotal role in all this by granting tax holidays to pioneer industries. The Tariff Advisory Board was set up in 1963 to grant tariff protection, and the Federal Industrial Development Authority (FIDA) was established in 1967 to administer investment incentives. In 1970, the former was subsumed into the latter, which was subsequently renamed the Malaysian Industrial Development Authority (MIDA). The Pioneer Industries Ordinance of 1958 was replaced by the Investment Incentives Act of 1968, as Malaysia made a policy shift away from import substitution towards export orientation. The Industrial Coordination Act of 1975 was also passed to regulate investment activities in the country in accordance with the NEP. More recently, the incentive system was restructured, as contained in the Promotion of Investments Act, 1980.

Malaysia presently offers a rich assortment of incentives to both domestic and foreign investors. Among the investment incentives offered are pioneer status (tax holidays), investment tax allowance, abatement of adjusted incomes, accelerated depreciation allowance, reinvestment allowance, and a variety of export incentives. The last include export credit refinancing, export allowance, double deduction of export credit insurance premiums, double deduction of promotion of exports, industrial building allowance, and R & D allowance (MIDA, 1989).

All this notwithstanding, foreign investment is highly regulated in Malaysia. Even so, the federal government has not closed any industry to private foreign investment. Even the state governments, which exercise sole rights over natural resources, permit foreign investment in mining and forestry. Foreign investment in the oil and gas subsector is a federal matter and is managed by the National Petroleum Corporation (PETRONAS) through production-sharing arrangements.

The Industrial Coordination Act, 1975 (ICA) has imposed a licensing requirement, which can be used arbitrarily to ensure the 30 per cent Bumiputra equity participation in accordance with the NEP, on projects involving shareholders' funds of M$2.5 million and above or employing at least 75 full-time workers. In the face of severe public criticisms of the ICA, and in view of the declining interest shown by prospective foreign investors, the Malaysian government has pragmatically introduced several exemptions, as reflected in the current guidelines on foreign equity. Thus, for example, foreigners are allowed to hold 100 per cent equity if the company exports at least 80 per cent of its output; companies exporting 51–79 per cent of their production are allowed to have foreign equity ownership of up to 79 per cent; and 30–51 per cent foreign equity is permitted for projects exporting 20–50 per cent of their production. Under the existing guidelines, the equity structure for joint ventures depends also on whether the projects are initiated by foreigners, Bumiputras or non-Bumiputras.

The Malaysian Constitution provides a guarantee against nationalization of foreign assets without compensation. In addition, Malaysia has concluded investment guarantee agreements with sixteen countries, whereby the foreign investor is provided protection against nationalization and expropriation, prompt and adequate compensation in the event of nationalization or expropriation, freedom to transfer capital, profits, and other earnings, and legal redress under the Convention on Settlement of Investment Disputes.

Data Constraints

Reliable and comprehensive data relating to foreign investments in Malaysia are hard to come by. Portfolio investment figures, in particular, are extremely scanty, while DFI statistics are incomplete and their validity or reliability is rather limited. Malaysia is by no means unique in this respect. Other countries in the region display similar shortcomings. There are considerable variations with respect to definition, coverage, and time frame of foreign capital stocks and flows in the various national official statistics. All this tends to frustrate attempts at inter-country comparisons.

In Malaysia, DFI statistics are derived from MIDA. As mentioned, DFI data are not comprehensive in coverage. They exclude investment outside the promoted sectors and ignore reinvestments by the existing units. MIDA statistics cover investment in manufacturing and hotel industries; and information is limited to equity, loan capital, and employment only. MIDA statistics on direct foreign investment, more often than not, are based on approved investment.

These data can be misleading as there is bound to be a sizeable discrepancy between investment projects approved by MIDA and those actually implemented by the applicants. It is not unusual for an approved project to be abandoned, postponed, or trimmed down in the face of changing international, home, and host country circumstances. The MIDA data provide no clue regarding the proportion of approved DFI projects that actually get off the ground. According to MIDA, of the total investment projects (both local and foreign) approved during 1980–9, 46.3 per cent were in operation, 4.4 per cent were in the stage of plants being set up, and 29.4 per cent were in the initial stages of implementation as at 31 December 1989. In other words, 19.9 per cent of the approved projects had not been implemented. It is not clear whether DFI projects have a higher or lower implementation ratio than local ones. In any case, it is quite obvious that data on approved DFI significantly exaggerate foreign equity participation in the sectors covered.[7] This may not be exactly offset by omissions or incomplete coverage referred to earlier. It is therefore hard to judge the extent to which the official data understate or overstate the foreigners' stake in the Malaysian economy.

Given these weaknesses that characterize DFI data available in the host country, Malaysia, it would seem imperative that one should resort to home country sources. The latter is hardly a practical suggestion. For one thing, it is hard for a Malaysian researcher to put his fingers on data on all investing countries. For another, such data are often too aggregated, as they are intended to merely show capital outflows as registered by the central banks of the individual countries. Data on capital exports, sufficiently disaggregated to shed light on the sectoral distribution of capital outflows, are not readily available. One other caveat is that capital exports are sometimes channelled through particular countries for certain tax reasons, thus camouflaging the actual destination of capital transfers (Wagner, 1989).

DFI data provided by multilateral organizations like the International Monetary Fund (IMF) are not very helpful either, as such data are available only at a highly aggregated level. Moreover, international comparisons are hampered by dissimilar standards of compilation of data between countries and differences in accounting procedures and depreciation rules. Furthermore, there is no standard international classification for investment, unlike trade (SITC) and industry (ISIC).

These data problems have to be borne with when foreign investment stocks and flows are analysed. Needless to say, the scope of the analysis in what follows in the rest of this chapter is affected by data constraints of one kind or another. Accordingly, the conclusions based on the analysis will have to be treated with caution.

General Trends

By and large, direct foreign investment inflows are more important than those of portfolio foreign capital. But there have been times when the latter had exceeded the former as, for instance, in 1982–4. DFI inflows. have been growing rapidly, cresting in 1982 and declining thereafter until 1987. PFI inflows have followed a similar trend, peaking in 1982. But, portfolio investments exhibit a much higher degree of volatility compared with direct investments. This is not at all surprising since portfolio investment can be withdrawn without much financial loss and more easily than direct investments, which entail physical sinking of capital in the form of plants, machinery, and equipment. There have been significant net outflows of portfolio investment in 1987 and 1988 (Table 4.1).

Apparently, foreign portfolio investments are strongly influenced by the market conditions facing local stocks and shares. Thus, the substantial inflows of PFI during 1981–3 might have been due to the pull factor associated with the expansionary fiscal policies adopted by the government in the early 1980s. When the bubble burst in 1985 and the stock

TABLE 4.1

Malaysia: Capital Inflows and Current Account Balance of Payments,
1970–1988 (US$ million)

Year	DFI (1)	Portfolio (2)	Total (3) = (1+2)	Net Factor Payment Abroad (4)	B-o-P Current Account (5)
1970	94	−28	66	355	8
1971	100	87	187	363	−108
1972	114	67	181	378	−248
1973	172	−11	161	659	105
1974	571	11	582	997	−543
1975	350	267	617	727	−496
1976	381	50	431	1,097	580
1977	406	65	471	1,276	436
1978	500	79	579	1,700	108
1979	573	194	767	2,050	929
1980	934	−11	923	584	−285
1981	1,265	1,131	2,396	5,574	−2,486
1982	1,397	1,804	3,201	8,343	−3,601
1983	1,261	1,410	2,671	8,109	−3,497
1984	797	1,003	1,800	5,368	−1,671
1985	695	335	1,030	5,508	− 613
1986	489	599	1,088	4,780	52
1987	397	−948	−551	5,270	2,572
1988	611	−966	−355	5,423	1,184

Source: International Monetary Fund, *International Financial Statistics 1989*.

market remained sedated and dull with the prices of even the blue chips plunging to unprecedented lows, a withdrawal of foreign portfolio investment would have entailed huge capital losses for foreign investors. It must have made considerable sense to wait till the stock market recovered so as to minimize losses, before some funds were withdrawn in 1987 and 1988.

An alternative explanation would be that the negative net inflows were caused by massive outflows of local capital in search of higher returns elsewhere and/or to take advantage of anticipated exchange rate changes. The latter explanation sounds just as plausible as the former, since domestic interest rates were low and the ringgit was under severe speculative pressure in those years.

The extent of foreign-investor participation in the Malaysian economy is also reflected in the net factor payments abroad. The movement of net factor payments abroad roughly corresponds to that of foreign direct and portfolio investment flows, reaching the crest in 1982 (see Table 4.1); but these payments have been relatively more stable, which is understandable as factor payments arise largely from previous investments that are unrelated to new capital inflows shown in Table 4.1. Net factor payments have almost always exceeded net capital inflows. In other words, capital inflows have been insufficient to meet net factor payments in the form of profits, interests, and dividends sent to foreigners, which, however, constitutes no argument against foreign investment.

Net factor payments abroad have contributed to the country's current account deficits in the balance of payments in several years. Of greater significance is the fact that such payments are considerably larger than the current account deficits, which means that there would have been sizeable current account surpluses but for these payments. Equally significant is the observation that the deficits in the current account have been financed by private capital inflows, both direct and portfolio, rather than by the drawing down of reserves, as a comparison of columns 3 and 5 in Table 4.1 would suggest.

Figure 4.1 presents foreign investments and net factor payments abroad as percentages of GDP. The pattern of the graphs lends support to the preceding observations. Two additional observations are in order: (a) that foreign capital inflows account for only a small proportion of the GDP; and (b) that the proportion of factor payment to GDP is substantial. One may interpret the latter as the cost that Malaysia has to pay for the use of foreign capital.

Figure 4.2 presents graphs relating to domestic capital formation and foreign investment ratios. It appears that DFI inflows have little to do with domestic capital formation as the ratio of the former to the latter is not stable, which is not surprising since foreign investment and private domestic investment react to different sets of incentives. Direct foreign investment has increasingly gone into export-oriented activities where external factors play a critical role, whereas domestic investment is heavily influenced by such internal factors as domestic demand and public investment.

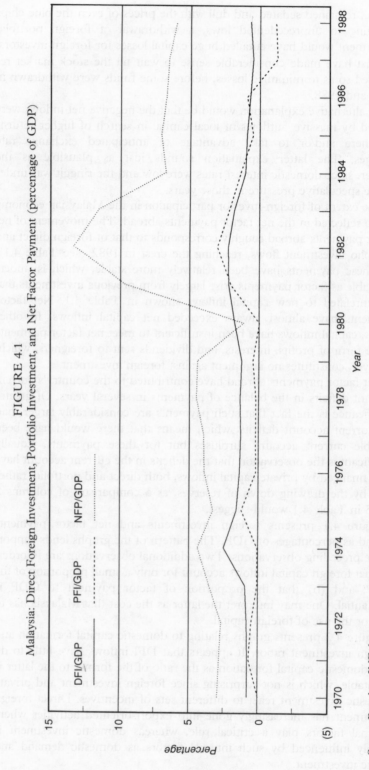

FIGURE 4.1

Malaysia: Direct Foreign Investment, Portfolio Investment, and Net Factor Payment (percentage of GDP)

Source: Based on IMF data.

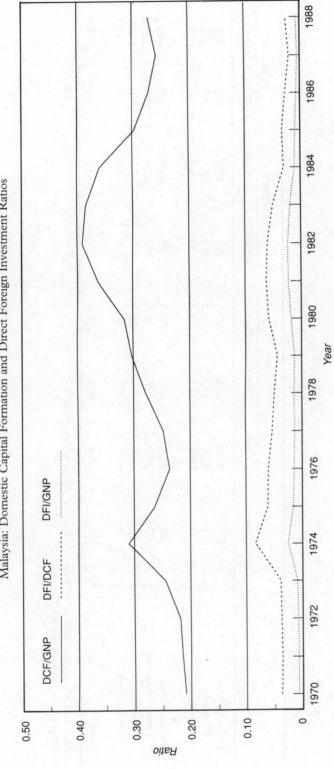

FIGURE 4.2

Malaysia: Domestic Capital Formation and Direct Foreign Investment Ratios

Source: Based on IMF data.

TABLE 4.2
External Capital Flows into Malaysia, 1976–1987 (annual average)

	1976–1978		1979–1982		1983–1985		1986–1987	
	US$m.	Per Cent	US$m.	Per Cent	US$m.	Per Cent	US$m.	Per Cent
Official Flows	171	68.0	238	29.5	397	35.0	173	163.2
Bilateral	81	32.4	115	14.2	319	28.1	163	153.8
Multilateral	90	36.0	123	15.2	79	7.0	10	9.4
Private Flows	80	32.0	570	70.5	736	64.9	−67	−63.2
Direct investment	87	34.8	35	4.3	200	17.6	137	129.2
Portfolio investment	−17	−6.8	217	26.9	430	37.9	−160	−150.9
Export credit	9	3.6	317	39.2	106	9.3	−44	−41.5
Total	250	100.0	808	100.0	1,134	100.0	106	100.0

Source: OECD, Geographical Distribution of Financial Flows to Developing
Countries, 1976/79 up to 1984/87 issues.

It can be seen from Table 4.2 that private capital inflows have over-taken official capital inflows into the country during the period 1976–85. However, there were substantial private capital outflows during 1986–7, mainly in the portfolio category which is highly sensitive to changes in stock market conditions. Private capital inflows in the form of direct investment have been relatively steady, notwithstanding variations in terms of annual averages.

The Structure of Direct Foreign Investment

Foreign investment in Malaysia exhibits a certain pattern, particularly in terms of market orientation and ownership structure. The bulk of DFI has gone increasingly into export-oriented manufacturing industries and has taken the form of 100 per cent foreign equity or majority foreign ownership. This section examines the structure of foreign investment in Malaysia by source and industry, highlighting investments from the Pacific region.

Ownership Pattern

Under the NEP, the Bumiputra share of corporate sector equity has increased from 4.3 per cent in 1971 to 19.4 per cent in 1988, while that of the foreigners has fallen from 61.7 per cent to 24.6 per cent over the same period, as shown in Table 4.3. In absolute terms, however, foreign equity in the Malaysian corporate sector has risen from M$4.0 billion in 1971 to M$24.1 billion in 1988.

Foreign equity is assuming greater importance especially in new projects and expansion of established projects in recent years. Thus,

TABLE 4.3

Malaysia: Ownership of Share Capital in the Corporate Sector, 1971–1988
(percentage)

	1971	1975	1980	1985	1988
Foreign	61.7	53.3	42.9	26.0	24.6
Share in Malaysian companies	32.9	31.3	24.0	16.2	15.8
Net assets of local branches	28.8	22.0	18.9	9.8	8.8
Malaysian	38.3	46.7	57.1	74.0	75.4
Bumiputra individuals	2.6	3.6	5.8	11.7	13.0
Bumiputra trust agencies	1.7	5.6	6.7	7.4	6.4
Other Malaysian residents	34.0	37.5	44.6	54.9	56.0
Total (M$ million)	6,564	15,084	32,420	77,964	97,971

Sources: Malaysia, 1981, 1983, 1986a, and 1989.

foreign equity in new projects has increased from 58.6 per cent in 1988 to 73.7 per cent in 1989. The increase in foreigners' stake was even sharper in the case of expansion of established projects: 74.8 per cent in 1989 compared with 40.0 per cent in the previous year. Even in terms of loans, the foreign share in the case of new projects has increased from 52.5 per cent to 74.1 per cent between 1988 and 1989 (Table 4.4).

Wholly foreign-owned projects are far more important than wholly Malaysian-owned ones. In 1989, the former accounted for 48.8 per cent of the total approved capital investment, compared with the latter's tiny share of 7.9 per cent. In the case of joint ventures, however, Malaysian-majority ownership is more important than other forms. In 1989, the latter formed 19.8 per cent of total approved investment compared with the former's 23.5 per cent (Table 4.5).

It is thus clear that foreign investment is playing an increasingly important role in the Malaysian economy. DFI in Malaysia is dominated by the Pacific region whose share of the equity in approved projects has increased from 64.5 per cent in 1982 to 82.8 per cent in 1987. By contrast, the EC share has fallen from 21.8 per cent to 8.1 per cent over the same period (Table 4.6). Japan, Singapore, and the United States have

TABLE 4.4

Malaysia: Ownership Structure of Manufacturing Projects
Granted Approval, 1988 and 1989

		New Projects		Expansion/ Diversification	
		1988	1989	1988	1989
Proposed Called-up Capital	(M$ million)	3,349.1	4,031.4	120.6	538.4
Malaysian equity	(M$ million)	1,386.8	1,061.4	72.4	135.7
Foreign equity	(M$ million)	1,962.3	2,970.0	48.2	402.7
Share of foreign equity	(per cent)	58.6	73.7	40.0	74.8
Loans[1]	(M$ million)	5,331.9	6,207.3	292.3	1,331.0
Local	(M$ million)	2,535.2	1,610.5	221.5	732.5
Foreign	(M$ million)	2,796.7	4,596.8	70.8	598.5
Foreign share	(per cent)	52.5	74.1	24.2	45.0
Total Proposed Capital Investment	(M$ million)	8,681.0	10,238.7	412.9	1,869.4
Local	(M$ million)	3,922.0	2,671.9	293.9	868.2
Foreign	(M$ million)	4,759.0	7,566.8	119.0	1,001.2
Foreign share	(per cent)	54.8	73.9	28.8	53.6

Source: MIDA.

[1]Loans attributed to foreign interest is apportioned from the total loan according to the percentage of foreign share in the equity of each project.

TABLE 4.5

Malaysia: Approved Projects by Ownership, 1988 and 1989 (M$ million)

	1988			1989		
	Equity	Loan	Capital Investment	Equity	Loan	Capital Investment
Wholly Malaysian-owned	778.8	1,562.2	2,341.0	220.5	739.7	960.2
	(22.4)	(27.8)	(25.7)	(4.8)	(9.8)	(7.9)
Wholly foreign-owned	1,215.7	1,481.0	2,696.7	2,233.2	3,677.1	5,910.3
	(35.0)	(26.3)	(29.7)	(48.9)	(48.6)	(48.8)
Joint ventures:						
Malaysian majority	680.0	819.5	1,499.5	1,120.1	1,723.7	2,843.8
	(19.6)	(14.6)	(16.5)	(24.5)	(22.9)	(23.5)
Foreign majority	540.3	851.1	1,391.4	892.1	1,282.1	2,174.2
	(15.6)	(15.1)	(15.3)	(19.5)	(17.0)	(18.0)
Equal ownership	254.9	910.4	1,165.3	103.9	115.7	219.6
	(7.3)	(16.2)	(12.8)	(2.3)	(1.5)	(1.8)
Total	3,469.7	5,624.2	9,093.9	4,569.8	7,538.3	12,108.1
	(100.0)	(100.0)	(100.0)	(100.0)	(100.0)	(100.0)

Source: MIDA.
Note: Figures in parentheses give percentage shares.

TABLE 4.6
Malaysia: Sources of Foreign Equity in Approved Projects, 1982–1987

	1982		1985		1987	
	M$ million	Per Cent	M$ million	Per Cent	M$ million	Per Cent
Australia	62.1	12.0	7.3	2.2	29.7	4.0
Canada	13.6	2.6	1.1	0.3	11.2	1.5
Hong Kong	4.9	0.9	18.4	5.7	27.8	3.7
Indonesia	28.2	5.4	5.1	1.6	0.8	0.1
Japan	136.9	26.4	81.7	25.1	230.8	30.8
Korea	0.3	0.1	10.4	3.2	2.0	0.3
New Zealand	0.8	0.2	1.6	0.5	–	–
Philippines	27.3	5.3	0.1	–	2.5	0.3
Singapore	9.4	1.8	47.2	14.5	135.4	18.1
Taiwan	1.6	0.3	14.7	4.5	118.5	15.8
Thailand	26.7	5.1	0.3	0.1	0.7	0.1
USA	22.9	4.4	36.8	11.3	61.3	8.2
Asia–Pacific	334.7	64.5	224.7	69.2	620.7	82.8
EC	112.9	21.8	28.3	8.7	61.0	8.1
Others	71.4	13.8	71.9	22.1	68.3	9.1
Total	519.0	100.0	324.9	100.0	750.0	100.0

Source: MIDA.

TABLE 4.7
Malaysia: Foreign Investment[1] in Approved Projects by Source,
1987–1989

	1987		1988		1989	
	M$ million	Per Cent	M$ million	Per Cent	M$ million	Per Cent
Australia	126.1	6.1	25.5	0.5	29.1	0.3
Canada	49.4	2.4	5.2	0.1	16.3	0.2
China	8.7	0.4	–	–	11.3	0.1
Hong Kong	88.9	4.3	298.4	6.1	352.1	4.1
Indonesia	1.6	0.1	23.2	0.5	78.0	0.9
Japan	715.1	34.7	1,222.0	25.1	2,682.2	31.3
Korea	3.6	0.2	41.8	0.9	188.9	2.2
New Zealand	–	–	2.5	0.1	–	–
Philippines	0.2	–	–	–	0.3	–
Singapore	258.5	12.5	419.6	8.6	910.9	10.6
Taiwan	243.0	11.8	829.6	17.0	2,119.4	24.7
Thailand	3.3	0.2	57.5	1.2	8.9	0.1
USA	162.7	7.9	535.2	11.0	309.6	3.6
Asia–Pacific	1,661.1	80.6	3,460.5	70.9	6,707.0	78.3
EC	196.8	9.6	899.0	18.4	1,250.9	14.6
Others	202.1	9.8	518.5	10.6	610.2	7.1
Total	2,060.0	100.0	4,878.0	100.0	8,568.1	100.0

Source: MIDA.
[1]Foreign investment comprises equity and loan components.

long been the most important sources of DFI. These three
countries jointly accounted for 57.1 per cent of the equity in approved
projects in 1987. Taiwan has emerged as a major source of foreign
investment in Malaysia since 1987.

The Asia–Pacific share of foreign investment (comprising both equity
and loans) in approved projects amounted to 78.3 per cent in 1989,
against the EC share of 14.6 per cent (Table 4.7). Taiwan ranks second
in terms of DFI inflows, accounting for as much as one-quarter. DFI
from Japan, Taiwan, Singapore and the United States together formed
70.2 per cent of foreign investment in projects approved in 1989.

Foreign investment projects have a higher equity–loan ratio compared
with the wholly Malaysian-owned projects—0.61 against 0.30 respectively, in 1989 (Table 4.8). DFI from the Asia–Pacific region as a whole
has a much higher equity–loan ratio than DFI from the European
Community.

It has been reported that more than 1,700 international companies
have located their projects in Malaysia.[8] These include Australia's Ansell
International, New Zealand's Wix Corporation, Hong Kong's Textile
Alliance Group, Japan's Matsushita Group of Companies, Toray
Industries, and Marubeni Corporation, and the United States' Motorola,
Hewlett Packard, and Texas Instruments.

Japan tops the list as the most important source of foreign investment

TABLE 4.8
Equity–Loan Ratio of Foreign Investment Projects in Malaysia,
1988 and 1989

	1988	1989
Australia	0.63	0.98
Canada	1.60	0.68
China	–	2.32
Hong Kong	0.77	0.46
Indonesia	0.95	0.27
Japan	0.85	0.65
Korea	1.26	0.72
New Zealand	0.19	–
Philippines	–	3.00
Singapore	0.70	0.42
Taiwan	0.86	0.88
Thailand	0.37	0.78
USA	0.89	0.65
Asia–Pacific	0.89	0.67
EC	0.44	0.48
World	0.70	0.65
Wholly Malaysian-owned	0.50	0.30
Wholly foreign-owned	0.82	0.61
Joint ventures	0.57	0.68

Source: MIDA.

for Malaysia. There has been a sharp increase in Japanese investment in Malaysia since 1985, as shown in Figure 4.3. In 1989, Malaysia ranked second to Thailand as Japan's favoured overseas investment venue in South-East Asia. Japanese investment in Malaysia has tended to flow in what may be termed 'waves'. The first wave, which took place during 1973–4, focused on light manufacturing. The second wave, which came during the early 1980s, headed mainly for the construction sector. The current third wave is largely concentrated on electronics-related activities. The main distinguishing feature of the third wave is that smaller Japanese companies are, for the first time, participating actively, quite unlike the previous waves which were totally dominated by giant corporations. The smaller companies are investing in Malaysia to produce components and parts which their big clients need, now that Japanese MNCs have found it costly to source their inputs from Japan due to appreciation of the yen. Japanese DFI in Malaysia is concentrated largely in the manufacturing sector, as shown in Table 4.9. Japanese companies in Malaysia produce a wide range of manufactures of varying technological levels, including radio-cassette players, stereos, television sets, and air-conditioners.

American DFI is concentrated mostly in the petroleum sector which accounts for roughly two-thirds of the total (Table 4.10). However, the bulk of the US investments since 1988 have been going into manufacturing activities, especially the electronics industry. Thus, in 1988, the Malaysian manufacturing sector absorbed over 60 per cent of DFI from the United States. US investments in Malaysia have yielded fairly high returns in the 1980s, ranging from 15.4 per cent (1986) to 35.7 per cent (1984), as shown in Table 4.11.

The fastest-growing foreign investments in Malaysia are from Taiwan. Taiwanese investments have been growing rapidly since 1987, reaching M$884 million in 1988: such investments jumped a remarkable 400 per cent in 1988. Taiwan, the second largest source in terms of DFI inflow, is already the fourth largest foreign investor in Malaysia in terms of 'stock'. Taiwanese investments have gone mainly into electronics

TABLE 4.9
Japanese Direct Investment in Malaysia by Sector, 1976 and 1986
(percentage)

Sector	1976	1986
Agriculture/fishery	4.5	2.3
Mining	28.7	11.5
Manufacturing	57.6	66.7
Banking/insurance	0.8	3.8
Other services	8.4	15.6
All industries (US$ million)	356	1,283

Source: Wagner (1989).

FIGURE 4.3

Trends in Japanese Overseas Investment in the Manufacturing Sector

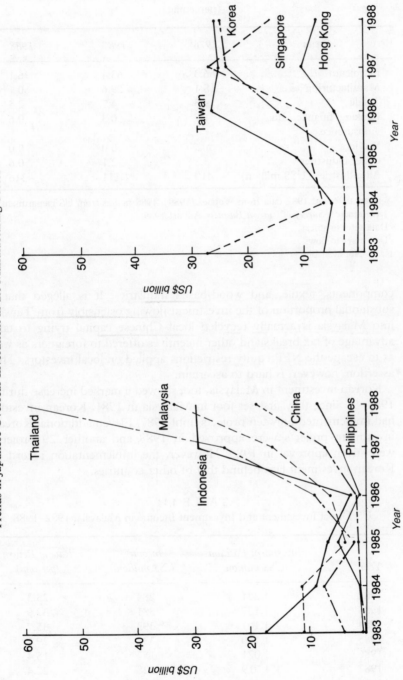

Source: JETRO, *Tradescope*, January 1990.

TABLE 4.10
US Direct Investment in Malaysia by Sector, 1976, 1987, and 1988
(percentage)

Sector	1976[1]	1987[1]	1988[2]
Petroleum	66.3	63.4	36.1
Manufacturing	18.1	29.6	60.1
Trade	9.3	4.7	2.5
Banking, finance, and insurance	1.7	0.3	0.6
Services	n.a.	0.0	0.0
Other industries	3.3	2.1	0.6
All industries (US$ million)	419	1,111	316

Sources: 1976 and 1987 data from Wagner (1989). 1988 figures from US Department of Commerce, Survey of Current Business, August 1989.
[1]Data refer to stocks.
[2]Data refer to flows.
n.a. = Not available.

components, textile, and wood-based industries. It is alleged that a substantial proportion of the investment flowing ostensibly from Taiwan into Malaysia is actually recycled local Chinese capital trying to take advantage of tax breaks and other incentives offered to foreigners as well as to escape the NEP equity restrictions applied on local investors. This assertion, however, is hard to ascertain.

Korean investment in Malaysia, too, showed a marked increase during 1988–9. Since they first set foot in Malaysia in 1981, Korean investors had implemented only ten projects until 1987. Eleven additional Korean investment projects were approved in 1988 and another 29 projects were given approval in 1989. However, the implementation record of Korean investment lags behind that of other countries.

TABLE 4.11
US Direct Investment and Investment Income in Malaysia, 1982–1988

Year	Investment Position (US$ million)	Income (US$ million)	Rate of Return (per cent)
1982	1,221	284	23.3
1983	1,157	381	32.9
1984	1,101	393	35.7
1985	1,140	332	29.1
1986	1,021	157	15.4
1987	1,019	228	22.4
1988	1,363	404	29.6

Source: United States Department of Commerce, Survey of Current Business, August 1987 and August 1989.

Singapore has always been a major source of DFI to Malaysia due to historical ties and physical proximity. Industrial restructuring in the Republic in the wake of rising wages and the strong Singapore dollar have forced many industries to move into Malaysia. Over 100 Singapore companies, producing goods ranging from rubber products to electronics, set up factories in Malaysia in 1988 compared with 58 in 1987. However, the Malaysian DFI statistics apparently overstate Singapore's share, since a significant proportion of foreign investment from Singapore is actually undertaken by MNCs operating in Singapore.

Sectoral Allocation

Foreign investments have gone into a wide spectrum of manufacturing activities ranging from simple food manufacturing to production of sophisticated scientific and precision instruments. None the less, electronics, chemicals, textile, and wood products have jointly accounted for as much as 62.9 per cent of the approved DFI in 1989 (Table 4.12).

Sectoral allocation of DFI in Malaysia, however, varies considerably between investing countries, as shown in Tables 4.13 and 4.14. In the case of the Australian DFI, non-metallic mineral products, fabricated metal products, and rubber products are the most important recipients, accounting for 61.5 per cent of the total paid-up capital. The beverages and tobacco, textiles, and electronics subsectors have absorbed 59.9 per cent of DFI in terms of paid-up capital from Hong Kong. Nearly 59 per cent of the Japanese investment (paid-up capital) in Malaysia is accounted for by three industries, viz. textiles, electronics, and basic metal products. The US investments (paid-up capital) in Malaysia are concentrated in the petroleum, chemicals, electronics, and paper, printing, and publishing subsectors which together form over 67 per cent of the total. By contrast, Singapore's overseas investments in Malaysia are far more diversified. The bulk of the Asia–Pacific investments (paid-up capital) in Malaysia have gone into textiles, electronics, non-metallic mineral products, basic metals, and food manufacturing which jointly account for 56.4 per cent of the total.

The sectoral pattern in terms of fixed assets corresponds closely to that in terms of paid-up capital, although fixed assets are considerably larger than paid-up capital in absolute terms (Table 4.14).

Some interesting comparisons between the Asia–Pacific region and the EC are brought out in Table 4.15. The EC investments dominate only two industrial subsectors: viz. petroleum and scientific and measuring equipment, in terms of both paid-up capital and fixed assets. In all other industrial groups, the Asia–Pacific region dominates, with the notable exception of leather and leather products.[9] Industries where the Asia–Pacific contributes over 90 per cent of foreign paid-up capital and/or foreign-owned fixed assets are (a) textiles and textile products, (b) paper, printing, and publishing, (c) plastic products, (d) basic metal products, and (e) machinery manufacturing.

TABLE 4.12

Malaysia: Foreign Participation in Approved Projects by Industry, 1988 and 1989

Industry	1988					1989				
	Foreign Equity			Foreign Investment[1]		Foreign Equity			Foreign Investment[1]	
	No.	M$ m.	Per Cent	M$ m.	Per Cent	No.	M$ m.	Per Cent	M$ m.	Per Cent
Food manufacturing	22	267.4	13.3	571.1	11.7	24	135.6	4.0	290.7	3.4
Beverages and tobacco	4	3.5	0.2	7.1	0.1	–	–	–	–	–
Textile and textile products	36	88.0	4.4	238.8	4.9	59	230.8	6.8	511.2	6.0
Leather and leather products	1	0.1	–	0.4	0.1	5	7.2	0.2	18.5	0.2
Wood and wood products	31	74.7	3.7	198.8	4.1	43	329.2	9.8	980.0	11.4
Furniture and fixtures	23	35.7	1.8	72.3	1.5	22	62.0	1.8	129.7	1.5
Paper, printing, and publishing	9	10.8	0.5	34.2	0.7	16	58.6	1.7	294.2	3.4
Chemicals and chemical products	17	261.7	13.0	763.5	15.7	29	448.7	13.3	993.6	11.6
Petroleum and coal	–	–	–	–	–	2	60.0	1.8	216.0	2.5
Rubber products	153	324.1	16.1	662.7	13.6	59	130.7	3.9	360.7	4.2
Plastic products	18	95.5	4.8	272.3	5.6	31	97.5	2.9	215.2	2.5

	No.	Value	%	Value	%	No.	Value	%	Value	%
Non-metallic mineral products	14	41.3	2.1	73.4	1.5	19	110.2	3.3	336.4	3.9
Basic metal products	10	127.5	6.3	612.7	12.6	27	153.7	4.6	439.4	5.1
Fabricated metal products	14	52.7	2.6	147.4	3.0	33	212.8	6.3	500.6	5.8
Machinery manufacturing	5	6.2	0.3	12.2	0.3	25	60.3	1.8	143.3	1.7
Electrical and electronic products	84	596.5	29.7	1,151.9	23.6	163	1,112.0	33.0	2,720.8	31.8
Transport equipment	15	7.3	0.4	22.4	0.5	19	61.4	1.8	136.8	1.6
Scientific and measuring equipment	13	4.1	0.2	13.9	0.3	5	52.7	1.6	209.9	2.4
Miscellaneous	11	13.3	0.7	23.1	0.5	19	49.2	1.5	70.9	0.8
Total	470	2,010.5	100.0	4,878.0	100.0	600	3,372.7	100.0	8,568.1	100.0

Source: MIDA.

[1]Foreign investment = foreign equity + foreign loan.

TABLE 4.13

Malaysia: Foreign Investment (Paid-up Capital) in Companies in Production by Source and Industry as of 31 December 1988 (M$ million)

	Australia	Hong Kong	Japan	Korea	Singapore	Taiwan	USA	Asia–Pacific	EC	Total
Food manufacturing	5.8	32.4	29.7		421.5	0.2	4.8	496.8	167.9	930.6
Beverages and tobacco		45.7			192.6		21.7	260.1	102.1	432.4
Textile and textile products	13.4	68.1	239.2		159.3	4.1	3.4	489.0	31.2	531.2
Leather and leather products					1.9			1.9		19.7
Wood and wood products	1.6	6.4	30.5	0.5	25.8	17.2	1.5	86.7	15.6	103.1
Furniture and fixtures		0.1		2.6	11.4	3.0		17.2	1.3	19.2
Paper, printing, and publishing	0.3	7.7	0.6		21.5		35.8	70.7	4.3	75.9
Chemical and chemical products	7.6	29.4	41.0		48.9	0.6	48.7	284.8	136.1	424.2
Petroleum and coal		0.5	105.2		24.0		87.8	217.8	297.2	515.4
Rubber products	25.8	2.4	13.5	1.5	100.0	1.9	14.5	170.5	51.2	237.4
Plastic products		6.2	21.2	0.9	14.3	0.8	1.3	45.0	3.7	49.4
Non-metallic mineral products	43.1	5.2	47.8	59.8	206.8	3.9	7.7	375.4	89.5	498.5
Basic metal products	7.8	0.3	131.1		116.1	5.7	0.6	313.8	10.7	327.1
Fabricated metal products	22.7	8.5	32.4		150.4	3.7	2.8	220.8	14.5	257.9
Machinery manufacturing	1.7		42.9		40.9	0.7	12.2	99.4	7.9	112.3
Electrical and electronic products	18.4	43.8	323.0		94.7	16.0	35.7	535.9	155.0	716.0
Transport equipment		5.1	101.8		60.6		7.8	175.6	37.1	221.7
Scientific and measuring equipment	0.6	1.2	12.4	0.2	2.7	1.6	8.5	24.8	38.0	71.2
Miscellaneous			9.4		4.3		13.9	31.0	12.3	48.1
Total	148.9	263.0	1,181.8	65.6	1,703.6	59.7	308.9	3,917.7	1,177.4	5,591.3

Source: MIDA.

TABLE 4.14

Malaysia: Foreign Investment (Fixed Asset) in Companies in Production by Source and Industry
as of 31 December 1988 (M$ million)

	Australia	Hong Kong	Japan	Korea	Singapore	Taiwan	USA	Asia–Pacific	EC	Total
Food manufacturing	8.4	44.4	33.7		343.2	0.1	9.4	442.3	121.7	871.2
Beverages and tobacco		18.9			201.8		32.9	253.7	101.0	427.4
Textile and textile products	14.0	87.4	224.0		65.2	2.7	3.1	397.4	26.1	442.9
Leather and leather products					2.4			2.4		24.6
Wood and wood products	10.0	4.6	10.7	0.5	21.3	23.4	7.4	87.9	47.3	136.5
Furniture and fixtures				3.0	6.4	3.0		12.5	0.8	16.4
Paper, printing, and publishing	3.1	19.4	0.9		30.9	0.1	48.4	104.1	1.8	106.7
Chemical and chemical products	10.6	27.7	41.1		37.3	0.2	68.9	361.1	160.3	525.4
Petroleum and coal	0.1	1.2	356.3		41.2	0.1	92.9	492.3	665.2	1,157.9
Rubber products	100.5	3.9	24.2	3.2	84.8	3.3	177.9	399.1	71.6	522.5
Plastic products		6.5	26.6	2.0	16.8	1.3	4.3	57.6	2.1	61.1
Non-metallic mineral products	58.3	5.2	130.4	180.5	249.5	4.5	14.6	644.6	155.5	879.4
Basic metal products	4.6	0.2	151.7		83.8	10.4	0.5	323.3	5.6	332.0
Fabricated metal products	11.6	7.4	29.3		132.9	1.6	3.1	186.2	14.7	225.1
Machinery manufacturing	0.5	0.2	95.5		34.2	1.0	19.1	151.6	6.1	161.9
Electrical and electronic products	12.8	178.1	693.7		128.5	24.2	534.9	1,582.7	228.5	1,926.2
Transport equipment		8.6	188.3		14.9		10.4	223.1	17.4	254.2
Scientific and measuring equipment		0.5	16.0		7.9		3.4	27.8	51.9	98.7
Miscellaneous	2.6	0.4	19.7	0.1	4.0	1.6	31.1	59.8	14.6	75.7
Total	237.1	417.0	2,042.1	189.4	1,506.9	77.8	1,062.2	5,811.8	1,692.4	8,245.7

Source: MIDA.

TABLE 4.15

Malaysia: Foreign Investment by Industry and Region as of 31 December 1988 (percentage share)

	Asia-Pacific		EC		Others	
	Paid-up Capital	Fixed Assets	Paid-up Capital	Fixed Assets	Paid-up Capital	Fixed Assets
Food manufacturing	53.3	50.8	18.0	14.0	28.7	35.2
Beverages and tobacco	60.2	59.4	23.6	23.6	16.2	17.0
Textile and textile products	92.1	89.7	5.9	5.9	2.0	4.4
Leather and leather products	9.6	9.8	–	–	90.4	90.2
Wood and wood products	84.1	64.4	15.1	34.7	0.8	0.9
Furniture and fixtures	89.6	76.2	6.8	4.9	3.6	18.9
Paper, printing, and publishing	93.1	97.6	5.7	1.7	1.2	0.7
Chemical and chemical products	67.1	68.7	32.1	30.5	0.8	2.6
Petroleum and coal	42.3	42.5	57.7	57.4		
Rubber products	71.8	76.4	21.6	13.7	6.6	9.9
Plastic products	91.1	94.3	7.5	3.4	1.4	2.3
Non-metallic mineral products	75.3	73.3	18.0	17.7	6.7	9.0
Basic metal products	95.9	97.4	3.3	1.7	0.8	0.9
Fabricated metal products	85.6	82.7	5.6	6.5	8.8	10.8
Machinery manufacturing	88.5	93.6	7.0	3.8	4.5	2.6
Electrical and electronic products	74.8	82.2	21.6	11.9	3.6	5.9
Transport equipment	79.2	87.8	16.7	6.8	4.1	5.4
Scientific and measuring equipment	34.8	28.2	53.4	52.6	11.8	19.2
Miscellaneous	64.4	79.0	25.6	19.3	10.0	1.7
Total	70.1	70.5	21.1	20.5	8.8	9.0

Sources: Derived from Tables 4.13 and 4.14 above.

Market Orientation

In the early stages of industrialization, under the import-substitution strategy, foreign investments in Malaysia were concentrated in domestic market-oriented manufacturing activities. More recently, however, new DFI inflows have gone mostly into export-oriented industries partly in response to Malaysia's export promotion policy 'bias' and partly in conjunction with the massive industrial restructuring exercises in the home countries, where labour-intensive activities are losing their comparative advantage. Besides, Malaysia's investment guidelines call for majority Malaysian ownership for projects that are substantially dependent on the domestic market.

In the Malaysian context, therefore, the Kojima hypothesis (Kojima, 1977 and 1990)—according to which Japanese overseas investment is 'trade-creating' in contrast to American overseas investment—is irrelevant or invalid. Kojima contends that Japanese overseas investment is 'trade-creating' as it facilitates the relocation of labour-intensive industries in which the home country is losing its comparative advantage to labour-abundant host countries, and that American overseas investment is 'anti-trade' as it concentrates on import-substituting, high-technology activities in the host countries. Contrary to the Kojima hypothesis, available evidence suggests that the Japanese affiliates in Malaysia were selling the bulk of their output in the local market, while American affiliates in Malaysia exported the bulk of theirs in the 1970s.[10] The picture must have changed significantly in the 1980s, as DFIs, regardless of sources, have been channelled largely into export-oriented Malaysian manufactures. Indeed, DFI is essentially a supplement, not necessarily a substitute for trade flows in a dynamic world. For, DFI plays a catalytic role in the evolution of dynamic comparative advantage which apparently forms the basis of international trade.

The Impact of Foreign Investment Activities

As mentioned earlier, direct foreign investment in Malaysia has a fairly long history. In the beginning, DFI was concentrated in import-competing industries partly in response to the investment incentives provided by the Malaysian government and partly to maintain their share of the Malaysian market for consumer goods. With the saturation of the small domestic market, attention shifted from import substitution to export orientation. This shift has caused changes not only in the role that foreign investment plays in the country but also in the impact it has on the host economy. It appears that externalities through forward and backward linkages, technological diffusion, and skill transfers in the case of export-oriented projects differ markedly from those of domestic market-oriented activities. However, it is hard to observe the impact of DFI, let alone quantify it, given the lack of visibility that often surrounds the externalities of foreign investment projects. Nevertheless, it will be useful to take a close look at some of the identifiable effects of DFI, especially from the Pacific sources.

Technology Transfer

Arguably, Malaysia needs foreign technology more than foreign capital *per se*, for, as seen earlier, Malaysia has a fairly high domestic savings rate, and the DFI inflow, after all, accounts for only a small proportion of the gross domestic capital formation. It is technology that the country lacks, and Malaysia lags way behind in R & D. Seen from this angle, it is clear that Malaysia is really after the technology that foreign investment brings with it rather than foreign capital itself. Although in theory it is possible to separate the technology and equity components so as to obtain foreign technology without foreign equity participation, it is difficult in practice to do so if the absorptive capacity, especially technical know-how, is limited. Besides, most MNCs are unwilling to part with their technology unless they have an equity interest attached to it. DFI is thus viewed in Malaysia as a major conduit for technology transfer.

Malaysia has a clear policy on the transfer of technology, with well laid-out guidelines for technology agreements between local and foreign counterparts, and provides protection for intellectual property rights (MIDA, 1989). Curiously, joint ventures accounted for only 11.9 per cent of the total agreements approved during the period 1970–87, and over one-half of the total involved technical assistance (Table 4.16). Turnkey engineering agreements, where technology suppliers are responsible for all technical decisions, account for a negligible proportion of the total. In terms of industry groups, electrical/electronics, chemicals, fabricated metals, and transport equipment industries dominate, jointly accounting for more than one-half of the total number of technology agreements (Table 4.17). The number of such agreements increased in absolute terms for all industry groups with the exception of paper products between 1970–8 and 1979–87.

The Asia–Pacific region figures prominently as a source of technology for Malaysia. Japan, the United States, and Australia have jointly accounted for nearly one-half of the total technology agreements that Malaysia entered into during 1970–87 and more recently in 1989. Hong Kong, Singapore, and Korea are the other major Pacific sources of technology for Malaysia (Table 4.18).

It is difficult to assess how much technology transfer has actually transpired, but it is clear that there are considerable inter-industry variations. One might only expect a meagre technology transfer in the electronics sector which is dominated by a few MNCs. The electronics companies are generally turnkey projects which have relied entirely on the parent companies for all technology inputs and technical decisions. It has been found that technological spin-offs were minimal, given the 'enclave' nature of the entire operations located in FTZs with the training of the work-force being limited to on-the-job or in-plant experience (Cheong et al., 1981). This, however, does not mean that there have been no externalities emanating from the electronics industry. There have been significant learning effects associated with export manufacturing, given

TABLE 4.16

Malaysia: Approved Technology Agreements by Type, 1970–1989

	1970–1978		1979–1987		1970–1987		1989	
	Number	Per Cent	Number	Per Cent	Number	Per Cent	Number	Per Cent
Joint venture	45	10.2	130	12.6	175	11.9	15	7.6
Technical assistance	245	55.4	503	48.8	748	50.8	64	32.3
Know-how	–	–	11	1.1	11	0.8	13	6.6
Licence and patent	10	2.3	95	9.2	105	7.1	35	17.7
Management	59	13.4	105	10.2	164	11.1	12	6.1
Services	55	12.4	35	3.4	90	6.1	12	6.1
Trade mark	28	6.3	19	1.8	47	3.2	18	9.1
Turnkey	–	–	25	2.4	25	1.7	–	–
Supply and purchase	–	–	2	0.2	2	0.1	6	3.0
Sales/Market/Distribution	–	–	21	2.0	21	1.4	6	3.0
Others	–	–	85	8.3	85	5.8	17	8.5
	442	100.0	1,031	100.0	1,473	100.0	198	100.0

Sources: Malaysia, Ministry of Trade and Industry, and MIDA.

TABLE 4.17

Malaysia: Distribution of Technology Agreements by Industry, 1970–1989

Industry	1970–1978		1979–1987		1970–1987		1989	
	Number	Per Cent	Number	Per Cent	Number	Per Cent	Number	Per Cent
Electrical and electronics	100	22.6	166	16.1	266	18.1	40	20.2
Chemicals	61	13.8	126	12.2	187	12.7	27	13.6
Fabricated metal	52	11.8	110	10.7	162	11.0	7	3.5
Transport	43	9.7	117	11.3	160	10.9	15	7.6
Textiles	27	6.1	36	3.5	63	4.3	4	2.0
Paper products	27	6.1	8	0.8	35	2.4	–	–
Non-metallic minerals	24	5.4	84	8.1	108	7.3	10	5.1
Food	23	5.2	94	9.1	117	7.9	21	10.6
Basic metal	21	4.8	49	4.8	70	4.8	6	3.0
Rubber	16	3.6	66	6.4	82	5.6	18	9.1
Plastic and petroleum	12	2.7	28	2.7	40	2.7	6	3.0
Hotel	7	1.6	36	3.5	43	2.9	6	3.0
Others	29	6.6	111	10.8	140	9.5	38	19.2
Total	442	100.0	1,031	100.0	1,473	100.0	198	100.0

Sources: Malaysia, Ministry of Trade and Industry, and MIDA.

TABLE 4.18

Malaysia: Approved Technology Agreements by Country of Licenser, 1970–1989

Country	1970–1978		1979–1987		1970–1987		1989	
	Number	Per Cent	Number	Per Cent	Number	Per Cent	Number	Per Cent
Japan	152	34.4	313	30.4	465	31.6	87	43.9
United States	68	15.4	110	10.7	178	12.1	23	11.6
Australia	21	4.8	52	5.0	73	5.0	2	1.0
Hong Kong	11	2.5	43	4.2	54	3.7	9	4.5
Singapore	9	2.0	38	3.7	47	3.2	3	1.5
Korea	2	0.5	17	1.6	19	1.3	3	1.5
Sub-total	263	59.5	573	55.6	836	56.8	127	64.1
Others	179	40.5	458	44.4	637	43.2	71	35.9
Total	442	100.0	1,031	100.0	1,473	100.0	198	100.0

Sources: Malaysia, Ministry of Trade and Industry, and MIDA.

the wide variety of jobs within the electronics assembly industries in FTZs (Lester, 1981). A more interesting piece of evidence relates to the diffusion of skills from the electronics industry to the domestic economy. It has been found that the level of sophistication in the local machine shop industry has increased as a result of the industry's contacts with electronics companies, while employees leaving the electronics factories have found the skills they had acquired useful in their new occupations (Lester, 1981).

In the rubber industry, the Rubber Research Institute of Malaysia (RRIM) has stepped up its R & D activities on technological development in tyre manufacturing. Malaysian subsidiaries of Goodyear and Dunlop have benefited from their parent companies not only in terms of technical assistance but also from technological innovations such as radialization. There have also been other spin-offs. For example, the trend towards radialization has led the RRIM to invent epoxidized (chemically modified) natural rubber with such special qualities as wet grip and rolling resistance that are ideal for radial tyres (Fong et al., 1988).

There is evidence of effective transfer of technology relating to the production of oleochemicals, which is much more sophisticated than palm-oil refining (Fong et al., 1988). There are five joint ventures engaged in the manufacture of oleochemicals, with foreign-majority ownership. It has been forecast that by 1995 Malaysia will supply about one-fifth of the world's oleochemical requirements.[11] The oleochemical industry, unlike the electronics industry, is not footloose since Malaysia has an inherent raw material advantage. Given the bright long-term prospects of the industry, it is not surprising that serious efforts to transfer technology are underway. As in the case of rubber tyres, the presence of oleochemical industry has spawned new local R & D efforts. For instance, the Palm Oil Research Institute of Malaysia (PORIM) has stepped up its search for new industrial uses for palm oil.

Readily available case studies (Fong, 1987 and Fong et al., 1988) provide interesting insights into the extent of technology transfer through DFI. All these case-studies, by sheer coincidence, relate to DFI from Asia–Pacific sources and therefore are highly relevant. A couple of these case-studies refer to American MNCs which assemble electronics components in FTZs for export to their parent companies in the United States or other subsidiaries elsewhere. In both cases, technology and equipment were supplied by the parent company, which also patented the basic technology. Although some efforts were made to transfer technology and skill to the local work-force through on-the-job training at home and abroad, the core processes involved in electronics manufacturing were jealously guarded under the guise of patented technology. The training given to local engineers in the parent companies was apparently not sophisticated enough to enable the locals to take on greater responsibilities than supervising assembly operations on the shop floors. Interestingly, these companies also perceived employment generation and export, and not the transfer of technology and skill, as their major function.

Four case-studies concern Japanese MNC subsidiaries: one producing electrical consumer products, another manufacturing iron and steel products, and two others producing textiles. The company producing consumer electronics, mostly for the domestic market, has a technical collaboration agreement with its parent company in Japan which charged technology fees including a 4.0 per cent royalty payment. Although the technology agreement entitled the local company to have access to all technology deemed 'relevant', the parent company had ruled the core processes as being not relevant, and the expertise passed on to the local work-force was confined largely to the adaptation of manufacturing processes to the local conditions. The story is very much the same for the Japanese MNC subsidiary in the iron and steel business. In spite of the fact that the firm's production processes consist mainly of low-level iron and steel fabrication activities, little technology transfer has taken place.

One of the Japanese MNC subsidiaries in the textile business represents a part of the Japanese offshore network of man-made fibre plants; Korea, Taiwan, Hong Kong, and Thailand represent the other locations. Consequently, there have been extensive linkages between the Malaysian plant and its counterparts in the region through importation of capital equipment, raw materials, and components. The study shows that although the parent company sheltered its polyester-staple making technology, it was generous in diffusing yarn-making, garment-weaving, dyeing, and printing technologies. The other Japanese DFI in the case-study produces yarn and fabric using fairly up-to-date technological processes. This firm has its own R & D unit, although its role has been somewhat limited to the adaptation of Japanese technology to the local conditions. There have been some breakthroughs in the adaptation of the spinning and weaving processes to suit Malaysian humidity. But the 'core' processes of spinning and weaving are all innovated in Japan and have been well guarded.

Two other case-studies relating to a Malaysian–Singapore joint venture and a Malaysian–Taiwanese joint venture merit some attention. The former runs a number of textile mills in the country, with machinery and equipment sourced from Britain, Japan, West Germany, and the United States. The textile mills are among the most highly automated, requiring a relatively small work-force. Considerable transfer of technology appears to have occurred, as workers have acquired skills in various aspects of textile manufacturing such as spinning, knitting, printing, dyeing, bleaching, and garment making, and in the maintenance and operation of highly sophisticated machinery and equipment. The Malaysian–Taiwanese joint venture produces copper and aluminium power cables, telephone cables, and underground cables. This may be cited as a case in point where technology has been successfully transferred, as the Malaysians not only understand the wire and cable technology and operate advanced machinery and equipment but also undertake R & D activities which have led this joint venture to diversify its products mix.

It may be gleaned from all this that the American and Japanese MNCs are generally alike in so far as technology transfer to the host country is concerned. The accent in their training programmes, more often than not, seems to be on 'show-how' rather than 'know-how'. By comparison, the NIEs are relatively more willing to transfer their technological skills. The difference is primarily due to cost considerations: developed-country MNCs invest heavily in R & D for purposes of technological innovation, whereas the technology transferred by the NIEs, and other developing countries, is generally copied or represents older technology acquired from advanced countries at much less cost.

However, the extent of technology transfer depends not only on the willingness of the foreigners to impart their knowledge but also on the readiness of the local staff to absorb it. Shortage of skilled personnel seems to be the main cause of low technological absorptive capacity. Nevertheless, the direct transfer of technology from the parent in the home country to the subsidiary in the host country represents only a part of the story. The very presence of MNCs with modern technology often has positive demonstration effects on domestic firms, which also represent an important feature of the overall technological impact of DFI on the host country, apart from the adoption of the management and labour practices of foreign firms.

The role of DFI as a source of technology transfer should not, however, be downplayed. Many semiconductor plants in Malaysia have upgraded themselves: in addition to assembly operations, they also test plastic leaded chip carriers (PLCCs) including fine pinch, small outline integrated circuits (SOICs), pin grid arrays, quad flat packs, and other state-of-the-art packages (O'Connor, 1989). In the textiles industry, air-jet looms are replacing conventional weaving machines (Rasiah, 1989).

One should not disparage technology transfer in the electronics sector. In fact, the human capital in advanced integrated circuit (IC) design and masking has been so well developed in Malaysia that American companies seem to have little choice but to locate prospective increases in production in Malaysia, for no other country in South-East Asia comes close. Even Korea has developed this ability only recently.

Domestic Linkages

Reference must be made to the forward and backward linkages associated with DFI, since many foreign firms source most of their primary factors and raw materials inputs as well as a significant proportion of their intermediate inputs locally, while their output is used as input in domestic firms. However, the domestic linkages of FTZ firms tend to be rather weak, as they have strong external linkages, given the enclave nature of their assembly operations, and their duty-free access to imported raw materials and intermediate inputs. Nevertheless, domestic linkages are not totally absent even in the case of FTZ firms. Thus, for example, local purchases by the Penang FTZ firms in 1982 accounted for about 5 per cent of their total purchases of raw materials and capital goods.[12] Many new domestic industries have come into existence mainly

to serve the FTZs. These include insurance, freight, ?
and die-making, and packaging activities.

Two local engineering firms supply high-precision
ment, spare parts, and machines to semicondu
Malaysia, Singapore, Taiwan, and Korea (Singh, 1.
such medium- and small-scale support industries in Penan
36 of them cater to the MNCs in the three FTZs (Rasiah, 1988).
things remaining equal, local sourcing is preferred so that inventories
can be kept at low or zero level as a cost-cutting measure.

The Japanese subsidiaries, in particular, have begun to source their
inputs locally in recent years, thanks to the appreciation of the yen,
which has rendered imports from Japan expensive. It has been reported
that in 1986 the percentage of local purchases by Japanese manufacturing firms in Asia stood at 66.8 per cent, which is higher than the
59.3 per cent registered by Japanese firms in the United States and
60.9 per cent in Europe.[13] There is evidence to suggest that Japanese
electrical appliance manufacturers in Malaysia have the largest local sub-
contract for sourcing printed circuits, switches, thermostats, etc.[14] By
contrast, the American MNCs hardly resort to local subcontracting.
Nevertheless, both Japanese and American MNCs have increased their
in-company purchases from their factories throughout the region.

It is also of relevance to note that a recent econometric study using
simultaneous equations has revealed foreign investment to be the most
important variable determining both market concentration and
profitability (price–cost margin) in the Peninsular Malaysian manufacturing sector (Kalirajan, 1989).

Employment and Wages

DFI has created substantial employment opportunities for the locals,
notwithstanding the bias in favour of capital-intensive operation, which
may be attributed partly to the structure of investment incentives. FTZ
firms in particular have played an important role in employment generation, as they constitute mainly labour-intensive assembly activities.
Total FTZ employment stood at 70,000 in 1982; the number had
increased to more than 110,000 by 1988. Although breakdown of
employment by home country is not available, a rough estimate suggests
that nearly 90 per cent of it is attributable to DFI from the Asia–Pacific
region, of which more than two-thirds is associated with Japanese and
US investments.

A striking feature of FTZ employment is the high ratio of female
labour. Female workers account for over 75 per cent of the total FTZ
employment. Outside the FTZs, however, the employment pattern
seems much less skewed. While it is no secret that most MNCs have
come to Malaysia to take advantage of low wages, there is no evidence
of workers being 'exploited'. Casual empiricism, based on a random survey, suggests that wages paid by the US and Japanese MNCs are quite
comparable to those paid by local firms.[15]

Regional Development

Some parts of Malaysia are more developed than others. The more developed areas are located in the west coast of Peninsular Malaysia, while the east coast of the peninsula and the Borneo states of Sabah and Sarawak remain relatively underdeveloped. Industries tend to agglomerate regionally, with several states (especially Selangor, Johore, and Penang) accounting for a disproportionate share of the total. Foreign investors have aggravated industrial congestion by clustering around areas where infrastructural facilities are most developed. However, significant dispersions of industries have taken place in recent years. Direct foreign investment, notably from the Asia–Pacific sources, has contributed in no small measure to this process by responding to the call.

The construction of economic and social infrastructure[16] has rendered the industrial estates in the less developed areas attractive. Two other factors have expedited the process. One of these relates to the new-born interstate competition to attract foreign investment,[17] which has fortunately coincided with the recent influx of small- and medium-scale Japanese, Taiwanese, Hong Kong, and Korean ventures which are suited for the less congested locations. The other factor is the emergence of specialized investment zones which cater to particular groups of foreign investors or particular lines of manufacturing: for example, the Selangor state government has delineated a 40-hectare site as a Taiwanese Industrial Park and a 200-acre industrial estate for furniture makers.

Problems and Prospects

Foreign direct investment plays a critical role in the industrial development of Malaysia. Malaysia could not have initiated its industrialization programme without foreign participation, as it lacked the industrial technology, know-how and experience, and managerial expertise at the time of Independence. Over the years, Malaysia has acquired some of these essential ingredients. This does not, however, imply that Malaysia is already in a position to do away with foreign investment, for the character and role of foreign investment have been changing over time. The focus of foreign investors has shifted from import-substitution industries to export-oriented activities. There are also indications that foreign investment is moving away from simple assembly operations towards sophisticated manufacturing of components, parts, and other intermediate inputs.

Policy Considerations

Available data, albeit scanty, give a clear indication of the importance of foreign investment to Malaysia, especially in the industrial sector. These data also reveal the strong Pacific orientation in the structure of foreign investment as well as of the concentration of DFI in a few industries. Shifts in the sectoral allocation pattern in favour of export-oriented industries in recent years are also evident. Although new forms of foreign investment are emerging, DFI still represents by far the most important form of foreign investment in the country.

There are many reasons as to why Malaysia has been actively seeking foreign investment, in addition to its long-cherished open-economy traditions. Modernization of the economy, diversification of the production structure, employment creation, technology transfers, industrial dispersion, and export orientation of the manufacturing sector have been some of the important policy goals. Investment incentive schemes have been designed to achieve these policy objectives. However, the contribution of foreign investment in these areas has apparently been limited, presumably because of a built-in bias in favour of large-scale, capital-intensive projects and policy conflicts.

Despite the active encouragement given to foreign investment, the NEP has imposed limits on the role of DFI, as it sought to reduce foreign equity share in the corporate sector to 30 per cent. Although this is not necessarily inconsistent with an absolute increase in foreign investment, provided that domestic investment can grow sufficiently faster, the NEP did act as a constraint. On the one hand, the NEP called for reduced foreign equity share in the economy, while on the other, the NEP strategy required substantial injections of foreign capital as well as of technical and managerial know-how. This contradiction can be resolved by resorting to 'new' forms of foreign investment such as licensing and franchising agreements and management contracts, but the access to such avenues is severely constrained by Malaysia's limited technological absorptive capacity. In other words, these alternatives are no substitutes for DFI.

Much as the NEP sought to limit foreign ownership, the trends in the balance of payments might have rendered such a policy simply untenable. It was seen in Chapter 2 that Malaysia ran into huge deficits in the current account in the early 1980s and that a large part of the deficit was financed by foreign capital inflows. There are signs that such deficits are reappearing. After three consecutive years of surplus in the current account, balance-of-payments deficit resurfaced in 1989. It seems likely that Malaysia will continue to experience balance-of-payments deficits, as the anticipated trade surplus would not be sufficient to offset the growing deficit in the services account. The fact that much of the latter is due to the outflow of investment income is no argument against foreign investment, for, in the absence of foreign investment, there might be no trade surplus in the first place, given the export orientation of DFI. Besides, foreign investment is preferable to foreign debt, as the latter will need to be serviced regardless of the country's export performance, whereas foreign investments in export-oriented activities will have to generate sufficient foreign exchange earnings before profits can be repatriated. In this sense, foreign debt is a burden, while foreign investment is not. Additionally, risks associated with exchange rate changes are borne by the creditor in the case of foreign investment, whereas in the case of foreign (creditor) currency-denominated debt, such risks more often than not fall entirely on the debtor.

Moreover, the new emphasis on heavy industrialization has also introduced a new dimension. This policy tends to increase the country's dependence on foreign capital and technology significantly, at least in the short and medium terms. Thus, it is extremely difficult to reconcile the NEP equity objective neatly with other national aspirations.

In fairness, it must be pointed out once again that pragmatism has led the government to temporarily shelve the NEP in the wake of the difficult times of the mid-1980s, and that many exceptions for foreign equity participation especially in the export-oriented industries have been granted.

However, it is difficult to ascertain whether the various investment incentives given to foreigners are really necessary. In any case, it is dangerous to make generalizations in this regard as conditions differ greatly between industrial projects and between industrial locations. There are undoubtedly enormous social costs involved in the tax concessions and other exemptions. Although tax incentives are rarely cited by foreign investors as the main reason for investing in the country, there is little doubt that such incentives are viewed as compensation for disincentives. The latter, which imply additional costs and inconvenience for investors, include politically engineered regulations. The first-best solution would therefore be to remove the disincentives and not to compensate. Thus, it may be argued that deregulation and decontrol would make more economic sense than additional tax incentives for purposes of attracting foreign investment.

Future Outlook

It is hard to imagine Malaysia maturing into the NIE status without foreign participation in the industrialization process. In this regard, the role of the Pacific actors is crucial, not only because the market for Malaysian industrial output lies mainly in the countries which are investing heavily in the country, but also because the industrial experiences of some of the major Pacific investors, especially those of the NIEs, are particularly relevant to Malaysia, as the country is apparently trailing the footsteps of those who have succeeded.

Structural changes, especially the de-industrialization process, in the developed countries of the Pacific, augur well for countries like Malaysia which are striving to deepen their industrialization. By the same token, industrial restructuring taking place in the newly industrializing economies also provides opportunities for near-NIEs like Malaysia which aspire to upgrade themselves industrially. DFI from these sources can provide capital, technology, and the marketing network, all of which are crucial for the export-oriented industrialization of host countries.

Of course, Malaysia will have to compete with other developing countries for DFI. Malaysia already has an edge over many others in this respect. It has political stability, infrastructural facilities, efficient administration, an educated and disciplined labour force, Schumpeterian entrepreneurs and, above all, the will to succeed. Its immediate rivals vying for DFI are China, Indonesia, the Philippines and Thailand. None of them can really match what Malaysia can presently offer. Even Thailand, which has been ranked above Malaysia as a DFI venue in recent times, is experiencing difficulties in absorbing foreign capital and technology. All this may mean that Malaysia can effectively compete with other prospective host countries for foreign investment without having to offer additional fiscal incentives to foreign investors, provided that it continues to be pragmatic about its equity goals.

A country's 'revealed comparative attractiveness' as a venue for DFI in manufacturing may be measured by means of an index[18] which expresses the host country's ratio of manufacturing investment to total investment as a proportion of the home country's ratio of its overseas investment in manufacturing to total investment (Montes, 1990). A value of more than unity reveals that the country is more advantageous as a manufacturing location than the overall average, while a value of less than unity suggests the opposite. Table 4.19 presents indices, based on the pattern of Japanese investment, for each country in the Asia–Pacific region versus all developing nations, versus developing Asia, and versus the world. Malaysia's index has increased from 1.47 in 1978 to 2.74 in 1988 by developing country standards, and from 1.87 to 2.75 by world standards. It is also significant to observe that Malaysia's index in 1988 exceeded that of Indonesia, the Philippines and Thailand, regardless of the standards used.

Notwithstanding all these, there are some 'disquieting' signs which one must not lose sight of. The trend towards closer economic integration in Western Europe and the democratization of the Eastern European states are likely to change the DFI equations to the detriment of countries like Malaysia. As a result, the EC may become increasingly Euro-centric and in the worst possible scenario may withdraw from the rest of the world. If the EC becomes a 'fortress', as will be discussed in Chapter 5, exporters to the EC will step up their direct investments in the EC and establish production units there to protect their market share. This might mean less capital inflow into Malaysia from countries like Japan, the United States, and Korea. Recent political developments in Eastern Europe also may lead to a diversion of international resources in the future at the expense of the Third World countries. While such possibilities should be recognized, one must hasten to add that there is no basis for alarm. For one thing, as will be discussed in the next chapter, it is by no means certain that there will be a Fortress Europe after 1992. For another, East European countries have a long way to go before they can shed their hangups and be on par with the eclectic South-East Asian countries in the eyes of foreign investors who tend to cautiously equate Eastern Europe with Latin America. In any case, the effect of all this on Malaysia in terms of DFI flows may well be no more than marginal, given Malaysia's competitive edge *vis-à-vis* other developing countries.

There are also the threats emanating from technological developments

TABLE 4.19

Japanese Overseas Investment and Manufacturing Advantage (Cumulative Approvals) by Country/Region, 1978–1988

Region	Year	Direct Investment		Manufacturing/ Total (per cent)	Manufacturing Advantage Index		
		Total (US$ m.)	Manufacturing (US$ m.)		vs. Dev. Regions	vs. Dev. Asia	vs. World
World	1978	26,809	9,174	34.2			1.000
	1983	53,131	16,952	31.9			1.000
	1988	186,356	49,843	26.7			1.000
Developing Regions	1978	15,150	6,619	43.7	1.000		1.277
	1983	28,390	10,536	37.1	1.000		1.163
	1988	71,786	19,307	26.9	1.000		1.006
Developing Asia	1978	7,668	3,410	44.5	1.018	1.000	1.300
	1983	14,552	5,800	39.9	1.074	1.000	1.249
	1988	32,227	12,371	38.4	1.427	1.000	1.435
Hong Kong	1978	715	145	20.3	0.464	0.456	0.593
	1983	1,825	215	11.8	0.317	0.296	0.369
	1988	6,167	492	8.0	0.297	0.208	0.298
Korea	1978	1,007	697	69.2	1.584	1.556	2.023
	1983	1,312	839	63.9	1.723	1.604	2.004
	1988	3,248	1,589	48.9	1.819	1.274	1.829

Country	Year						
Singapore	1978	2.134	1.642	1.671	73.0	395	541
	1983	2.287	1.830	1.966	73.0	1,009	1,383
	1988	1.952	1.360	1.941	52.2	1,990	3,812
Taiwan	1978	2.737	2.106	2.144	93.7	266	284
	1983	2.872	2.299	2.470	91.6	439	479
	1988	3.075	2.143	3.058	82.2	1,473	1,791
Indonesia	1978	0.910	0.700	0.713	31.1	1,166	3,745
	1983	0.863	0.691	0.742	27.5	2,001	7,268
	1988	1.127	0.785	1.121	30.1	2,955	9,804
Malaysia	1978	1.874	1.442	1.468	64.1	302	471
	1983	2.187	1.750	1.880	69.8	533	764
	1988	2.754	1.919	2.738	73.6	1,350	1,833
Philippines	1978	1.023	0.788	0.802	35.0	152	434
	1983	1.261	1.009	1.084	40.2	290	721
	1988	1.703	1.186	1.693	45.5	510	11,200
Thailand	1978	2.204	1.696	1.726	75.4	233	309
	1983	2.346	1.878	2.017	74.9	390	521
	1988	2.733	1.904	2.718	73.1	1,456	1,992

Source: Montes (1990).

in advanced countries which may effect dramatic factor intensity reversals in manufacturing production (Hoffman, 1985; Hoffman and Rush, 1987). As a result, comparative advantage in major industries of export importance to Malaysia may shift back to developed countries. This danger is exacerbated by the narrow export specialization of Malaysian manufactures in electronics and textiles.

The output structure of the Malaysian electronics industry is dominated by components which account for over 80 per cent of total output; and semiconductors form nearly 90 per cent of the components subsector. This is hardly surprising since the industry itself is dominated by multinational semiconductor firms. The medium-term prospects for the semiconductor industry are unclear, as the industry seems vulnerable to cyclical fluctuations as shown by the experience of the early 1980s. The comparative advantage of Malaysia in the assembly of semiconductors based on cheap labour is being eroded by automation, especially in the case of dynamic random access memory chips (DRAMs). The trend towards the use of application-specific integrated circuits also favours supply locations nearer to the market as it requires close co-ordination between consumers and producers. In addition, Malaysia faces stiff competition from other countries especially in the production of 64K and 256K semiconductors.

All these clearly point to the need for diversification and upgrading. Branching into consumer and industrial electronics, however, is by no means easy. The established firms have a clear edge over the new entrants, as the cost of producing a new generation of products tends to fall sharply with experience. It has been shown that the cost differential between industry leaders and followers tends to be small when the learning rates are very fast or very slow (Spence, 1981). Thus, a steep learning curve would help reduce the disadvantage of the newcomer, as in the case of Korea's semiconductor industry. However, much would depend on (a) the starting point on the learning curve, which for a newcomer is typically higher, and (b) the length of the product cycle, which in the case of electronics is rather short, with new products displacing the old ones at short intervals (Mody and Wheeler, 1989). All these seem to suggest that it is not going to be easy for Malaysia to upstage itself in the electronics sector.

The Malaysian textile industry is also beset with similar predicaments. It is the garment subsector which predominates, successfully commissioning work for foreign clients on the strength of its efficient and low-cost labour force. In the garment industry, new technologies offer major possibilities for cost reduction, especially in the pre-assembly stage. Recent studies have shown that significant productivity gains are possible in developed countries through automation (Hoffman, 1985; Hoffman and Rush, 1987). The growing trend towards high-quality, high-fashion textiles and garments with high inventory turnover also tends to detract from the advantage of cheap labour (Hoffman, 1985). The industry also faces tighter quotas under the MFA. However, Malaysia's 6 per cent annual export volume growth permitted under the

MFA is generous compared with the 1 per cent growth granted to Japan, Korea, and Hong Kong. This should help divert investment from these countries to Malaysia. If, however, textile quotas are globalized under the Uruguay Round, it is almost certain that Malaysia will lose out to countries like China, India, Pakistan, and Bangladesh, where wages are much lower, unless Malaysia upgrades the industry by moving out of simple labour-intensive operations. Admittedly, the argument that an elimination of MFA quotas would hurt the relatively high-wage countries is tenuous. In this regard, it is pertinent to point out that high-wage Hong Kong maintained its market share in Norway where clothing imports were regulated by only global (not country-specific) arrangements during 1978–82 (Abreu, 1989).

In the automotive sector, important changes are taking place, which may alter the industry equations drastically. The US manufacturers have been badly shaken by Japanese inroads into the small and mid-size markets, while Korea is enjoying some competitive success in the US compact market. The prospects of newcomers like Malaysia will depend critically on what Japan chooses to do. Although there are indications that Japan will step up the manufacture of upscale products, it is by no means certain that Japan will cede entry-level sales to the newcomers. What is certain is that the market for automobiles is in for rapid technological change and intense competition. The major Japanese and US firms are investing heavily on factory automation. Simulation analyses have indicated that robotically produced Japanese motor vehicles will cost less than the Korean substitutes, while the US robotic production would yield unit costs comparable to that of imports from Korea (Mody and Wheeler, 1989). The implication is that the competitive environment for Korea will be much tougher than it was for Japan a decade ago. Needless to say, it is going to be an uphill task for Malaysia's Proton Saga in the international market.

It may be inferred from the preceding discussion that DFI inflows into Malaysia in the long term will move towards industries where Malaysia has an inherent comparative advantage. This underscores the need for Malaysia to develop a 'niche' strategy with accent on high-quality, high value-added, Malaysian resource-based products. Since such production invariably entails capital-intensive and technology-intensive processes, the role of DFI will be critical. Japan and the United States are expected to show increased interest in such activities as they are likely to phase out resource-based manufacturing for a variety of reasons including environmental considerations. In so far as the electronics and machinery industries are concerned, developed-country investors seem to prefer the NIEs on account of their strong industrial skills and technological sophistication. However, there is little doubt that DFI from the NIEs will continue to flow into Malaysia's 'traditional' export-oriented manufacturing activities, as this would form an integral part of their strategy to reduce trade frictions with developed countries, especially the United States.

Malaysia may lose its competitive edge as an investment centre, as the current influx of DFI is placing increasing demands on physical infra-structure. A recent report by Japan's Overseas Economic Cooperation Fund (OECF) has argued that Malaysia's physical infrastructure would reach its limit by 1993, if no new infrastructural development projects were undertaken.[19] It is encouraging to note in this regard that the Malaysian Government has set up a special Cabinet Committee headed by the Prime Minister himself to look into the country's infrastructural development. A total of M$2.9 billion (one-third of the 1990 develop-ment budget) was allocated for roads, highways, airports, and electricity and water supplies.

Investment–Trade Linkages

The link between trade and investment is readily obvious, given the fact that the bulk of DFI in Malaysia is accounted for by export-oriented activities which in turn have duty-free access to imports of machinery, equipment, raw materials, and intermediate inputs.

A vivid case in point is the Mitsubishi brand-to-brand car parts com-plementation scheme involving Malaysia, the Philippines, and Thailand, which has important implications for both intra-regional and intra-industry trade. This involves a regional division of labour, with Malaysia concentrating on the production of door panels and other stamped parts, Thailand specializing in the manufacture of fuel tanks, consoles, bumpers, windshields, etc., and the Philippines, transmission parts.

Already, the Mitsubishi group is sourcing automobile parts and com-ponents from a network of affiliates and subsidiaries in ASEAN, Australia, and Canada. In fact, all major Japanese automotive producers, including Toyota, Honda, Nissan, Isuzu, Mitsubishi, and Mazda, have formed networks of affiliates and subsidiaries which span ASEAN and the East Asian NIEs (Phongpaichit, 1990). Several Japanese firms in the electronics industry are developing complex production networks span-ning several countries in the Asia–Pacific region. All these bode well for intra-firm trade among Japanese subsidiaries and between subsidiaries and parent companies.

A finding of considerable importance, as seen in Chapter 3, is that intra-industry trade is on the increase. This is particularly pronounced in the case of Malaysia's trade with industrialized and newly industrializ-ing economies. And there are reasons to believe that the bulk of the intra-industry trade consists of intra-firm sales. The latter is intimately related to direct foreign investments in Malaysia's manufacturing sector in general and export-oriented industries in particular. More specifically, the role of multinationals and the presence of transfer pricing in intra-firm sales have rendered the structure of trade in manufactures so com-plex that it cannot be analysed within the simple framework of traditional theory. In other words, comparative advantage cannot be adequately explained in terms of factor and resource endowments. Thus, for example, it would seem inconsistent with the factor propor-tions theory that Malaysia should export labour-intensive products since

wages in Malaysia are relatively high. The real explanation may well be that Malaysia outsmarted its neighbours by taking a lead in the establishment of FTZs. Perhaps, higher labour costs have been outweighed by 'other' things which Malaysia can offer better than its neighbours whose wages are lower.

An important policy implication of the above discussion is that Malaysia has little choice in the direction of its external trade in manufactures, given the structure of direct foreign investments in the country. It would then follow that the Malaysian trade policy is heavily influenced by, or dependent on, its foreign investment policy and not the other way around. To put it differently, Malaysia can bring about changes in its trade structure only via changes in the structure of foreign investments in the country.

1. Joint ventures may take the form of majority foreign interest (more than 50 per cent foreign equity), minority foreign interest (less than 50 per cent foreign equity), or equal participation joint ventures (50–50 foreign–local equity).
2. Wholly owned foreign companies operate with 100 per cent foreign equity.
3. Turnkey projects involve the setting up of plants and industrial complexes complete with supply of equipment by foreign investors.
4. See Saham (1980).
5. See Ali and Rani (1984).
6. Malaysia (1983), Table 3-14, p. 62.
7. Langhammer and Gross (1986) and Wagner (1989) have also made references to the discrepancy between realized and approved foreign investment in Malaysia.
8. MIDA, *Malaysia: Your Profit Centre in Asia* (undated).
9. According to MIDA statistics, Bermuda dominates foreign investment in the Malaysian leather industry, accounting for 89.4 per cent of foreign paid-up capital and 89.7 per cent of foreign-owned fixed assets.
10. Japanese firms in Malaysia sold 87.3 per cent of their output in the local market in 1973 whereas American companies in Malaysia exported 76.2 per cent of their output. See Hill and Johns (1984).
11. See Malaysia (1986b), *Industrial Master Plan 1986–1995*.
12. See Arif (1986c).
13. JETRO (1990), *Tradescope*, 10(1), January, p. 10.
14. See Fong et al. (1988).
15. See Arif (1984).
16. These include highways, telecommunication networks, and port facilities and institutional arrangements.
17. Individual states have been (a) sending missions abroad to lure foreign investment into their respective states, and (b) participating in international trade fairs.
18. Formally:

$$\frac{M_{ij}}{I_{ij}} \Big/ \frac{M_j}{I_j}$$

where M_{ij} = manufacturing investment in host country i by home country j;
I_{ij} = total investment in host country i by home country j;
M_j = overseas manufacturing investment by home country j; and
I_j = total overseas investment by home country j.

19. The OECF report was quoted in the *Asian Intelligence* published by Political and Economic Risk Consultancy Ltd., Hong Kong, 16 May 1990.

5
Moving into the Pacific Century

THERE are ominous signs that the centre of gravity is shifting slowly but surely from the Atlantic to the Pacific. The dawning of the Pacific Age by the turn of the century, it is anticipated, will bring with it both opportunities and challenges which will have important implications not only for the countries in the Pacific Basin but also for those on the periphery and in the rest of the world. Malaysia occupies an important position in the Pacific and will have much to contribute to, and to benefit from, the Pacific dynamism.

The vast literature on the Pacific region raises more questions than it answers. How realistic is this prophecy about the Pacific Era in the twenty-first century? What will it mean for the major actors in the centre stage? Will Pacific countries be able to organize themselves to meet the challenges of the Pacific Age? What are the implications of all this for the vibrant, albeit small, economy of Malaysia? An attempt is made in this chapter to address these and other related issues.

Economic Dynamism

The Pacific Basin is the home of some of the most dynamic economies in the world. It is only the Pacific developing countries which have made a successful transition to developed-country status within a short span of time in recent history. The spectacular economic performance of Japan is by no means an exception. Indeed, the East Asian NIEs have also become show-pieces of the Pacific. The performance of the ASEAN economies has been splendid by developing-country standards. In fact, East Asia has now become the world's 'economic powerhouse'.[1] Continuous expansion of the US economy through the 1980s has facil-itated the economic success of the region.[2] Structural changes taking place in the Pacific developed economies, including Australia, Canada, and New Zealand, have also spurred adjustments elsewhere in the Pacific.

The Asia–Pacific region is particularly well endowed with a variety of natural resources. Nearly all minerals required by industry are found in sufficiently large quantities. Energy resources of the region are sub-stantial and agricultural and forest resources are abundant. The region has a sizeable food surplus, with the United States, Canada, Australia,

TABLE 5.1

Asia–Pacific Countries: Basic Indicators, 1988

Group/Countries	Population[1] (million)	Population Growth (%) (1965–1988)[2]	Area (1 000 sq. km)	GDP[3] (US$m.)	GDP[3] Per Capita (US$)	Merchandise Exports (US$m.)[4]
Developing countries						
NIEs						
Hong Kong	5.7	2.4	1	53,195	9,332	63,161
Korea	42.0	1.7	99	150,382	3,581	60,697
Singapore	2.7	1.6	1	23,875	8,843	39,324
Taiwan	19.7	2.0	36	112,828	5,727	60,502
ASEAN						
Brunei	0.2	n.a.	6	3,422	15,421	1,798
Indonesia	175.2	2.2	1 919	69,667	409	17,135
Malaysia	16.9	2.7	330	34,634	2,049	21,110
Philippines	58.7	2.7	300	38,959	664	7,074
Thailand	54.6	2.5	542	56,140	1,028	15,869
Other Asia–Pacific						
China[5]	1,087.3	1.8	9 561	300,341	278	47,540
Cook Islands[6]	<0.1	n.a.	<1	33	1,916	7
Fiji	0.7	1.9	18	1,081	1,517	307
Kiribati	n.a.	n.a.	1	23	350	2
Papua New Guinea	3.6	2.3	462	3,565	990	1,420
Solomon Islands	0.3	3.2	28	141	487	64

(continued)

TABLE 5.1 (continued)

Group/Countries	Population[1] (million)	Population Growth (%) (1965–1988)[2]	Area (1 000 sq. km)	GDP[3] (US$m.)	GDP[3] Per Capita (US$)	Merchandise Exports (US$m.)[4]
Tonga	0.1	n.a.	1	78	822	7
Vanuatu	0.1	3.1	12	120	826	17
Western Samoa	0.2	1.1	3	109	678	15
Developed countries						
Australia	16.5	1.6	7 687	193,785	11,925	32,910
Canada	26.1	1.2	9 976	417,700	16,285	114,632
Japan	122.7	0.9	372	2,384,458	19,530	264,856
New Zealand	3.3	1.0	269	35,092	10,699	8,832
United States	246.1	1.0	9 363	4,461,200	18,301	321,600

Sources: Asian Development Bank, *Key Indicators of Developing Member Countries of ADB*, July 1989; Brunei, Ministry of Finance, *Brunei Statistical Yearbook 1984/1985*; Far Eastern Economic Review, *Asia Yearbook 1989*; Hong Kong, Census and Statistics Department, *Hong Kong Monthly Digest of Statistics*, August 1988; International Monetary Fund, *International Financial Statistics*, Yearbook 1988 and June 1989; Population Reference Bureau, *1988 World Population Data Sheet*; Republic of China, Directorate-General of Budget, Accounting and Statistics, Executive Yuan, *Statistical Yearbook of the Republic of China 1987*; United Nations, *Demographic Yearbook 1970*; World Bank, *World Development Report 1989*; Naya et al. (1989b).

[1] 1985 for Brunei.
[2] 1961–1988 for Hong Kong.
[3] 1983 for Tonga; 1985 for Brunei; 1986 for Cook Islands, Kiribati, and Western Samoa; and 1987 for China, Indonesia, Solomon Islands, and Vanuatu.
[4] 1987 for Brunei, Cook Islands, Indonesia, Kiribati, Solomon Islands, Tonga, and Vanuatu.
[5] Gross national product.
[6] Population for Cook Islands is 17,300 and area is 236 sq. km.
n.a. = Not available.

and New Zealand accounting for the bulk of it. Many of the developing countries in the region have also made impressive gains in food production during the 1980s. Even if North America were excluded, the Western Pacific region alone accounts for about one-sixth of the world's exports of wheat, two-thirds of mutton and lamb, and two-fifths of rice exports. The Western Pacific provides more than 80 per cent of the world's exports of natural rubber, over 90 per cent of palm-oil exports, about 70 per cent of tropical hardwood exports, nearly 80 per cent of exports of coconut oil and copra, and about 70 per cent of wood exports. The Asia–Pacific region has a high degree of self-sufficiency in natural resources. In other words, the regional pattern of resource endowments provides a viable basis for a high degree of intra-regional complementarity and interdependence within the Pacific Basin.

A profile of the Asia–Pacific economies is presented in Table 5.1, which underscores the point that the region represents a heterogeneous 'grouping'. Japan has the highest per capita income, followed by the United States. The NIEs constitute the middle-income category, with some ASEAN countries and South Pacific islands trailing behind. The Asia–Pacific region accounts for more than one-half of the world output (Table 5.2). A striking observation is that Japan's share of the world output trebled between 1965 and 1987, while that of the other developed countries in the region declined. The shares of the NIEs and ASEAN also increased creditably during this period.

TABLE 5.2
Asia–Pacific Share in World Output, 1965 and 1987

	1965		1987	
	US$ billion	Per Cent	US$ billion	Per Cent
Australia, Canada, and New Zealand	75.2	4.3	590.5	3.9
United States	701.8	40.1	4,496.6	29.7
Japan	91.0	5.2	2,377.0	15.7
NIEs[1]	8.8	0.5	272.5	1.8
ASEAN-4[2]	17.5	1.0	181.7	1.2
China	64.8	3.7	287.7	1.9
Asia–Pacific	959.0	54.8	8,205.9	54.2
EC	453.3	25.9	4,148.4	27.4
Others	337.7	19.3	2,785.8	18.4
World	1,750.0	100.0	15,140.0	100.0

Sources: Asian Development Bank, Key Indicators of Developing Member Countries of ADB, July 1989; Republic of China, Statistical Yearbook of the Republic of China 1987; World Bank (1989b).
[1] Includes Korea, Taiwan, Hong Kong, and Singapore.
[2] Includes Indonesia, Malaysia, the Philippines, and Thailand.

TABLE 5.3
Average Annual Rates of Growth of Real GDP in the Asia-Pacific, 1960–1988

Country/group	1960–1969[1]	1970–1979[2]	1980–1987[3]	1985	1986	1987	1988
Developing countries							
NIEs							
Hong Kong	10.0	9.4	8.1	-0.1	11.8	13.5	7.4
Korea	8.5	9.8	7.2	5.4	11.7	11.1	11.0
Singapore	8.9	9.6	6.4	-1.6	1.8	8.8	11.0
Taiwan	11.6	10.1	7.4	4.3	10.6	11.1	6.8
ASEAN							
Brunei	n.a.	12.2	-3.7	-0.3	n.a.	n.a.	n.a.
Indonesia	3.5	7.7	4.9	1.9	3.2	3.6	3.8[4]
Malaysia	6.5	8.1	5.0	-1.1	1.2	5.4	8.9
Philippines[5]	4.9	6.3	1.0	-4.1	2.0	5.7	6.4
Thailand	8.3	7.0	5.1	3.2	3.5	6.3	11.0
Other Asia–Pacific							
China[6]	2.9	7.5	9.2	17.4	8.0	10.3	12.2[4,7]
Fiji	7.4	5.3	0.5	-4.6	8.8	-7.8	-2.5
Papua New Guinea	4.5	5.4	2.0	4.8	5.0	4.8	5.2

Developed countries						
Australia	5.1	3.3	3.4	1.8	4.3	3.0
Canada	5.7	4.7	2.9	4.0	5.2	4.5
Japan[5]	12.1	5.2	3.9	4.7	5.7	5.7
New Zealand	4.1	2.2	1.0	1.5	0.4	0.4
United States[5]	4.1	2.8	2.3	3.4	-2.3	2.9

Sources: Asian Development Bank, Key Indicators of Developing Member Countries of ADB, April 1983 and 1984, and July 1987, 1988, and 1989; Brunei, Ministry of Finance, Economic Planning Unit, Statistics Section, Brunei Statistical Yearbook, 1978/1979, 1981/1982, 1982/1983, 1983/1984, and 1984/1985 issues; Far Eastern Economic Review, 31 August 1989; International Monetary Fund, International Financial Statistics, Yearbook 1987 and 1988, and June 1989; Malaysia, Ministry of Finance, Economic Report 1990/91; Pacific Economic Cooperation Conference, Pacific Economic Outlook 1989–1990; Republic of China, Council for Economic Planning and Development, Taiwan Statistical Data Book 1988; World Bank, World Development Report 1982; Naya et al. (1989b).

[1] 1960–70 for Hong Kong and Malaysia; 1961–9 for Singapore and Indonesia; 1962–9 for Canada; 1966–9 for Fiji; and 1967–9 for Papua New Guinea.
[2] 1971–9 for Malaysia; and 1975–9 for Brunei.
[3] 1980–5 for Brunei.
[4] Preliminary estimates.
[5] Real GNP.
[6] Real national income.
[7] Estimate of real GDP.
n.a. = Not available.

The Asia–Pacific region has been growing economically from strength to strength at a much faster pace than the rest of the world. Thus, for example, in the 1970s, many Pacific economies registered an average annual growth rate of 6 to 8 per cent, while Western Europe averaged 3 to 4 per cent.[3] Although the growth rates in the 1980s paled in comparison with those of the 1970s due to the impact of the world-wide recession, the Pacific countries did return to their growth path in the second half of the decade. On the whole, the developing countries in the Asia–Pacific have fared better than the developed ones in terms of their real GDP growth. This is particularly evident in the case of the NIEs and China (Table 5.3).

The Pacific dynamism is reflected even more visibly in the trade figures. The share of the Asia–Pacific in world trade increased from 34 per cent in 1965 to 38 per cent in 1987. The share of the developed countries in the region, with the notable exception of Japan, in world exports declined between 1970 and 1987, but the shares of the NIEs, ASEAN and China increased significantly (Table 5.4). What is particularly striking is the fact that almost all countries in the region increased their Pacific orientation, as the share of the Asia–Pacific destinations in the exports of Asia–Pacific countries rose significantly during 1970–87. Thus, the share of Asia–Pacific destinations in the total Asia–Pacific exports increased from 54 per cent in 1970 to 66 per cent in 1987. Figure 5.1 illustrates the growing volume of trade flows among Asia–Pacific countries between 1980 and 1988.

This trend is further corroborated by the import figures in Table 5.5. In 1987, the Asia–Pacific absorbed 39 per cent of the world imports, compared with 33 per cent in 1970. Most countries in the region, notably the developing ones, increased their share of world imports during the same period. Even more interesting is the observation that nearly all of them are sourcing their imports from within the region rather than without. Thus, in 1987, Asia–Pacific countries obtained 64 per cent of their imports from Asia–Pacific sources, as against 59 per cent in 1970.

It can be inferred from all these that Asia–Pacific trade interdependence is growing markedly. This message is brought out even more clearly in Table 5.6 which provides an insight into the intra-Pacific trade. The volume of intra-regional trade, in terms of both imports and exports, increased more than ten times during 1970–87. The contributions of the NIEs, in particular, to the intra-regional exports and imports increased sharply between 1970 and 1987, while those of Australia, New Zealand, and Canada declined. The US contribution to intra-regional exports has declined, but its share of intra-regional imports has increased, while the reverse has been the case for Japan and ASEAN. To put it differently, the United States is importing more from the region than it is exporting to it, while Japan and ASEAN are exporting more to the region than they are importing from it.

TABLE 5.4

Asia–Pacific Exports in Relation to World Exports, 1970 and 1987 (percentage)

Country	1970		1987	
	Share of World Exports	Share of Asia–Pacific Destinations in Country's Exports	Share of World Exports	Share of Asia–Pacific Destinations in Country's Exports
Australia	1.7	64.3	1.1	68.9
Canada	5.9	70.0	4.2	82.6
Japan	6.8	61.3	9.8	66.7
New Zealand	0.4	43.1	0.3	63.4
United States	15.3	40.1	10.6	49.7
Hong Kong	0.9	60.7	2.1	70.7
Korea	0.3	85.5	2.0	71.3
Singapore	0.6	59.3	1.2	71.7
Taiwan	0.5	76.9	2.3	76.9
Brunei	0.0	100.0	0.1	97.0
Indonesia	0.4	80.5	0.7	87.0
Malaysia	0.6	68.1	0.8	76.6
Philippines	0.4	89.8	0.2	76.8
Thailand	0.3	67.7	0.5	61.3
China	0.6	55.3	1.7	66.6
Pacific Islands[1]	0.1	60.8	0.1	60.2
Asia–Pacific	34.8	54.4	37.6	65.6
World exports (US$ billion)	282.6		2,354.4	

Source: East–West Center database, Honolulu.
[1] Includes Fiji, Kiribati, Papua New Guinea, Solomon Islands, Tonga, Vanuatu, and Western Samoa.

FIGURE 5.1
Expansion of Intra-regional Trade in the Asia–Pacific Region
(US$ billion)

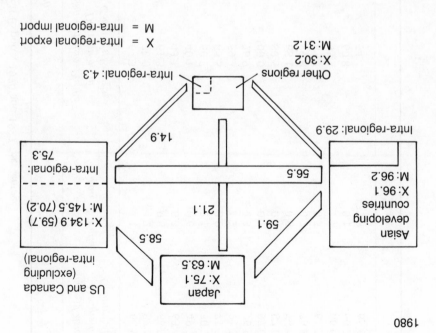

1980

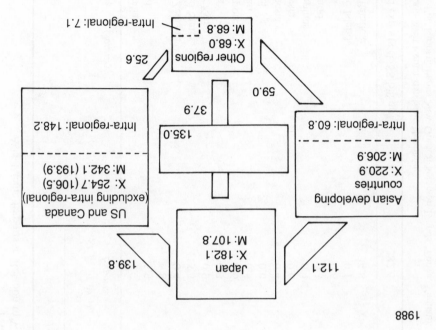

1988

X = Intra-regional export
M = Intra-regional import

Source: JETRO (1990).

Note: Other regions include Australia/New Zealand, the Oceanian developing countries, and the Asian socialist nations.

TABLE 5.5

Asia-Pacific Imports in Relation to World Imports, 1970 and 1987 (percentage)

Country	1970		1987	
	Share of World Imports	Share of Asia-Pacific Origin in Country Imports	Share of World Imports	Share of Asia-Pacific Origin in Country Imports
Australia	1.5	50.4	1.1	64.5
Canada	4.6	75.6	3.7	78.7
Japan	6.4	57.5	6.2	61.2
New Zealand	0.4	51.8	0.3	67.0
United States	14.4	51.8	17.4	57.4
Hong Kong	1.0	68.4	2.0	81.6
Korea	0.7	81.8	1.7	70.6
Singapore	0.9	69.1	1.4	71.2
Taiwan	0.5	81.2	1.4	71.0
Brunei	0.0	84.8	0.0	52.7
Indonesia	0.3	66.7	0.4	70.4
Malaysia	0.5	65.1	0.5	77.4
Philippines	0.4	74.8	0.3	71.4
Thailand	0.4	63.8	0.5	68.7
China	0.6	51.8	1.8	65.7
Pacific Islands[1]	0.1	80.3	0.1	88.1
Asia-Pacific	32.8	59.2	38.9	64.2
World imports (US$ billion)	297.1		2,435.2	

Source: East–West Center database, Honolulu.
[1] Includes Fiji, Kiribati, Papua New Guinea, Solomon Islands, Tonga, Vanuatu, and Western Samoa.

TABLE 5.6
Intra-Pacific Trade, 1970 and 1987

	Share of Regional Exports (per cent)		Share of Regional Imports (per cent)	
	1970	1987	1970	1987
Australia and New Zealand	7	4	5	4
Canada	22	14	18	12
USA	32	21	38	40
Japan	22	27	19	15
NIEs[1]	8	22	12	19
ASEAN-4[2]	6	7	9	5
Others	3	5	2	5
Total Intra-Pacific Trade (US$ billion)	53.5	581.3	57.7	607.8

Sources: As for Table 5.2.

[1]Includes Korea, Taiwan, Hong Kong, and Singapore.

[2]Includes Indonesia, Malaysia, the Philippines, and Thailand.

In 1976, for the first time in history, the US trade with the Western Pacific exceeded that with Western Europe.[4] This trend has gathered momentum in recent years. The manufactured exports of Pacific developing countries find a more open market in the United States than in Japan. The latter has been more readily absorbing primary products of the developing countries in the region. Australia has also been serving as a major source of primary products and minerals.

What makes all this all the more interesting is that the protectionist forces in the Pacific Basin have not been able to stop the expansion of intra-regional trade. Although tariff barriers have been generally reduced through the various multilateral trade negotiations, there has been a proliferation of measures such as quantitative import restrictions, voluntary export restraints, and organized marketing arrangements. Japan and the East Asian NIEs have been affected most by these measures. Of particular concern to developing countries in the region are NTBs on textiles and clothing. This sector has been systematically squeezed by the Multifibre Arrangements. Countervailing duty represents another major hardcore NTB. The US record in this respect is distressing, particularly for developing countries against whom much of the US trade investigations have been levelled. The adverse effects of all these, especially on developing countries in the region, could not be offset by the nominal preferential treatment accorded to them through the Generalised System of Preferences. The latter is circumscribed in a number of ways, including narrow product coverage and the 'competitive need limit' rule, as was seen in Chapter 3.

Equally interesting are the ways in which the developing countries of the region have 'overcome' some of these barriers. Korea and Taiwan have responded to the VERs, in the case of differentiated products by upgrading their products, changing the export routes and shifting the production locations. For undifferentiated products like textiles and steel, transhipment (cheating on rules of origin) has been increasingly resorted to. Such avenues for circumventing or bypassing trade restrictions have rendered some of the trade barriers somewhat ineffective.[5] For a long time South Korea and Taiwan have also successfully used exchange rate policy to promote their exports and, at times, to thwart the protectionist forces.[6] Thus, intra-regional trade has increased sharply, despite the protectionist tide, although it cannot be denied that it would have flourished in the absence of trade restrictions.

Trade disputes in the region have increased and intensified, especially between the United States on the one hand and Japan and the East Asian NIEs on the other, for closer interdependence also implies increased friction of sorts. Some of these disputes may be attributed to the protectionist forces which are relentlessly at work. In particular, CVD investigations and anti-dumping actions have caused considerable anxiety and uneasiness. Central to all these is the huge US trade deficit with Japan, Korea, and Taiwan. The US pressure on these countries to revalue their currencies led to a sharp appreciation of the Japanese yen, the Korean won, and the New Taiwan dollar in the late 1980s, but it appears that exchange rate corrections alone would be inadequate to redress the trade imbalance. Arguably, the situation calls for fundamental structural adjustments, especially in the US economy. Japan and Australia have been taken to task by some ASEAN countries for not opening their markets sufficiently to ASEAN manufactures. The US–Japan trade disputes have affected other countries in the periphery that get caught in the crossfire. The major players often ignore the implications of their dispute settlement for others in the region. An example of this danger was manifested when Japan agreed to import more American plywood at the expense of ASEAN plywood, and American beef at the expense of Australia and New Zealand.

Not surprisingly, growing interdependence in Asia–Pacific trade has been accompanied by rising intra-regional investment flows. However, the directions in which such investments flow within the region have been somewhat uneven. As the United States has emerged as a net importer of capital in recent years, its role as a major source of foreign direct investment for other Pacific countries has dwindled, in relative terms. The Asia–Pacific share of US foreign investment had declined from 35.8 per cent in 1966 to 31.8 per cent in 1977, although subsequently it increased marginally to 32.3 per cent in 1981.[7] Besides, the bulk of the US investment in the region (about 86 per cent) has gone to the developed countries, while the balance has gone almost entirely to ASEAN and the East Asian NIEs.[8] Japan, a major source of international capital, has been investing

heavily in the Asia–Pacific countries. It is no accident that more than 40 per cent of the capital inflows into the United States was accounted for by Japan in 1988; nor is it insignificant that the Japanese investments of US$84 billion in the United States far exceed the US$56 billion it has invested in the European Community.[9] Japan is also a major, often the largest, investor in the NIEs and ASEAN countries. In recent years, the Asian NIEs themselves have emerged as important sources of foreign capital, especially in the ASEAN subregion. Some NIE investments, particularly Korean and Taiwanese, have also found their way into the developed countries of the Pacific, especially the United States and Canada. They have set up plants in these countries in their attempts to overcome the trade barriers, after having been graduated out of the developing-country preferential status.[10]

Exchange rate realignments in recent years have also contributed immensely to the building of new investment networks in the Pacific Basin. The strong appreciation of the yen, the New Taiwan dollar, and to a lesser extent the Korean won, has set in motion a train of offshore investments in the direction of South-East Asia. Japanese, Taiwanese, and Korean firms are investing heavily in manufacturing facilities in ASEAN to cut down production costs so that they can compete effectively in the international market and maintain their market shares.

Rapid structural changes taking place in developed countries in the wake of the changing patterns of international division of labour have also contributed significantly to the intra-regional movement of capital in the Pacific Basin.[11] As a result, 'sunset' industries in one part of the Asia–Pacific have re-emerged as 'sunrise' industries in another part of the region. In the dynamic setting of the Pacific, it is not unusual to find some countries losing their comparative advantage in certain activities to some others, and replacing them with new products and new processes.[12] Indices of revealed comparative advantage[13] presented in Table 5.7 reflect the shifts in comparative advantage taking place in the Asia–Pacific region.

Evidently, Japan and the United States have lost their comparative advantage in labour-intensive manufactures while maintaining their competitive lead in technology-intensive manufactures. The NIEs enjoy strong comparative advantage in unskilled labour-intensive manufactures and have also gained new competitive strengths in human capital-intensive manufactures. In ASEAN, agricultural resource-intensive manufactures have a strong showing in terms of comparative advantage. Indonesia and Malaysia, in particular, and presumably Australia, too, have tremendous comparative advantage in mineral resource-intensive activities as well. Singapore has lost its comparative advantage in resource-intensive manufactures (since Indonesia and Malaysia have developed their own capabilities in these areas) but has gained comparative advantage in technology-intensive activities.

In a dynamic situation, the pattern of comparative advantage is constantly changing. While some industries 'migrate' from the more advanced industrialized countries to the industrializing ones in the

TABLE 5.7
Asia–Pacific Manufactures: Revealed Comparative Advantage

Country	Agricultural Resource-intensive			Mineral Resource-intensive			Unskilled Labour-intensive			Human Capital-intensive			Technology-intensive		
	1970	1980	1986	1970	1980	1986	1970	1980	1986	1970	1980	1986	1970	1980	1986
Japan	0.22	0.11	0.07	0.17	0.10	0.12	1.70	0.78	0.51	1.75	2.42	1.73	1.21	1.71	1.55
United States	0.99	1.53	1.13	0.54	0.32	0.43	0.44	0.62	0.42	1.02	1.02	0.91	1.40	1.59	1.34
Korea	0.79	0.60	0.38	0.39	0.11	0.21	5.62	4.74	3.40	0.21	1.33	1.07	0.29	0.79	0.79
Taiwan	1.13	0.68	0.52	0.24	0.12	0.21	4.22	5.49	4.06	0.33	0.60	0.54	0.65	1.06	0.90
Hong Kong	0.23	0.30	0.39	0.36	0.17	0.20	5.88	5.70	4.42	0.22	0.33	0.25	0.59	1.25	0.97
Singapore	2.13	1.20	0.84	1.33	1.02	1.34	0.79	0.85	0.76	0.30	0.39	0.26	0.39	1.11	1.32
Indonesia	2.60	1.43	1.09[1]	2.30	2.44	3.22[1]	0.00	0.11	0.79[1]	0.01	0.00	0.00[1]	0.01	0.02	0.03[1]
Malaysia	2.93	3.07	2.50[2]	1.53	1.13	1.40[2]	0.29	0.56	0.46[2]	0.11	0.07	0.10[2]	0.05	0.46	0.63[2]
Philippines	3.32	2.78	2.19[1]	1.19	0.72	0.53[1]	0.45	1.60	1.40[1]	0.05	0.10	0.07[1]	0.00	0.12	0.31[1]
Thailand	3.55	3.82	3.85[1]	0.86	0.54	0.43[1]	0.18	1.40	1.98[1]	0.02	0.12	0.11[1]	0.00	0.23	0.33[1]

Source: Computed from the East-West Center database statistics.
[1] Data for 1985.
[2] Data for 1984.

region, as the former move up the ladder, in what has been characterized as the 'flying geese pattern' in the Japanese international economics
literature, a reverse movement has also been made possible by technological innovations. Some recent studies have suggested that productivity and competitiveness can increase substantially through the
appropriate use of new micro-electronic technologies and automation.[14]
Although there is no evidence of any major reverse movement of industries in the Asia–Pacific region, such a possibility cannot, of course, be
ruled out. Even if it does take place, it is unlikely that countries like the
ASEAN members will return to square one, since there are bound to be
significant ratchet effects. Besides, possibilities for new products and
new processes are almost infinite, and it will certainly take many countries in the region to orchestrate the dynamic forces that are at play.

The competitive dynamics of the Pacific requires a sound macroeconomic environment to manifest itself. There is a general consensus
among economists that unless a country gets its macroeconomic policy
right, other policies, no matter how well conceived and implemented,
would be of no avail. Macroeconomic management in the Asia–Pacific
generally appears to be on an even keel, with reasonably low rates of
inflation and unemployment, and high growth rates of real GDP in
most countries. However, internal and external imbalances have posed
serious problems in some countries. External debt constitutes a major
problem for some countries in the region, but the problem is not as
widespread as in Latin America.

The growing economic interdependence in the Asia–Pacific tends to
dilute or eat into the 'sovereignty' of the economies of the region by
reducing the scope for unilateral or independent policy actions, especially on the part of the smaller entities. Economic openness brings with
it not only prosperity through more efficient resource allocations, but
also problems associated with exposure to external fluctuations.
Although such problems can be handled via an appropriate policy mix,
the task is by no means easy.

In this regard, the United States plays a critical role, given its dominant position. For example, the huge twin deficits of the United States
have caused problems not only for the US economy but also for others
which maintain close economic relations with the United States. As is
well known, the US twin deficits have led to both increased interest
rates in the United States, causing massive diversion of international
capital flows away from other countries, and increased protectionist
measures with adverse consequences for its trading partners. The manner in which the United States handles its problems also has implications for other economies. For instance, the US attempts to correct its
external imbalance through trade interventions have not augured well
for others in the region and arguably amounted to treating the symp-
toms rather than the disease.

The US problem, it seems, has its roots in its expansionary fiscal
policy, which led to increased budget deficits, private consumption, and
imports on the one hand, and reduced private savings and sluggish

exports on the other, all of which added up to extremely severe and persistent balance-of-payments strains.

The inflow of foreign capital, lured by high interest rates, caused the US dollar to appreciate, which only served to exacerbate the country's external deficit problem. It was the Plaza Agreement in September 1985 which resulted in the depreciation of the US dollar and the sharp appreciation of the Japanese yen.

Recent experience has shown that the above exchange rate realignments, while helpful, cannot correct the chronic external imbalance problem which in the Asia–Pacific context simply boils down to the US–Japan bilateral trade gaps. Expenditure switches via exchange rate changes by themselves cannot cure the US trade deficit, when domestic macroeconomic imbalance is the main cause of the deficit.[15] Economies which benefited most from this dollar–yen realignment seem to be those whose products replaced the Japanese products in the US market by virtue of the fact that their currencies did not appreciate as much against the dollar as the yen.

However, recent policy changes and structural adjustments which are underway in the United States are serving to reduce the tension. Structural reforms include substantial budget expenditure cuts— especially the drastic reductions in defence—increase in domestic savings, and emergence of export consciousness among the US producers. It is encouraging to note that the US exports grew at a 30 per cent rate in 1988 to record levels, and that the imports by Japan and the East Asian NIEs from the United States grew by 30–40 per cent in 1988.

The region, in general, appears to be in much better shape now than it was in the early 1980s. The deep-seated world recession of the early 1980s did hurt some countries badly. Attempts by some resource-rich countries to ride out the recession by pursuing counter-cyclical macroeconomic policies led to other problems including soaring external debts. As was seen in Chapter 2, Malaysia has managed its external debts remarkably well. It is Australia, Indonesia, and the Philippines which are saddled with the heaviest debt burdens in the Western Pacific. Overall, Asia–Pacific countries seem to have weathered the recessionary crisis of the 1980s just as well as they did the oil shocks of 1973 and 1979, by adopting reasonably sound macroeconomic policies. The region has demonstrated its resilience and its ability to adjust and adapt to changing economic circumstances in a pragmatic fashion.

The future economic prospects of the Asia–Pacific region are tremendous. It is envisaged that the share of the Asia–Pacific in world output will increase to 48.0 per cent by the year 2000, from 44.0 per cent in 1981 (Table 5.8). Much of this increase is likely to come from developing countries in the Western Pacific, whose share of world output is expected to more than double from 4.5 per cent in 1981 to 10.0 per cent by 2000. The North American share is projected to shrink a little by 1.5 percentage points to 27.0 per cent during this period, while that of the other developed countries in the region is likely to remain unchanged at 11.0 per cent.

The developing countries of the region, i.e. the East Asian NIEs, ASEAN, and China, would generate most of the heat, growing at an average rate of about 7.5 per cent per annum. The projections in Table 5.8 suggest that the developed countries of the region would grow at a much slower rate, which, however, would surpass that of the European Community. The latter's share of world output is expected to fall from 24.5 per cent in 1981 to 20.8 per cent in 2000. Table 5.9 presents the sources of growth under three possible scenarios.

The 1990s may witness spectacular changes in the regional division of labour, with developed countries de-industrializing and developing economies filling the vacuum. Already, there are indications that the share of manufacturing in total output in Japan is falling. This downtrend is likely to gather momentum in the coming years. Japan is likely to specialize increasingly in products that are characterized by high levels of design and technology and find a niche for itself in the production of sophisticated items of light weight and small size, a phenomenon which is described as *keihaku-tansho* (higher and thinner, shorter and

TABLE 5.8
Projected Growth Rates and Distribution of World GNP, Year 2000

	Per Cent Share in 1981	Projected Average Real Growth, 1981–2000	Per Cent Share in 2000
USA	24.0	3.0	22.0
Canada	2.5	3.5	2.5
Mexico	2.0	5.0	2.5
Australia and New Zealand	1.5	3.0	1.5
Japan	9.5	3.5	9.5
China	2.0	7.5	4.5
Korea, Hong Kong, and Taiwan	1.0	7.8	2.5
ASEAN	1.5	6.8	3.0
European Community	24.5	2.0	20.8
Soviet Bloc	14.0	2.5	11.8
Others	17.5	5.0	19.5
World	100	3.4	100
Reference			
Asia–Pacific[1]	44.0		48.0
North America	28.5	3.2	27.0
Asia OECD	11.0	3.4	11.0
Developing Asia	4.5	7.3	10.0

Source: Rasmussen (1988), Table 4, p. 154.
[1]Excludes the United States and Canada.

TABLE 5.9
GNP Growth and Contributing Factors by Country/Region, 1985–2000

	Baseline			Low Growth			High Growth		
	1985–1995	1995–2000	1985–2000	1985–1995	1995–2000	1985–2000	1985–1995	1995–2000	1985–2000
USA	2.0	1.6	1.8	0.9	0.7	0.8	2.5	2.0	2.3
Domestic demand	1.8	1.8	1.8	1.0	0.8	1.0	2.3	2.3	2.3
Export	4.0	1.5	3.1	2.1	3.8	2.7	4.0	1.6	3.2
Import	0.9	2.5	1.5	1.2	0.5	1.0	2.0	4.2	2.7
Japan	3.4	4.2	3.6	2.4	3.9	2.9	4.4	5.0	4.6
Domestic demand	3.9	3.8	3.9	2.9	3.6	3.1	5.1	4.6	4.9
Export	2.3	3.4	2.7	0.5	5.5	2.1	3.0	4.1	3.4
Import	6.9	0.7	4.8	5.1	3.0	4.4	8.0	1.5	5.8
Other OECD	2.0	1.8	1.9	1.5	2.0	1.7	2.7	2.9	2.8
Domestic demand	2.0	1.5	1.8	1.4	1.4	1.4	2.6	2.3	2.5
Export	2.6	3.0	2.8	1.8	4.6	2.7	3.3	4.5	3.7
Import	2.9	0.0	1.9	1.7	-0.8	0.9	2.9	-0.1	1.9

(continued)

TABLE 5.9 (*continued*)

	Baseline			Low Growth			High Growth		
	1985–1995	1995–2000	1985–2000	1985–1995	1995–2000	1985–2000	1985–1995	1995–2000	1985–2000
China	5.4	4.2	5.0	5.3	3.5	4.7	6.0	5.3	5.8
Domestic demand	5.3	4.5	5.1	5.3	4.3	4.9	5.9	5.7	5.8
Export	5.2	1.1	3.8	3.2	3.8	3.4	5.0	-0.2	3.2
Import	4.9	3.3	4.3	3.2	8.1	4.8	4.5	2.1	3.7
Asian NIEs	7.0	3.2	5.7	6.9	1.9	5.2	8.3	6.0	7.5
Domestic demand	7.2	3.5	5.9	6.7	3.5	5.6	8.4	6.0	7.6
Export	5.6	3.3	4.8	4.2	4.6	4.4	6.0	3.9	5.3
Import	5.7	3.9	5.1	3.0	8.8	4.9	5.9	3.5	5.1
ASEAN	5.6	3.2	4.8	5.6	1.6	4.3	6.2	4.6	5.7
Domestic demand	5.5	3.2	4.8	5.2	2.6	4.3	6.1	4.3	5.5
Export	4.7	1.3	3.6	3.4	2.0	2.9	5.3	2.1	4.3
Import	4.5	1.6	3.5	1.5	6.7	3.2	5.1	0.8	3.6
Rest of World									
Export	3.2	0.6	2.4	2.3	0.4	1.6	3.5	0.9	2.7
Import	3.6	3.8	3.7	2.1	6.8	3.6	3.7	5.0	4.1

Source: F. C. Lo et al., 1989, Table 2, p. 100.

smaller).[16] This means that Japan will move away from raw material-intensive production, as the new products and processes tend to reduce the raw material content of its manufactures. The commodity producers in ASEAN will be exporting increasingly resource-intensive manufactures rather than commodities in primary forms. This scenario suggests that intra-regional trade in the Asia–Pacific will be increasingly characterized by intra-industry trade rather than inter-industry trade in the twenty-first century.

The process of de-industrialization in Japan and the other developed countries in the region, leading to a relative decline of manufacturing and an expansion of the services sector, would only serve to complement industrial deepening in the developing countries of the region. A major contributor to the dynamism of the region would be the youthfulness of the population in the western corridor of the Pacific Basin. This is in sharp contrast to the ageing population of Japan and other developed countries in the region. Recent demographic projections show that by the year 2025 the number of Japanese below the age of 40 will decline by 7 per cent, and those below the age of 20 will decline by 23 per cent.[17] The economic implications of these demographic changes are reduced labour supplies, increased household propensity to save, increased social security burden for the state, and slow economic growth.[18] None the less, technological innovations will help offset some of the negative effects of the changing population structure on Japanese productivity and competitiveness so that Japan would continue to be a major growth pole of the region in the next century.

The East Asian NIEs are likely to capitalize on their industrial lead over ASEAN and continue to upgrade themselves, moving from labour-intensive light manufactures into technology-intensive heavy manufactures. It would pay ASEAN countries to concentrate on labour-intensive and resource-intensive manufactures in which the NIEs would develop a comparative disadvantage given the rising wage levels. This may bring some ASEAN countries into direct competition with China, which also may find it advantageous to specialize in light manufactures.

That China is potentially a major factor in the Asia–Pacific economy is an undeniable fact. Some writers even go as far as to suggest that China will pose a major threat to ASEAN exports in the international markets.[19] One must not, however, lose sight of the fact that China lags behind ASEAN countries in many ways and that ASEAN has a clear edge over China in terms of infrastructure, institutions, organizational structure, industrial experience, international exposure, and entrepreneurship. To suggest that China would develop all these quickly after the 'opening' would only amount to wishful thinking. It is not even certain that China will keep its door fully open or just leave it slightly ajar. Besides, ASEAN countries are in an enviable position to capitalize on their lead to move into higher tiers of manufacturing activities. Even if China successfully resolves its internal problems so that it can enter the international arena with a high degree of confidence, a collision course between China and its ASEAN neighbours is *not* inevitable. A complementary China–ASEAN relationship would seem more likely, with China specializing in unskilled labour-intensive manufacturing and ASEAN countries focusing on skill-intensive processes, with considerable intra-industry and inter-industry trade prospects among them. Since China is a vast country with many provinces effectively cut off from one another, it would be easier for the coastal areas of China to develop closer economic linkages with ASEAN than with their own hinterland.

All in all, the economic outlook for the Asia–Pacific region, in both the medium and long term, appears to be excitingly bright. Barring unforeseen political developments and disruptive changes in the international economic environment, countries of the region, both developed and developing, can confidently look forward to developing a mutually rewarding symbiotic relationship with one another in their economic pursuits by the year 2000 and beyond.

Economic Regionalism

The rapidly changing geopolitical equations and economic matrices in the Pacific after the end of the Cold War lend support to the belief that the Pacific Basin will soon become the new epicentre of the world economy. Realizing this, the more eclectic countries of the region are preparing to take advantage of the rising Pacific economic tide. The growing economic interdependence among the Asia–Pacific countries may be taken as a prelude to the emergence of a fairly close-knit Pacific community of nations in the next century, although the notion of the Pacific Community still remains no more than a dream. Efforts are already underway to translate the vision of Pacific economic co-operation into a reality.

It is argued that Pacific countries should organize themselves not only to make the most of the growing interdependence in the region but also to resolve the accompanying problems, for, economic interdependence implies not only profitable opportunities but also problematic conflicts. Geopolitical disputes of the region will probably be dwarfed by economic conflicts as the Pacific nations compete with one another in the international market.

The Pacific Basin is culturally, ethnically, linguistically, geographically, and anthropologically far more diverse than Europe. The political forces which drove Western Europe into cohesion in the post-war years are totally absent in the Pacific. Economic linkages in the Pacific pale in comparison with those in Western Europe. Despite all this, there is an emergent trend towards economic regionalism in the Pacific. Unlike regionalism in other parts of the world, the wider Pacific regionalism is propelled primarily by market forces rather than by political currents, although the experience of ASEAN has been quite different.

As is well known, ASEAN came into existence because of security and strategic reasons. Nor can it be denied that regional economic co-operation played a secondary role in ASEAN affairs during the 1970s and 1980s. Notwithstanding all this, it may well be argued that ASEAN will grind to a halt unless primacy is accorded to private sector interests in regional initiatives. To demonstrate this, one needs to retrace the regional economic co-operative efforts of ASEAN since its inception in 1967.

Economically, ASEAN as a regional organization was dormant for ten years until the Bali Summit in 1976. The private sector and the general public had no idea of what was going on in the intergovernmental meetings of ASEAN foreign ministers, the proceedings of which were treated as classified information. ASEAN demonstrated to the rest of the world (mainly to appease Vietnam) that it was not a military pact but an economic alliance by unveiling its programme of economic co-operation at Bali. ASEAN Industrial Projects (AIPs), ASEAN Industrial Complementation (AIC), and Preferential Trading Arrangement (PTA) were the three main instruments of regional economic co-operation. The AIP scheme was designed to establish large-scale industries on an intergovernmental basis, one in each member country, while the AIC scheme was formulated to create linkages among existing industries. The PTA scheme was intended to promote intra-regional trade through preferential tariff reductions.

A systematic evaluation of all these schemes is beyond the scope of the present section. The failure of these programmes and the reasons for their failure are discussed elsewhere.[20] The absence of private sector involvement constituted the single most important explanation for their failure. In retrospect, it appears that the Bali package was put together in haste, and industries were handpicked and allocated rather arbitrarily without the private sector being consulted. The PTA did get off the ground, but its progress was stultified by the cumbersome item-by-item approach to tariff reduction in the initial stages. Across-the-board tariff cuts, introduced at a later stage, were heavily circumscribed by the unduly long exemption lists.

The Manila Summit in December 1987 breathed new life into ASEAN economic co-operation by introducing important changes in its modalities.[21] The PTA was deepened and widened with a firm timetable to increase the depth of tariff cuts and to shorten the exclusion lists. Likewise, the framework for industrial co-operation was revamped, paving the way for active private sector participation in regional industrial projects through the ASEAN Industrial Joint Ventures (AIJV) scheme. The latter was made more attractive for the private sector by loosening the rules of the game, by allowing an increased margin of preferences (MOP) for their products and by giving them local content accreditation in the participating countries.

The role of ASEAN subregionalism in the wider context of Pacific regionalism is reflected in the spillover effects of ASEAN economic co-operation. Of special significance is the fact that the revamped AIJV programme allows up to 60 per cent foreign participation. Some East

Asian economies are already taking advantage of this. The spillover of ASEAN economic co-operation is exemplified in the ongoing brand-to-brand complementation in the manufacture of automotive components and parts in the ASEAN region, reference to which was made in Chapter 4.

It would be incorrect to speak of ASEAN as a separate entity that is detached from the rest of the Pacific, for ASEAN is not an inward-looking subregional organization. On the contrary, ASEAN represents a group of open economies with trade regimes that are very liberal by developing-country standards. Even more liberal are their foreign exchange regimes and policies towards foreign investments. The irony, in fact, is that ASEAN countries have stronger economic ties with the rest of the Pacific than among themselves! Thus, whatever goes on in the ASEAN region in the name of regional co-operation is bound to have wider Pacific implications in one way or another.

Japan has been directly participating in the ASEAN co-operative endeavours by providing funds to finance some of the regional industrial projects. Japanese Prime Minister Takeo Fukuda made available US$1 billion to finance the AIPs in 1977 under the Overseas Development Assistance (ODA), although only a part of the sum was used in the two urea projects, one in Aceh (Indonesia) and the other in Bintulu (Malaysia). More recently, Japan has helped create, through its ODA funds, agencies such as the US$2 billion ASEAN–Japan Development Fund (AJDF), the ASEAN–Japan Development Corporation (AJDC), and the Japan–ASEAN Investment Corporation (JAIC), all of which provide special and differential treatment for ASEAN investment.

Intra-ASEAN trade accounts for much less than one-fifth of all ASEAN trade. There has been only a marginal increase in the share of intra-regional trade in the total from 13.9 per cent in 1973 to 15.8 per cent in 1985.[22] Moreover, a large proportion of the intra-ASEAN trade (about two-thirds) is simply bilateral, i.e. between Singapore and Malaysia.[23] Such empirical evidence is often cited by critics to show that ASEAN economic co-operation lacks substance.

It is very wrong to jump to such conclusions on the basis of the intra-regional trade figures for two entirely unrelated reasons. For one thing, the official trade statistics understate the actual intra-ASEAN trade flows, since they do not include the large volume of illegal trade transactions that take place within the region. It is an open secret that the illegal trade traffic is heavy, especially between Singapore and its neighbouring islands. Sumatra (Indonesia) and Mindanao (the Philippines), in particular, have strong and well-organized bases for smuggling activities. For another, intra-regional trade, no matter how well documented, provides only a partial picture of a very complex phenomenon.

It is not difficult to explain why intra-regional trade within ASEAN has been relatively small. ASEAN countries' factor and resource endowments are somewhat similar and they have been producing goods, both primary commodities and manufactures, that are very similar, if not identical. Put another way, ASEAN economies by and large are competitive and not complementary. Under these circumstances, any attempt to increase intra-regional trade through discriminatory tariff reductions would probably result in substantial trade diversion, shifting the sources of imports from low-cost third countries to high-cost partners. Trade creation effects are likely to be weak, since the cost differentials among members presumably are not large enough to cause a shift from a higher-cost domestic source to a low-cost partner source. ASEAN countries would have been worse off, had they gone all out to increase their intra-regional trade through discriminatory trade measures. It can therefore be argued that the low volume of intra-ASEAN trade is not a bad thing after all.

Singapore has always been different from the rest. Since it has no natural resources of its own, the rest of ASEAN had served as its hinterland long before ASEAN was formed. Singapore is also more industrialized than any other ASEAN country. Thus, the Singapore economy has always played a complementary role in the South-East Asian region, which also explains why Singapore has had stronger intra-regional trade linkages than any other ASEAN country.

Important structural changes are taking place in the ASEAN economies. These changes may affect the production and trade matrices of ASEAN significantly in the foreseeable future. Malaysia and Thailand are quickly climbing up the ladder in terms of manufacturing. Indonesia is successfully reorientating its manufacturing sector towards the global market through bold liberalization measures. The Philippine economy has bounced back to growth. Brunei is diversifying its economy in an attempt to reduce its dependence on oil exports. Singapore is moving away from manufacturing into technology- and skill-intensive services, while Malaysia is losing its comparative advantage in labour-intensive manufacturing operations. All these will no doubt alter the character of ASEAN economic co-operation in the 1990s and beyond. There is a trend towards increased complementarity within ASEAN, which will have a favourable impact on intra-ASEAN trade flows, especially in terms of intra-industry trade, in the years ahead.

ASEAN countries have traditionally been highly outward-oriented, with exports and imports accounting for substantial proportions of their gross domestic products. Their outreach goes far beyond the ASEAN subregion to the wider Pacific region. That ASEAN countries have more trade with East Asia and North America than among themselves, suggests that it is economic imperatives and not political expediency that determines the scope and limits of regionalism in South-East Asia. Seen in this light, ASEAN regionalism appears to be essentially a subset of Pacific regionalism in economic and commercial terms.

Reference may also be made to what is sometimes termed 'soft regionalism'[24] which connotes the absence of a formal structure. Such de facto regionalism without legal status is brought about not by political processes but by market forces. This is exemplified in the kinds of economic relations that revolve around the Asian NIEs (South Korea,

Taiwan, Hong Kong, and Singapore) which are also sometimes referred to as the 'Gang of Four', 'Asian Tigers', 'Four Dragons', or 'G-4' in the literature. This 'grouping' exhibits common characteristics and its members are linked to one another by market forces through trade, investment, credit, and technology transfers, notwithstanding the high degree of competition and rivalry among them. Such soft regionalism in the Western Pacific also represents another subset of Pacific regionalism, not only because the countries involved have extensive linkages with the wider Pacific region but also because linkages tend to crisscross across subregional 'groupings', formal or otherwise. Thus, for instance, Singapore is recognized as a member of G-4 just as it is a member of ASEAN; in fact, it is not uncommon to see Singapore being lumped together with the East Asian NIEs and taken out of ASEAN for purposes of statistical analysis in recent empirical studies.[25] This observation, however, should not be overstretched, since it is ASEAN but not the 'Gang of Four' which has legal standing. None the less, the above characterization serves to underscore the need to redefine economic regionalism broadly in the Pacific context.

A broad definition of economic regionalism would enable one to see the undercurrents that are dragging the Pacific countries in a certain direction. However, one has to draw a line between regionalism and bilateralism and must be careful not to mix bilateral arrangements with multilateral or plurilateral arrangements in the Pacific. By the same token, one must also draw a distinction between bilateralism and bilateral arrangements. This is particularly pertinent in the Pacific context. For instance, the US bilateral trading arrangements with various countries in recent times can be interpreted in many ways: they may be ascribed to the historical roots and geographic proximity as in the case of the US–Canada Free Trade Area (FTA), or to the US concerns over its domestic politics and foreign policy as in the case of the US–Israel FTA, or to a genuine US desire to promote economic development in less developed countries that have friendly relations with the United States, as in the case of the US–Caribbean Initiative. They may also be taken as indicators of a general shift in the US policy away from multilateralism in favour of bilateralism or as evidence of a US attempt to create a trade bloc of its own in response to the 1992 European designs.

Bilateral FTA schemes are, of course, vastly inferior to multilateral trading arrangements, as they entail discrimination against third countries and hence trade diversion (Arndt, 1989 and Schott, 1989). If regional FTAs are considered second-best, bilateral ones can only be third-best or worse, to say the least.

Nevertheless, one might notice in all these the presence of elements that do facilitate what may be termed the 'Pacific process'. For example, free trade area arrangements which the United States has with Canada and Mexico, *if* extended to other countries in the Pacific, can help enhance the economic interdependence of the Pacific economies, especially if Canada and Mexico also enter into similar bilateral FTA arrangements with one another. In other words, bilateral ties between two countries can be plurilateralized if one of them enters into similar arrangements with several others, and multilateralized if its bilateral partners also undertake similar initiatives among themselves. This would lead to more trade creation and less trade diversion.

There are some signs that such a process is underway in the Pacific. The United States is reportedly considering special trading arrangements with several countries in the Pacific, including ASEAN, Japan, and South Korea, while Japan seems keen to enter into special trading arrangements with ASEAN. If the process catches on, the bilateral FTAs can provide the building blocks for the construction of a Pacific Community.

Admittedly, it is not clear at this point in time how realistic the above scenario is. But there are encouraging signs which suggest that such an eventuality is not too far-fetched. Some prominent political leaders in the region have supported such ideas. For example, former US Ambassador to Japan Mike Mansfield has long been advocating a US–Japan FTA, and former US Trade Representative William Brock has proposed a US–ASEAN FTA. A feasibility study on the US–ASEAN initiative is already in place.[26]

It is also of relevance to note that Australia and New Zealand have already established what is called Closer Economic Relations (CER) under a pact signed in 1983 which was further expanded in 1988 in what seems to be one of the most comprehensive agreements in the world. Under the expanded agreement, both countries have agreed to waive anti-dumping actions against each other, to include many sensitive items (e.g. steel and automobiles) which were previously excluded from the CER, and to harmonize customs procedures, business laws, quarantine arrangements, and technical barriers to trade. It is also significant to note that July 1990 was set as the deadline for free trade in merchandise with a commitment to eventual free trade area in services as well between the two countries. Equally significant is the South Pacific Regional Trade and Economic Cooperation Agreement (SPARTECA) which removes import controls on exports from the South Pacific islands to Australia and New Zealand, subject to some qualifications such as rules of origin.[27]

Several multilateral forces have been set in motion in the Pacific that help energize the Pacific process, with the private sector and academia playing the leading roles and governments responding positively to their calls. One of these is the conference series mounted by the Pacific academic community in the field of international economics under the banner of Pacific Area Free Trade and Development (PAFTAD) which began in 1968. PAFTAD has been acting as an intellectual forum on policy issues relating to Pacific trade and development, whose deliberations have attracted the attention of policy-makers and practitioners in the region. The idea of a Pacific free trade area comprising the United States, Canada, Japan, Australia, and New Zealand was first mooted in

1965 when Kojima came up with the proposal.[28] The idea subsequently became the subject of much intergovernmental and private sector discussion, which led to a variety of proposals with institutional structures differing in function and membership.

As early as 1967, the Japanese government threw its weight in support of the idea of some kind of Pacific regional organization. In retrospect, it appears that the Japanese had jumped the gun, as the Japanese motives were then suspect in the eyes of many countries in the Pacific Basin. It was not until 1980 that the idea was revived, with the Japanese and Australian governments jointly setting in motion a series of meetings, the first of which was held in Canberra, Australia. Like PAFTAD, the new series, now called Pacific Economic Cooperation Conference (PECC), has become a major Pacific event that takes place at regular intervals. Unlike PAFTAD, which is purely academic in nature and substance, PECC is tripartite in character with the participation of governments, private sector interests, and the academia of the region, and down-to-earth in its approach, focusing on specific issues of common interest to the participating countries: e.g. energy, the development of human resources, and environmental protection. Such issues have been handled by specific functional task forces.

PECC is a loosely structured forum whose role is simply consultative, and it has been made clear that it is not a negotiating body and that its recommendations are not binding on the governments of the countries which are represented in it. None the less, PECC is in the centre stage in so far as the Pacific process is concerned, as it has successfully mobilized forces that really count in the region to chart out a new course towards what the participating countries believe to be the Pacific Century.

Another serious effort at high-powered multilateral Pacific economic co-operation is what has been labelled the 'Hawke initiative', named after Australian Prime Minister Bob Hawke who played an instrumental role in organizing the 'inaugural' ministerial meeting in Canberra in November 1989. The essence of the Hawke initiative was to create an inter-governmental regional body, the Asia Pacific Economic Cooperation (APEC), comprising the major market economies of the Pacific, with an institutional structure similar to that of the Organization for Economic Co-operation and Development (OECD). But, unlike the OECD which is regarded as the rich men's club, APEC is designed to have a North–South axis, with developed and developing countries joining hands as equal partners in the Pacific venture.[29] The geographical spread of APEC and the complexity of the various issues involved underscore the horrendous difficulties its architects will have to come to terms with. What is important is that a new, promising process has begun, with a commitment to keep it going through regular ministerial meetings.

PAFTAD, PECC, and APEC are moving in the same direction, almost in tandem. They do not compete with but complement one another. They seem to blend remarkably well, having a common purpose and sharing a common dream. Reference must also be made in this context to the Malaysian initiative to form an East Asian economic grouping (EAEG), comprising ASEAN, Japan, China, Korea, and the Indo-Chinese states, which may well complement other Pacific initiatives if it materializes.

As alluded to earlier, the main forces behind the emergent trend towards regionalism in the Pacific Basin are not political but economic. The fairly high degree of cohesion that already has gained some visibility in the region is largely a response to the imperative of the marketplace. Private sector interests in the Pacific constitute the main driving force in the whole exercise, as they are more sensitive to market signals than any other. It is therefore hardly surprising that private sector interests have assumed a particularly high profile in the San Francisco-based Pacific Basin Economic Council (PBEC), yet another chip in the Pacific game.

To complete the discussion of this section, attention must be drawn to two vexing issues which are somehow interrelated. One of these concerns the question of membership in Pacific regional organizations, while the other revolves around the position of ASEAN as a subregion in the wider Pacific regional network.

The question of membership of a Pacific regional organization is the trickiest of them all, given the vastness of the Pacific Basin, the heterogeneity and plurality of the Pacific society, and the intricacies of the various vested interests at work. The Pacific Rim resembles a huge crescent that envelopes a large number of countries stretching from New Zealand in the Western Pacific to Chile in the Eastern Pacific. Needless to say, these Pacific countries are divided by cultural, ideological, historical, and linguistic differences. They are also at unequal and disparate stages of economic development and industrialization, with divergent interests and perceptions. Nothing short of a miracle could bring them together and make them agree on a common programme. Besides, such a huge regional organization would be extremely unwieldy. A pragmatic approach initially would be to have a narrower focus on those economies which already have extensive Pacific trade and investment linkages. This would preclude the Latin American countries.

The need for a sharper focus has led to various geographical delineations in the Pacific literature. The term 'Western Pacific' is often used to cover the region stretching from Japan and Korea to Australia and New Zealand. In the same vein, the term 'Asia–Pacific' has a slightly wider coverage than that of 'Western Pacific' by bringing North America into the fold. Pacific economic discussions have tended to focus on the market economies and to leave out the centrally planned ones. The only notable exception to this has been China, by virtue of its extensive involvement in Pacific economic affairs. China is by far economically more integrated with the rest of the Pacific than any other communist country, including the Soviet Union, although the latter has similar aspirations.

Of all the Pacific organizations mentioned earlier, it is PAFTAD which has the widest coverage, with the participation of individuals from many countries, including Mexico in the East and China and the Soviet Union in the West. Being an academic organization, PAFTAD has found it relatively easy to handle the ideological polemics of such a 'membership' structure. Even so, the 'membership' of Taiwan has proved to be a thorny issue in political terms. A compromise was finally struck to admit both China and Taiwan, with the latter being treated *de jure* as a province of the Republic of China. Taiwan has been referred to in recent times by such terms as the 'Taiwan Province', 'Chinese Taipeh', and 'Chinese economy on Taiwan'.

The tripartite character of PECC has also rendered its membership structure fairly flexible, although the presence of the government component has made it less flexible than PAFTAD. China's much publicized open-door policy has legitimized its candidacy in PECC, which, however, has led to Taiwan being edged out. The Soviet Union seems to have thus far disqualified itself by virtue of its low profile in the Pacific economy.

The membership structure of the APEC is constrained by the fact that it is a high-powered intergovernmental forum with ministerial representations. It was apparent that the membership of countries like China and the Soviet Union would have made countries like Indonesia and Malaysia uncomfortable in the APEC. Even though the APEC agenda is purely economic in content, the governments do take political costs and benefits into account. It is for these and other reasons that the APEC comprises only the major market economies in the Western Pacific together with Canada and the United States.

That ASEAN has an important role to play in Pacific economic co-operation is readily recognized.[30] ASEAN probably holds the key to the formation of a Pacific Community in the long run for a number of palpable reasons. First, ASEAN represents the most viable and promising subregional grouping in the Pacific. Secondly, the ASEAN economies are among the most dynamic economies of the Pacific. Thirdly, the ASEAN countries have strong and extensive economic linkages with the rest of the Pacific. Fourthly, the ASEAN countries have established cordial relations with the major players in the Pacific. Last but not least, ASEAN represents an eclectic group of countries with a high propensity for moderation in their views on global issues.

However, ASEAN has apparently been reluctant to stick its neck out. Several explanations have been put forward in the recent writings on the subject. It has been pointed out, for instance, that ASEAN countries fear that an economic organization of the Pacific Basin would be dominated by Japan or the United States, or, worse still, by both in concert.[31] It also appears that ASEAN is concerned that its participation in a Pacific Basin organization would dilute ASEAN's cohesion and loosen the bond among the member countries.[32] Finally, it has been postulated that ASEAN would eventually lose out to China if the Pacific Community materializes.[33] These and other issues are examined in the Malaysian context in the next section.

Implications for Malaysia

The strength of the Malaysian economy stems in no small measure from its strategic location along the sea lane that links the Atlantic with the Pacific (Map 5.1). It is this geographic factor that gives Malaysia considerable leverage in its dealings with the major economic powers. It is in the interest of the major countries of the world, as well as in Malaysia's own interest, that the international sea route remains open to inter-regional trade flows.

Malaysia may also have benefited from the political instability of East Asia in three main ways. First, it could receive special and differential treatment from the major economic powers which saw Malaysia as a moderate and stabilizing force in a strategic but turbulent part of the world. In a sense, a prosperous Malaysia was in the self-interest of major trading nations. Secondly, the 1950–1 Korean War provided a shot in the arm for Malaysia (then Malaya) through increased demand for natural rubber and tin which were then strategic raw materials. The Korean War boom of the early 1950s enabled the Malaysian economy to leapfrog. Thirdly, the Indo-Chinese debacle and the internal strife in Burma seem to have given Malaysia (and indeed the other ASEAN countries as well) a terrific advantage by default. While the Indo-Chinese states were locked in battles and turmoil and Burma went into self-imposed isolation, it must have been relatively easy for Malaysia to upstage itself in the international market. It is pertinent to remember that, in the 1950s, it was Rangoon and Saigon, not Kuala Lumpur, which were the better-known commercial epicentres of South-East Asia. Kuala Lumpur has, of course, overtaken them all, leaving these competitors way behind, due partly to its own strength and partly to the unfortunate events which put the clock back for its rivals.

The circumstances which thus acted in Malaysia's favour in the past are definitely changing. As alluded to earlier, the geopolitical equations of the region may look quite different by the year 2000 and beyond, with South-East Asia shedding the last vestiges of its past bi-polar character. The new strategic equilibrium may well accord primacy to economic pursuits in a relatively tension-free geopolitical environment in all countries, regardless of their ideological predilections. A totally new ball game is apparently in the making, a game in which military rivalry and security considerations will be replaced by economic competition and concerns for material welfare.

Trade has been the lifeblood of the Malaysian economy for many centuries. Peninsular Malaysia had thriving trade with the Indian sub-continent, the Middle East, and its own immediate neighbours, long before the Europeans appeared on the scene. It was trade that transformed Malaysia from a sleepy hamlet of villages into a throbbing modern economy. Outward orientation has paid off very handsomely for Malaysia. Of course, there were—and still are—negative sides in all this, the most serious being the economy's vulnerability to externally induced fluctuations.[34] Trade has been transmitting the booms and

MAP 5.1

Sea Routes through the Straits of South-East Asia

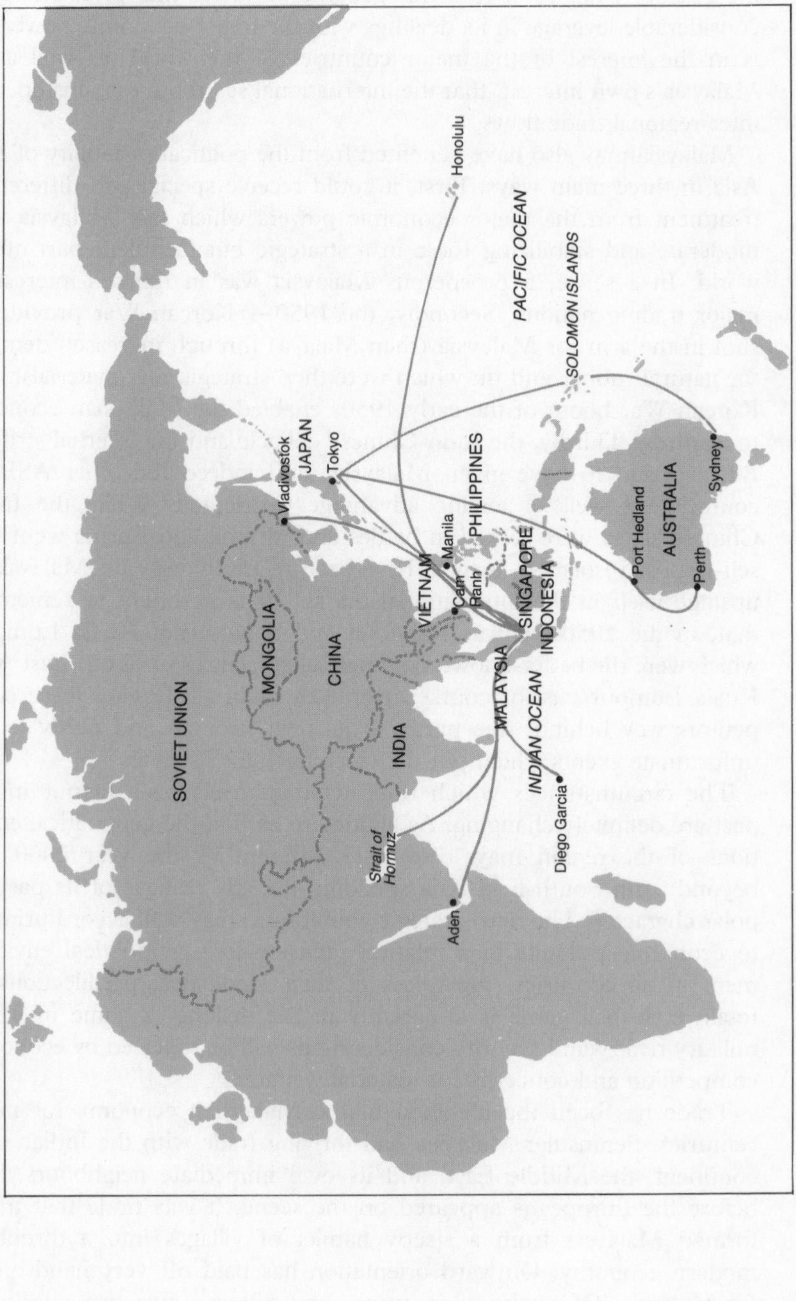

recessions of the advanced countries to the Malaysian economy in an almost symmetrical pattern, with occasional painful adjustments. Malaysia seems to have learned, through experience, to ride the surf. No one can deny that trade has brought Malaysia more perks than problems, and that Malaysia would have been a lot worse off had it remained inward-looking.

As was seen in Chapter 3, Malaysia's external trade has undergone dramatic changes in the post-war period in terms of both composition and direction. Malaysia has moved away from excessive export concentration in natural rubber and tin—once considered the 'twin pillars' of the economy—to a broad-based merchandise pattern, with a variety of primary commodities including palm oil, pineapple, cocoa, and pepper, and, above all, manufactures. Of particular significance is the remarkable increase in the share of manufactures in total exports in recent years, a clear indication of the modernization of the Malaysian economy. Likewise, the composition of Malaysian imports has changed over time, with intermediate and capital goods accounting for an increasingly larger proportion of the total.

In the same vein, the direction of Malaysia's trade flows, in terms of both import sources and export destinations, has been shifting in a discernible, albeit gradual, fashion. The shift away from the Atlantic to the Pacific is noticeable, with Malaysia's trade with the European Community shrinking in relative terms and that with Japan, the United States, and the East Asian NIEs expanding both relatively and absolutely, as was seen in Chapter 3.

Fundamental changes are also taking place in the pattern and structure of direct foreign investments in Malaysia, as was observed in Chapter 4. The bulk of the new foreign investments has been flowing into the manufacturing sector in sharp contrast to the previous pattern that favoured primary and extractive activities. By the same token, as in the case of trade, the origins of foreign capital have shifted from the Atlantic to the Pacific, with the European Community becoming progressively less important and Japan and the East Asian NIEs emerging as the dominant sources.

It is important to note that the changes in the direction of trade and investment flows are by no means peculiar to Malaysia, as such trends are readily observable in other ASEAN countries as well. What Malaysia has been experiencing in its trade and investment relations with the outside world is simply a reflection of the fundamental shifts taking place at the global level, as discussed earlier. There is no doubt that Malaysia is benefiting from all this, as the country's recent impressive economic performance, in terms of GDP growth, export growth, and other economic indicators, discussed in Chapter 2, can be largely attributed to the Pacific phenomenon.

As alluded to earlier, significant structural changes and adjustments are occurring in the world economy, as the latter gravitates gradually from the Atlantic toward the Pacific. Therein lie many opportunities which Malaysia can take advantage of. By looking at the changes in the structure, composition, and growth of manufacturing value-added (MVA), it is possible to identify broad industry groups in which significant changes are taking place. The MVA of the Asia–Pacific region as a whole has been growing at a much faster rate (4.2 per cent per annum) than Western Europe (1.6 per cent per annum) during the period 1975–85 (Table 5.10). The Western Pacific has registered an even more impressive MVA growth rate of 5.6 per cent per annum. Nevertheless, it is East and South-East Asia which posted the highest MVA growth rate of 10.2 per cent per annum.

The Asia–Pacific share of world MVA has increased from 35.3 per cent in 1975 to 38.8 per cent in 1985, while that of Western Europe has fallen by 5 percentage points from 36.3 per cent in 1975. The Western Pacific has increased its share of world MVA from 13.2 per cent in 1975 to 16.3 per cent in 1985. Even more significant is the observation that the East and South-East Asian countries have doubled their share of world MVA during this period as shown in Table 5.10.

A recent analysis (1988) by the United Nations Industrial Development Organization (UNIDO) has provided some interesting insights into the shifting pattern of dynamic comparative advantage. According to this study,[35] the fast-growing industries are:

paper and paper products	(ISIC 341)
industrial chemicals	(ISIC 351)
other chemical products	(ISIC 352)
plastic products	(ISIC 356)
non-electrical machinery	(ISIC 382)
professional goods	(ISIC 385)
electrical machinery	(ISIC 386)
'other' manufactures	(ISIC 390)

Industry branches in which developing countries as a whole grew more than twice as fast as developed countries during the period 1980–5 include the following:

food products	(ISIC 311)
beverages	(ISIC 313)
tobacco	(ISIC 314)
textiles	(ISIC 321)
footwear	(ISIC 324)
wearing apparel	(ISIC 322)
wood products	(ISIC 331)
glass and glass products	(ISIC 362)
pottery and china	(ISIC 361)
other non-metal mineral products	(ISIC 369)
industrial chemicals	(ISIC 351)
petroleum refineries	(ISIC 353)
petroleum and coal products	(ISIC 354)
iron and steel	(ISIC 371)
non-ferrous metals	(ISIC 372)

TABLE 5.10

Regional Share of World MVA and Regional MVA Growth Rates, 1975–1985 (percentage)

Item	1975	1980	1985	Annual Average Growth Rate		
				1975–1980	1980–1985	1975–1985
Total MVA	2,220[1]	2,701[1]	3,016[1]	4.01	2.23	3.12
Developing countries	10.33	11.18	11.89	5.68	3.49	4.58
Caribbean and Latin American	5.70	6.00	5.37	5.07	0.01	2.51
Tropical Africa	0.44	0.42	0.40	2.81	1.18	1.99
North Africa and Western Asia	1.29	1.20	1.58	2.62	8.04	5.29
Indian Subcontinent	1.23	1.13	1.27	2.36	4.68	3.52
East and South-East Asia	1.67	2.43	3.26	12.14	8.38	10.24
Developed countries	89.67	88.82	88.11	3.81	2.06	2.93
North America	22.10	22.38	22.53	4.28	2.36	3.31
Western Europe	36.33	34.05	31.34	2.67	0.54	1.60
Eastern Europe	19.75	20.03	21.26	4.31	3.45	3.88
Japan	9.47	10.55	11.36	6.28	3.74	5.00
Other Developed	2.03	1.80	1.63	1.54	0.24	0.89
Asia-Pacific	35.27	37.16	38.78	5.22	3.18	4.23
Western Pacific	13.17	14.78	16.25	5.66	4.31	5.64

Source: UNIDO database.

[1]Billions of 1980 constant US dollars.

Industries which are declining in developed countries and rapidly expanding in East and South-East Asian developing countries include:

food manufacturing	(ISIC 311)
tobacco	(ISIC 314)
textiles	(ISIC 321)
rubber products	(ISIC 355)
non-ferrous metals	(ISIC 372)
metal products	(ISIC 381)
'other' manufactures	(ISIC 390)

It appears that Malaysia has potential or actual comparative advantage in many of these products. Much would, of course, depend on Malaysia's resource and factor endowments and the factor intensity of the products in question. Much would also depend on how Malaysia's resource and factor endowments compare with those of its major trading partners. There is considerable diversity within the Asia–Pacific region for Malaysia to complement its production with that of others.

Figures 5.2–5.6 show the general trends in the regional division of labour through revealed comparative advantage indices by factor or resource intensity of manufactures. The ASEAN-4 tend to cluster together, just like the Asian NIEs, especially with respect to unskilled labour-intensive and human capital-intensive products. Likewise, Japan and the United States appear to have similar export production 'paths' with regards to technology-intensive goods. Malaysia's comparative advantage in technology-intensive goods seems better developed than that of Indonesia, the Philippines, or Thailand. However, Malaysia's strength seems to lie mainly in the agricultural resource-intensive and mineral resource-intensive products, as shown in Figures 5.2 and 5.3 respectively.

Revealed comparative advantage indices need to be interpreted with caution, since they represent 'proxies' and portray 'ex-post' situations. Simple extrapolation of the indices may well be misleading, especially if one's time frame is measured not in years but in decades. None the less, one may be able to see opportunities for Malaysia by looking at the indices of *other* countries in the region. There is a downward trend in recent years in Japan, the United States, and the Asian NIEs with respect to both unskilled labour-intensive and human capital-intensive goods, as shown in Figures 5.4 and 5.6 respectively, which suggests that there are some openings for newcomers in the production of these goods. However, upon close scrutiny, it appears that Malaysia will soon lose out to Indonesia, the Philippines, and Thailand in the unskilled labour-intensive category, since wages in Malaysia are considerably higher than those in the other countries. Malaysia presently has a slight edge over the other three in human capital-intensive or skill-intensive manufactures, which it can exploit further to gain a significant lead over its neighbours.

FIGURE 5.2
Index of Revealed Comparative Advantage:
Agricultural Resource-intensive Goods

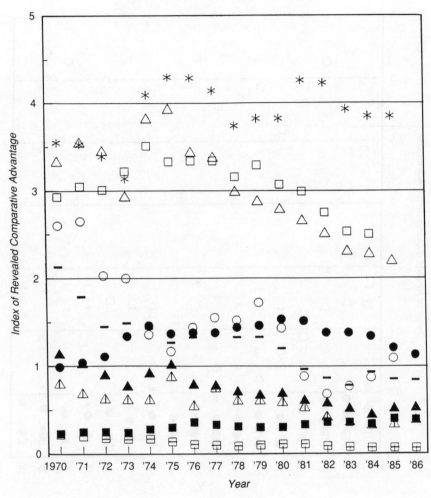

Legend:

Hong Kong	Indonesia	Japan	Korea	Malaysia
■	○	⊟	△	□

Philippines	Singapore	Taiwan	Thailand	United States
△	–	▲	*	●

Source: East–West Center database.

FIGURE 5.3
Index of Revealed Comparative Advantage:
Mineral Resource-intensive Goods

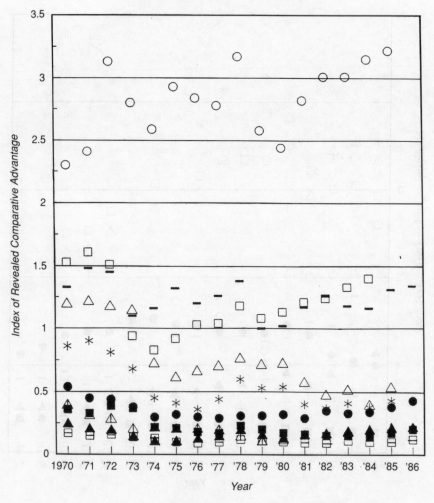

Source: East–West Center database.

FIGURE 5.4
Index of Revealed Comparative Advantage:
Unskilled Labour-intensive Goods

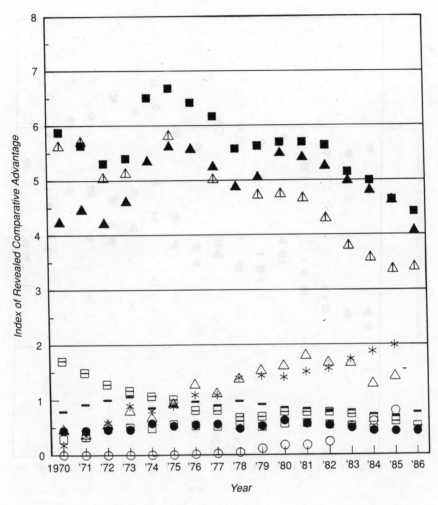

Source: East–West Center database.

FIGURE 5.5
Index of Revealed Comparative Advantage:
Technology-intensive Goods

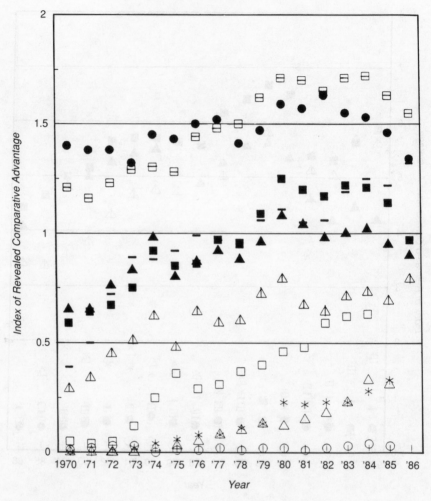

Source: East–West Center database.

FIGURE 5.6
Index of Revealed Comparative Advantage:
Human Capital-intensive Goods

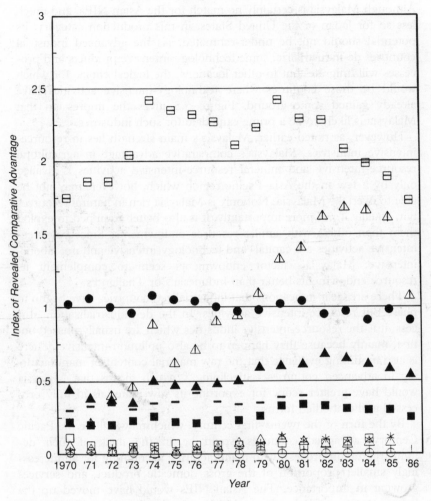

Legend:

Hong Kong	Indonesia	Japan	Korea	Malaysia
■	○	⊟	△	□

Philippines	Singapore	Taiwan	Thailand	United States
△	—	▲	✳	●

Source: East–West Center database.

Malaysia already has a tangible lead among the ASEAN-4 in technology-intensive goods. In fact, Malaysia seems to cluster with the Asian NIEs in so far as this category of products is concerned. Although Malaysia is certainly no match for the Asian NIEs, and much less so for Japan or the United States, in this production category, its potential should not be under-estimated. As the advanced industrial countries de-industrialize, some technology-intensive products and processes will 'migrate' out to other locations, the logical choice for which would be those countries where technology-intensive activities have already gained some ground. Figure 5.5 gives the impression that Malaysia is likely to be a prime candidate for such industries.

However, as noted earlier, Malaysia's main strength lies in resource-intensive industries. Malaysia's comparative advantage in agricultural resource-intensive and mineral resource-intensive activities is rivalled only by a few in the Asia–Pacific region which, however, may not be able to overtake Malaysia. Not only is Malaysia rich in natural resources but, equally if not more importantly, it is also better equipped to exploit them than others with similar resource endowments. Since resource-intensive activities are capital- and technology-intensive and not labour-intensive, Malaysia's factor endowments seem to complement its resource endowments better than Indonesia's or Thailand's.

There are clear indications that industrialized countries have begun to phase out resource-intensive activities. In the de-industrialization process, it is the resource-intensive industries which are usually phased out first, mainly because they happen to be also pollution-intensive. There is also mounting evidence that the raw material content of manufacturing in advanced countries is declining,[36] which means that Malaysia would have greater scope for exporting its raw materials in fully processed and embodied forms.

By the turn of the twenty-first century, which may well be the Pacific Century, advanced countries would be in the thick of their de-industrialization process, with manufacturing accounting for an increasingly smaller proportion of the gross domestic product, and services growing in importance. The Asian NIEs would have moved up the ladder, leaving behind activities which countries down below could take up.

It may be gleaned from the foregoing analysis that Malaysia stands to benefit from the structural changes that are in the offing, as the Asia–Pacific glides towards the next century. Much would, however, depend on how Malaysia plays its cards. Malaysia already has extensive trade and investment linkages in the Pacific Basin. It is investing heavily in human resource development through human capital formation. It has also begun to expand its R & D capabilities. By keeping its doors wide open, Malaysia can maximize its gains associated with the Pacific process. Closer Pacific integration will also imply increased risks which, however, can be minimized by continuing to have healthy trading and investment relations with other regions, especially Western Europe.

It would undoubtedly be in Malaysia's interests to have a world trading regime based on multilateralism, for such a system would enable a country to buy its imports from the cheapest possible source and to sell its products in the most lucrative market. The present system under the GATT, in spite of its many shortcomings, does serve the cause of multilateralism to a considerable extent, although its future seems to hinge precariously on the outcomes of the Uruguay Round. Thus, Malaysia, like other ASEAN countries, is playing an active role in the multilateral trade negotiations.

Concomitant with the above approach, Malaysia has been wary of formations of trade blocs. Like other ASEAN countries, Malaysia has been reluctant to participate in the regional attempts at institutionalizing the Pacific process, even though these attempts, referred to earlier, had nothing to do with the building of trade blocs. The main reasons for this reluctance seem to centre around the fear about possible US–Japanese domination, and concerns about the loosening of ASEAN ties.

Upon close examination, these explanations are not unassailable.[37] The strong influences exerted by the United States and Japan by virtue of their accomplishments can only be taken as given and must be factored in, regardless of whether the Asia–Pacific were to be structured or not. By participating in the process, Malaysia can help mould the structure so that it can find a comfortable niche and profit from it. ASEAN as a subregional group should be able to assert its position in a wider regional grouping—which could serve to strengthen rather than loosen the subregional ties.

In the light of the preceding discussion, it is not difficult to foresee Malaysia's elevation to the rank of the Asian NIEs by the turn of the century. Indeed, Malaysia is envisaged to become a full-fledged developed country by the year 2020. In the first decade of the next century, the manufacturing sector should account for 35–40 per cent of Malaysia's GDP and the share of manufactures in its total exports should be in the region of 55–60 per cent. The 'graduation' would, of course, mean withdrawal of many 'concessions', including the GSP, which Malaysia presently 'enjoys'. However, as alluded to in Chapter 3, the so-called concessions may have been a bane rather than a boon to Malaysia which would probably have been much better off with most-favoured-nation tariff cuts in developed countries. This is not to deny that the GSP has served as an implement to ignite the export-oriented industrialization process. But it seems to have outlived its usefulness as it now tends to constrain further export expansion.

It is clearly in the interest of Malaysia to opt for an open trading system based on rules and discipline rather than a 'managed' trading system based on power play and discretions. This means that Malaysia should be prepared to compete internationally on the basis of price and quality. The dawning of the Pacific era by no means dilutes the arguments in favour of an open trading system. Seen from this angle, Pacific economic co-operation is not necessarily antithetical to or inconsistent with the GATT initiatives.

Malaysia may find it advantageous to be supportive of what may be termed 'open regionalism' in the Pacific, by which is meant a loosely structured regional arrangement that provides a platform for consultations, co-operative efforts, and dispute settlements. Increased economic interdependence within the Asia–Pacific would also imply increased friction, conflicts, and disputes, which can only be dealt with effectively at the regional level, and not at the bilateral level. Thus, 'open regionalism' is one that is devoid of autarkic sentiments. Such an arrangement in the Asia–Pacific would be consistent with the first-best approach outlined above.

An alternative scenario would be one in which the world economy is subdivided into trade blocs of sorts, with Western Europe becoming an impenetrable 'fortress'. Should the Asia–Pacific countries respond to this by forming a trade bloc of their own, Malaysia would be worse off if it does not join the bandwagon. In any case, a Pacific Free Trade Area would be theoretically superior to an ASEAN Free Trade Area, since gains from the trade-creation effects are larger and losses from the trade-diversion effects are smaller in a bigger regional framework.

Malaysia has put forward the EAEG idea referred to earlier. Although it is not clear what form the proposed grouping will eventually assume, it is unlikely to evolve into an inward-looking trade bloc, as it would hurt members whose trade interests are global, not regional. It could at best be used as a consultative forum without erecting trade barriers against the rest of the world. The latter option would be a retrogressive step to take, as it would divert trade from third countries and invite retaliatory moves by third countries.

The East Asian Economic Grouping advocated by Malaysia would make sense if it were used as an instrument that would serve the cause of the multilateral trading system, and not as a tit-for-tat measure against protectionism elsewhere. Be that as it may, the EAEG proposal represents yet another signal heralding the dawn of the 'Pacific era' that visionaries talk about, since East Asia forms an integral part of the Western Pacific.

In any case, it is extremely unlikely that the Asia–Pacific region will organize itself like the European Community, for the forces which are at play in Western Europe are quite different from those that are at work in the Pacific Basin. The Asia–Pacific is too heterogeneous to emulate the West European model. As observed earlier, it is market forces which are driving the Asia–Pacific countries towards one another, in sharp contrast to Western Europe, where political forces dominate. To put it in another way, the governments in the Asia-Pacific region may well be simply reacting to regional trends brought about by market forces, while in Western Europe the governments play a pro-active role in bringing about regional integration.

Since no government can really afford to ignore the market signals for too long, one may expect the Malaysian authorities to monitor the Pacific trends and to act on them. Since the Pacific phenomenon is propelled by market forces and since the private sector plays a dominant role in the Malaysian economy, it would only be appropriate that the Malaysian government accord priority to the Pacific. Perhaps, Malaysia's 'Look East' policy of the early 1980s was but a prelude to what may be labelled as the 'Look Pacific' policy of the 1990s and beyond.

1. Gordon (1988), p. 20.
2. Naya et al. (1989b), p. 1.
3. Gordon (1988), p. 11.
4. Rostow (1986), p. 96.
5. For an elaborate discussion of the 'inefficacy' of trade restraints, particularly NTBs, see Baldwin (1982).
6. Ariff (1990).
7. Tan (1988), pp. 64–6.
8. Ibid.
9. Naya et al. (1989b), p. 9.
10. Japanese and Korean investments in the United States to produce consumer electronics provide typical examples. See Ariff (1989b).
11. For a good discussion of the link between structural changes and foreign investments, see Hill (1990).
12. For a discussion of dynamic comparative advantage, see Ariff (1990).
13. Export specialization ratios are used here as a proxy for 'revealed comparative advantage' (RCA), assuming that relative costs as well as differences in non-price factors are reflected in the pattern of commodity trade which in turn reflect inter-country differences in competitiveness. This measure introduced by Balassa (1965) defines RCA in terms of a country's commodity composition of exports relative to the commodity's share in world exports. A ratio greater than unity indicates that a country has a revealed comparative advantage. See note 8 in Chapter 3.
14. See, for example, Hoffman and Rush (1987), and Mody and Wheeler (1989).
15. Naya et al. (1989b), pp. 17–26.
16. Rasmussen (1988), p. 155.
17. Ibid., p. 150.
18. Chia (1988), p. 171.
19. See, for example, Wong (1984), Rasmussen (1988), and Lorenz (1989).
20. See Ariff (1980), (1981), and (1989a).
21. See Ariff (1988).
22. See Rieger (1985).
23. The ratio of intra-ASEAN trade varies considerably among member countries: In 1977, intra-regional trade accounted for 12.0 per cent for Indonesia, 17.1 per cent for Malaysia, 5.5 per cent for the Philippines, 23.6 per cent for Singapore, and 10.7 per cent for Thailand (see Hai and Ng, 1982).
24. The term 'soft regionalism' is not new to the international relations literature. For further discussion, see Scalapino (1987), pp. 7–8.
25. For example, see Lorenz (1989), and Naya et al. (1989b).
26. A report prepared by the East–West Center in Honolulu and the Institute of Southeast Asian Studies in Singapore has been submitted to the US and ASEAN governments. See Naya et al. (1989a).
27. One of the conditions is that value-added in South Pacific Islands must be at least 50 per cent.
28. See Kojima (1971).
29. APEC comprises the six ASEAN countries, Australia, Canada, Japan, South Korea, New Zealand, and the United States.
30. See Patrick (1981).

31. Rostow (1986), p. 104.

32. Ibid.

33. See Patrick (1981), Mendl (1983), and Lorenz (1989).

34. For a discussion of Malaysia's export inability and its impact on the domestic economy, see Ariff (1972).

35. UNIDO (1988).

36. See Hirata and Nohara (1989).

37. See also Akrasanee et al. (1981).

6
Conclusion

A PRIORI reasoning, based on the preceding analysis, would lead us to the inescapable conclusion that Malaysia will drift into the Pacific orbit which is already in the making. Once that happens, Malaysia will have little control over itself in the sense that the Pacific orbit will determine the course Malaysia will have to follow, which may not be a bad thing, if the prophecy of the Pacific Century is true. The prognosis looks as pretty as a picture, with Malaysia emerging as an NIE—whether it likes the label or not—before the turn of the century, experiencing dramatic structural transformations, contributing significantly to Pacific dynamism, and benefiting substantially from it.

All this, however, raises a number of pertinent questions. What are the dangers and pitfalls that Malaysia has to watch out for? What role will the major actors play in the Pacific arena? What will be the responsibilities of Malaysia as a Pacific nation? What options does Malaysia have in formulating its policies and strategies? Admittedly, these are difficult questions, and answers are not readily available. Besides, there can be no simple answers to complex and interrelated questions. Nevertheless, this concluding chapter will try at least to scratch the surface in an effort to unravel the 'mysteries' of the Pacific.

The post-war world, which is polarized into the communist and capitalist camps, will probably wither away by the turn of the century, if the current geopolitical trends are anything to go by. The Cold War is over, with the United States and the Soviet Union beginning to dismantle the barriers between them. This has given birth to an unprecedented opportunity for arms-control agreements between the two superpowers. This means that defence expenditures will decline sharply, diverting the scarce resources to more productive uses.

The recent shifts in the US–Soviet relations are likely to have far-reaching effects on the two camps which still dominate the world. Both the United States and the Soviet Union may cease to play the role of the hegemon in their respective camps, as both are conscious of the costs involved in playing such a role which entails providing public goods and operating a series of rewards and penalties to enforce the rules of the game in their respective spheres.[1]

In the capitalist camp, the United States has shouldered a heavy

defence burden, kept its market fairly open for imports, supported international multilateral institutions, imposed no control on capital outflows,
and mounted massive aid programmes, as all these have helped promote
US security goals. The end of the Cold War would therefore mean that
the United States will stop supplying public goods to others at its own
expense.[2]

Thus, one implication of the end of the Cold War is that the West
may no longer be favourably disposed towards less developed market
economies. Countries like Malaysia, which have benefited from the Cold
War in the past, may find the developed capitalist countries more
demanding and less conciliatory in bilateral trade dealings. This notwithstanding, the end of the Cold War can also mean exciting economic
opportunities, as resources are diverted away from defence expenditures
to other uses. The latter outcome may overwhelm the former, especially
if the global economy expands at a rate sufficient to keep the protectionist forces at bay.

Dramatic changes taking place in Europe may not augur well for
countries like Malaysia. With many Eastern European countries break-
ing away from the Soviet camp and anxious to interact with market-
oriented economies, more and more resources are likely to be funnelled
into these countries at the expense of others. In particular, the
reunification of Germany may strengthen the current tendency in
Western Europe to be even more Euro-centric, which would amount to
openly flouting the post-war golden rule of non-discrimination. The
possibility of some East European countries emerging as rivals to South-
East Asian countries in the West European market is real and cannot
be discounted altogether, although the threat is not imminent, since
East European countries will need time to set their own houses in order
first.

In the same vein, the proposed establishment of a single market
within the European Community by 1992 may have adverse implications for countries like Malaysia. Much will, however, depend on what
the term 'single market' means to the European Community and how
successful the European Community will be in its attempt. A single
market may simply amount to a removal of all barriers to the flow of
goods and factors among the EC members without new barriers being
erected against the third countries. If this were the case, a single market
in the European Community would not constitute a 'Fortress Europe' as
it has been caricatured.

It is by no means certain that the EC will be a single market by 1992.
The EC countries are not really homogeneous as they are at different
stages of development and have joined the grouping at different points
in time. It is unlikely that they will all act in unison come 1992. Even if
the European Community does not become a 'fortress', there may still
be some trade and investment diversions from developing countries like
Malaysia to the less developed EC members, namely Greece, Spain, and
Portugal, not to mention the adverse impact of the highly protectionist
Common Agricultural Policy (CAP) of the European Community. But,

on the other hand, structural changes taking place in the European Community after 1992 can have positive spillover effects on third countries. Thus, there may well be increased demand for Malaysian raw materials and resource-based manufactures emanating from the European Community even after 1992.

Far more dangerous is the possible trade war between the United States and Japan. While the US perception of the Soviet Union as a security threat has diminished, its perception of Japan as an economic threat has risen. The United States may have won the Cold War but is losing economic battles with Japan. If the United States gets desperate and strikes a bilateral deal with Japan, trade interests of third countries may be hurt badly. Getting caught in the crossfire is the last thing that countries like Malaysia would wish for. But the danger is real, especially since Japan has a high profile in terms of direct investments in Malaysia. Malaysian manufactured exports from production units owned or run by the Japanese may be viewed simply as offshore Japanese exports and treated as such.

It cannot be denied that East and South-East Asian economies have benefited immensely from the US budget and balance of payments deficits. The capacity of the United States to go on living beyond its means, incurring huge internal and external deficits, is not unlimited. The manner in which the United States handles its twin deficits will have serious trade repercussions. A 'hard landing' through rapid adjustments will result in a drastic contraction in world demand, whereas a 'soft landing' through gradual correction may lead to greater protectionist pressures. In either case, it is certain that countries like Malaysia will be adversely affected, although the latter approach would seem less painful.

In any case, the days of Japan as the 'supplier' and the United States as the 'absorber' are definitely over. Unless Japan takes up the slack left by the US correction process, there will be a serious contraction in world demand. A simulation exercise has shown that a 2 per cent contraction in the US GNP will cause a 4.4 per cent drop in Malaysia's GNP, while a 2 per cent expansion in Japan's GNP will lead to a 2.4 per cent increase in Malaysia's GNP.[3] In other words, Japan will have to grow almost twice as fast as the United States contracts in order to offset the negative impact of the US corrections on Malaysia's growth performance. It is, however, unlikely that Japan will compensate entirely for a decline in the US demand, not only because Japan's economy is less than two-thirds of the size of the US economy but also because Japan's marginal propensity to import is considerably less than that of the United States. The crippling deflationary effect of a contraction in the US economy can be averted only if Japan is prepared to undertake a bold and unprecedented reformation of its domestic economy through substantial deregulation, especially by dismantling its non-tariff barriers.

All this is by no means inconsistent with the bright long-term Pacific outlook presented in Chapter 5. The above discussion serves to underscore some of the dangers and pitfalls that Malaysia, as a Pacific nation, may have to come to terms with in the short and medium runs. Viewed in this light, there is a strong case for Malaysia not to place all its eggs in the Pacific basket.

Malaysia has a thriving trade with Western Europe and has established new viable trade linkages with the Middle East. It will be in the country's interest to strengthen these commercial relations, while the Pacific becomes increasingly and irresistibly attractive. The diminishing importance of the European Community as a trading partner and as a source of direct foreign investment for Malaysia, as seen in Chapters 3 and 4, is not necessarily irreversible. Malaysia is partly to be blamed for what might be viewed as a European retreat or withdrawal. Not only has Malaysia explicitly paid disproportionately less attention to Europe in comparison with the Pacific in its trade and investment initiatives in the past, but has also implicitly warded off potential European initiatives through its somewhat blunt Look East Policy. As mentioned, the situation is not irreversible. Remaining attractive to Western Europe would mean bigger Western European stakes in the Malaysian economy, for, the bigger the stake the greater the interest. Strong EC investment links, in particular, can act as corridors providing access to the vast EC market for Malaysian manufactures.

Malaysia's policy options with respect to external economic relations are rather limited. The inward-looking option is out of the question, as it would entail an enormous welfare loss. It would be an unambiguously retrogressive step for Malaysia to adopt autarkic policies in response to the uncertainties that characterize the current international trading environment.

The subregional economic co-operation that Malaysia has within the framework of ASEAN is necessary under the present circumstances but is not sufficient to ensure rapid economic growth. It is beyond the scope of this volume to delve deeply into the successes and failures of ASEAN as a regional grouping.[4] Suffice it to note that Malaysia's trade with its ASEAN partners has increased considerably in recent years, but the increase has very little to do with the preferential trading arrangement or the wider margin of preferences under the ASEAN industrial joint ventures. It will not be in Malaysia's interest to forge a closely knit subregional integration through discriminatory arrangements, as the trade diversion effects arising from it are likely to far exceed the trade creation effects, given the resource and factor endowments of the ASEAN region. Much of the increase in intra-ASEAN trade in recent years is attributable to the bold liberalization measures taken by individual countries in unilateral fashion outside the ASEAN framework. To say the least, the ASEAN market is no substitute for the global market. Nevertheless, ASEAN can play a supplementary role that is mutually beneficial to all its members.

Bilateral trading arrangements with major countries like the United States and Japan may be helpful under difficult circumstances but are clearly inferior to the multilateral system based on the principle of non-discrimination. Besides, bilateral deals often carry substantial political costs which defy quantification. The first-best policy option for Malaysia would therefore be to stay within the multilateral trading system and abide by the rules of the game. Malaysia's active participation in the Uruguay Round of multilateral trade negotiations under the auspices of the General Agreement on Tariffs and Trade is consistent with such a policy approach.

However, Malaysia acting alone cannot ensure that the GATT system will survive, let alone succeed. Should the multilateral trading system collapse and the world be divided into trade blocs, it would be in Malaysia's interest to align itself with the group that is most compatible; the bigger the group the better, other things being equal. As alluded to earlier, ASEAN represents too small a stage for Malaysia to upgrade or upstage itself. A wider Pacific grouping would be a viable proposition under such circumstances and would be the most logical choice for Malaysia to pick.

There is, however, no suggestion that the multilateral trading system is disintegrating or that the world is really being divided into trade blocs. These are just possibilities and there are no indications that they are unavoidable. The trends outlined in the preceding chapter in the Pacific context merely show that the Pacific is emerging as the new centre of world economic activity and do not purport to suggest that a Pacific trade bloc is actually in the making. Pacific regional organizations like the PECC and APEC are simply the region's responses to its own internal dynamism. Pacific regionalism, as was seen in the preceding chapter, is largely induced by anonymous market forces and not politically motivated, quite unlike regionalism elsewhere. Thus, there is no basis to believe that the Pacific Community, if at all it materializes, will emulate the EC model.

Dynamism implies intense interactions, and interactions in turn entail frictions of sorts. As Pacific countries become increasingly interdependent, issues relating to trade and factor flows are likely to surface, which cannot be effectively handled in a bilateral manner. Regional issues will warrant regional solutions; hence the need for regional organizations that would act as fora for airing grievances, discussing problems of common interest, exchanging information, providing early warning signals, and so forth. Seen from such an angle, Pacific organizations like the PECC and APEC do make considerable sense.

It will be in Malaysia's national interest to play an active role in such regional bodies right from the beginning so that it can influence the course they take and help mould them into a form in which it can find some comfort and profit. Conversely, a passive role will mean that Malaysia may have to put up later on with an outfit that could prove to be a strait-jacket. Malaysia should use these organizations to keep the multilateral trading system alive, as it can scarcely have any international impact acting on its own or even on the ASEAN platform.

At the same time, Malaysia must realize that its future is wedded to that of the Pacific. Malaysia has a tremendous locational advantage by being close to economies that are characterized as the 'high flyers'. What is more, Malaysia has all the prerequisites in place to take advantage of opportunities stemming from the structural changes and industrial adjustments taking place in these economies. Malaysia has abundant natural resources, excellent infrastructures, efficient administration, an educated and disciplined labour force, and a thriving entrepreneurial class. Thus, Malaysia seems all set to follow the footsteps of the East Asian NIEs, with industries that migrate from the latter finding a sanctuary in Malaysia whose resource and factor endowments match the factor intensities of the migrating industries. Can Malaysia really make it? Should Malaysia adopt the East Asian development model?

The second question is somewhat tricky, as the answer would depend crucially on what is meant by the term 'East Asian model'. To be sure, there is no single model that is representative of Japan and the East Asian NIEs. There are, in fact, as many models as there are economies, since every entity in a sense is unique. Japan, Korea, and Taiwan have pursued protectionist policies to promote their industries, while Hong Kong and Singapore have had very liberal trade regimes. In Japan and Korea, conglomerates have formed the backbone of the country's industrial sector, whereas in Taiwan, small and medium-size industries have played key roles. In Singapore, there has been considerable government support for industries through various incentives, whereas in Hong Kong there has been complete *laissez-faire*. Thus, there is no such thing as *the* East Asian model, although a common denominator in all these experiences has been their successful export drive. However, the essence of the so-called East Asian model lies not so much in the success of the East Asian export initiatives as in their success in eliminating the anti-trade bias present in their regimes. In other words, what is really at issue is the relevance of export promoting (EP) strategy to Malaysia.

Technically, an EP regime is one in which the effective exchange rates for exportables and importables are equalized (Bhagwati, 1988). Put another way, export promotion means nothing more than the removal of distortions caused by the structure of protection under an import-substitution regime without creating a bias in the opposite direction (Krueger, 1978). In other words, export promotion simply means the elimination of anti-export bias.

In Korea and Taiwan, where import-substituting and export-oriented industries have coexisted, the anti-export bias embedded in the structure of protection has been offset by various export promotion incentives. They have seemingly adopted a 'neutral' trade regime by neutralizing the distortions caused by their structure of protection. Of course, as noted earlier, the first-best solution would be to eliminate the distortions at the source instead of offsetting them with counter distortions. Although their trade regimes are thus not truly 'neutral', they have adopted liberal policies. Export orientation in all the NIEs has necessitated considerable deregulation and decontrol.

The lesson that Malaysia can learn from the East Asian experience is that there cannot be export promotion without liberalization and that liberalization pays. Liberalization can lead to both static and dynamic gains. Seen in such perspectives, it is not difficult to understand why export expansion has been a powerful 'engine of growth' for the East Asian NIEs. It is especially in this sense that the East Asian model is relevant to Malaysia. To remain competitive internationally, Malaysia must continue to deregulate its economy and liberalize its trade. There is no need, though, for Malaysia to copy the development pattern of the East Asian NIEs. Being resource-rich, it has other options which are not available to the resource-poor NIEs. Malaysia should therefore allow its primary production and manufacturing to expand simultaneously without a bias in favour of either. There is no reason why they cannot grow in parallel fashion, since manufacturing is essentially an extension of primary production in the downstream direction. There is a need to guard against excessive industrialization which could impose heavy social costs through damages inflicted on the environment and the quality of life.

The question of whether Malaysia can possibly work its way to the top through the export expansion route, given the current worrisome international trends, also warrants some discussion. Export-oriented industrialization has become an attractive policy option for many developing countries in South and South-East Asia, Latin America, and the Caribbean, following the meteoric rise of the East Asian NIEs. With so many countries joining the bandwagon, the chances of success for any individual country would seem rather slim. Moreover, the international trading environment facing these countries in the 1990s is much tougher than that which prevailed in the 1960s when Korea, Taiwan, and Hong Kong made their debut in the export markets. Such considerations have led some analysts to be sceptical about the workability of the EP option.

To be sure, 'export pessimism' is not a new doctrine. In 1950, Prebisch argued that export reliance would cause significant terms of trade deterioration, while in 1959 Nurkse postulated that foreign markets were so saturated that increased less developed country (LDC) exports could not be absorbed. They were later proven wrong by the East Asian NIEs which successfully launched and sustained their export drive. However, export pessimism has reappeared. This time around, it is argued that the emulation of the East Asian model by other LDCs would exert enormous pressure in developed-country markets, generating strong protectionist interventions (Cline, 1982). Although this argument sounds intuitively plausible, it crumbles upon close scrutiny.

As pointed out by Ranis (1985), one can only expect different LDCs to arrive at the substantial manufacturing export capacity at different points in time. Any increase in the pressure caused by the export initiatives of individual countries, if sufficiently staggered, may not be as spectacular as feared at any given point in time. Besides, such pressures may well be diffused over a wide range of activities, if exports are increasingly diversified. The LDC share in the industrial countries' consumption of manufactures is just over 2 per cent,[5] which suggests that there is considerable room for further expansion. To this must also be added the possible emergence of South–South trade. Since the EP strategy calls for a more open trading regime, we can reasonably expect increased South–South trade flows.[6] Furthermore, protectionist pressures in developed countries, caused by increased LDC exports, can be relieved to a considerable extent through increased LDC imports from developed countries.

Admittedly, protectionism is on the rise, but there is no basis to be unduly pessimistic about its prognosis. For one thing, some of the protectionist measures are so 'porous' that markets are kept more open than they seem.[7] For another, the growing trend towards globalization of industries, thanks to the multinationals, may also help contain the protectionist forces.[8] Finally, the GATT efforts to open up markets are likely to continue beyond the Uruguay Round which is expected to make tangible headway in that direction. Thus, the prospects for LDC manufactured exports are not as bleak as the export pessimism hypothesis suggests.

In the Malaysian context, there is even less room for export pessimism. Malaysia is not just an 'average' LDC. It already belongs to the league of advanced developing countries (ADCs) with a per capita income of over US$2,000. Malaysia has all the ingredients in place, as mentioned earlier. Besides, Malaysia is not really a newcomer. Trade has always been its lifeblood. Given the long tradition of a fairly liberal policy regime, and three decades of industrial experience, Malaysia has emerged as a prime candidate in the export game.

Already, Malaysia has a lead over many other LDCs which aspire to become exporters of manufactures. To upstage itself, Malaysia must continually adjust itself to changing circumstances with speed and dexterity. There is always room at the top for a country that aims high and is prepared to work hard at it. It appears that Malaysia has the courage and means to do just that. Malaysia's Pacific connections should pave the way, for Malaysia's economic relations with other countries in the Asia–Pacific region are essentially symbiotic.

1. See Krause and Sundberg (1989).

2. Ibid.

3. See Takenaka (1989), Table 3.

4. The author has written extensively on ASEAN. See, for example, Ariff (1980, 1981, and 1989a).

5. See Bhagwati (1988).

6. Ranis (1985) also makes a similar point. In this context, the experiences of Korea and Taiwan are particularly revealing: they have liberalized their trade regimes, and their trade with ASEAN countries has increased significantly in recent years.

7. See Baldwin (1982).

8. This is referred to as the 'spiderweb' phenomenon by Bhagwati (1988, p. 45).

Appendices

Appendix 1: Background

MALAYSIA is a federation of thirteen states, comprising eleven from the Malay Peninsula and two from the Borneo Island (Sabah and Sarawak), not to mention the two federal territories of Kuala Lumpur (Peninsular Malaysia) and Labuan (North-west Borneo). Nine of the eleven peninsular states are ruled by Sultans, while the others are headed by Governors appointed by the King who is elected by the Sultans from among themselves on a rotational basis to serve for a period of five years. The King, referred to as the Yang di-Pertuan Agong, is a constitutional monarch in a system based on parliamentary democracy, the twin pillars of which are the House of Representatives (Dewan Rakyat) and the Senate (Dewan Negara).

Malaysia was a British colony until independence was granted to Peninsular Malaysia (then known as Malaya) in 1957 and to Sabah and Sarawak in 1963 when they chose to join the peninsular component states to form the Malaysian federation. Singapore was a member of the federation briefly for two years (July 1963–August 1965) before it became an independent republic.

Malaysia covers a land area of 329 293 sq. km, of which Peninsular Malaysia accounts for 131 500 sq. km. Malaysia is a multiracial country with an estimated population of 17.4 million, of which Malays and other indigenous groups constitute about 54 per cent, Chinese about 35 per cent, and Indians roughly 10 per cent. For political purposes, the population is dichotomized into Bumiputras (literally 'sons of the soil' meaning the indigenous people) and non-Bumiputras (non-indigenous people of migrant stock). In Malaysian politics, the ethnic factor has always been a potent one. Indeed, most political parties are organized along communal lines and the ruling coalition itself represents an inter-ethnic political platform for the various communities.

The majority of the Bumiputras are in rural areas and engage in such traditional activities as farming and fishing, while the non-Bumiputras, particularly the Chinese, are concentrated in urban centres, focusing on modern sectors including manufacturing, commerce, and finance. Although poverty knows no racial boundaries and there are poor people in all communities, the Bumiputras are economically more backward, while the non-Bumiputras are economically far more advanced. Malaysians are pragmatic and have learned to live with stark realities, exhibiting considerable tolerance and the spirit of give and take. The racial riots of 13 May 1969 were really an aberration triggered by excessive communal politicking, which proved to be explosive in a situation marked by glaring economic disparities. The disturbances rammed home the point that such economic imbalance was totally antithetical to racial harmony and political stability, hence the formulation of the New Economic Policy (NEP) which was designed to redress the problem of ethnic inequities.

Appendix 2
The Planning, Co-ordination, and Evaluation Machinery

Parliament

Cabinet

National Action Council

National Security Council

National Planning Council

National Development Planning Committee (NDPC)

Committee on Socio-economic Study

National Development Administration Committee

Standards and Costs Sub-committee

Development Budget Sub-committee

Manpower Planning Sub-committee

Socio-economic Research Unit (SERU)

Malaysian Administrative and Modernization Planning Unit (MAMPU)

Implementation and Co-ordination Unit (ICU)

Economic Planning Unit (EPU)

Inter-Agency Planning Groups

Foreign Investment Committee

Economic Panel

Research and Evaluation

Modernization of Administration

Implementation

Planning

Ministries and State Governments

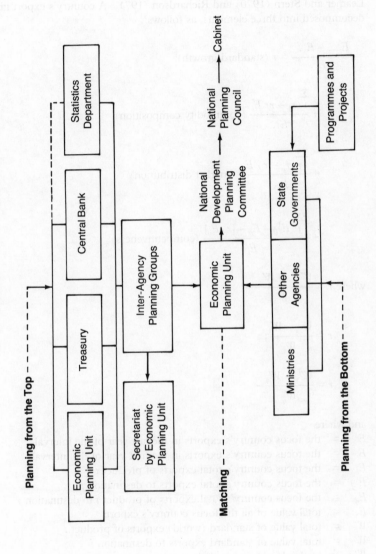

Appendix 3
The Planning Process

Planning from the Top - - - - -

| Economic Planning Unit | Treasury | Central Bank | Statistics Department |

Inter-Agency Planning Groups

Secretariat by Economic Planning Unit

National Development Planning Committee

Economic Planning Unit

National Planning Council → Cabinet

Matching - - - - -

| Ministries | Other Agencies | State Governments |

Programmes and Projects

Planning from the Bottom - - - - -

Appendix 4
A Formal Presentation of the Constant Market
Shares Model

THE CMS analysis employed in the section on trade performance in Chapter 3 is based on the methodology of Tyers and Phillips (1984), as adapted from Leamer and Stern (1970) and Richardson (1971). A country's export growth is decomposed into three elements, as follows:

$$\frac{E^1.. - E..}{E..} = r \text{ (standard growth)}$$

$$+ \frac{\sum_i (r_1 - r)\, E_i}{E..} \text{ (commodity composition)}$$

$$+ \frac{\sum_i \sum_j (r_{ij} - r_i)\, E_{ij}}{E..} \text{ (market distribution)}$$

$$+ \frac{\sum_i \sum_j (E^1_{ij} - E_{ij} - [r_{ij}\, E_{ij}])}{E_i} \text{ (competitiveness)}$$

where $r = \dfrac{W^1.. - W..}{W..}$;

$r = \dfrac{W^1_i - W_i}{W_i}$;

$r = \dfrac{W^1_{ij} - W_{ij}}{W_{ij}}$

and where
E^1 = the focus country's exports in the last year of the interval
E = the focus country's exports in the first year of the interval
E_i = the focus country's total exports of product i
$E_{.j}$ = the focus country's total exports to destination j
E_{ij} = the focus country's total exports of product i to destination j
$E..$ = total value of all the focus country's exports
W_i = total value of standard (world) exports of product i
$W_{.j}$ = total value of standard exports to destination j
W_{ij} = total value of standard exports of product i to destination j
$W..$ = total value of all standard exports

Appendix 5
SITC Classification of Trade in Manufactures

Code	Product
	(1) *Agricultural resource-intensive*
61	Leather, dressed fur, etc.
63	Wood, cork manufactures
	(2) *Mineral resource-intensive*
661–3	Non-metal building products and minerals
667	Pearls, precious, semiprecious stones
671	Pig iron etc.
	(3) *Unskilled labour-intensive*
54	Medical etc. products
65	Textile, yarn, fabric, etc.
664–6	Glass, glassware, pottery
695–7	Tools, cutlery, metal household equipment
729	Electrical machinery n.e.s.
735	Ships and boats
81–5	Plumbing, heating, lighting, etc. equipment; furniture; travel goods; clothing; footwear
893–5	Articles of plastic n.e.s.; toys; sporting goods; office suppliers, n.e.s.
899	Other manufactured goods
931	Special transactions
951	War firearms, ammunition
	(4) *Technology-intensive*
51	Chemical elements, compounds
52	Coal, petroleum etc. chemicals
56–9	Fertilizers, explosives, plastics, chemicals n.e.s.
71	Machinery, non-electric
722	Electrical powered machinery, switchgear
723	Electrical distributing machinery
726	Electro-medical, X-ray equipment
734	Aircraft
861– 3	Instruments, photo, cinema supplies, movies
	(5) *Human capital-intensive*
53	Dyes, tanning, colour products
55	Perfume, cleaning etc. products

(continued)

Appendix 5 (*continued*)

Code	Product
62	Rubber manufactures n.e.s.
64	Paper, paperboard and manufacturing
672–9	Iron and steel excluding 670–1
691–4	Metal manufactures excluding 695–9
698–9	Metal manufactures n.e.s.
724	Telecommunications equipment
725	Domestic electric equipment
731–3	Railway and road vehicles
864	Watches and clocks
891	Sound recorders, producers
892	Printed matter
896	Works of art etc.
897	Gold, silverware, jewelry

Sources: Krause (1982) and Tyers and Phillips (1984).

Appendix 6
GATT Illustrative List of Non-tariff Barriers

Group	Barriers
1	*Government participation in trade which either restricts imports from or subsidizes exports to Third World countries*
	Trade diverting aid
	Export subsidies
	Countervailing duties
	Government procurement
	State-trading in market-economy countries
	Other restrictive practices
2	*Customs and administrative entry procedures to discriminate against foreign products*
	Valuation
	Anti-dumping
	Customs classification
	Consular and customs formalities, fees, and documentation
	Samples requirements
3	*Standards which apply non-market quality or 'safety' standards as a 'cover' for inhibiting products*
	Standards
	Packaging, labelling, and marketing regulations
4	*Specific limitations on trade on particular countries*
	Quantitative restrictions (e.g. numerical import quotas)
	Discriminatory bilateral agreements (e.g. licensing requirements)
	Export restraints
	Minimum price regulations
5	*Charges on imports*
	Prior deposits
	Variable levies
	Fiscal adjustments at the border or elsewhere
	Restrictions on foreign wines and spirits
	Discriminatory taxes on automobiles
	Statistical and administrative duties
	Special duties on imports

Sources: Adapted from Golt (1974), p. 31; and Girling (1985), p 127.

References

Abreu, M.P. (1989), 'Developing Countries and the Uruguay Round of Trade Negotiations', Proceedings of the World Bank Annual Conference on Development Economics, World Bank, Washington, DC.

Akrasanee, N. et al. (1981), *ASEAN and the Pacific Community*, Centre for Strategic and International Studies, Jakarta.

Ali, A. and Rani, O. (1984), 'Malaysian Experience with MNCs', Universiti Kebangsaan Malaysia, Bangi (unpublished).

Anderson, D. (1982), 'Small Industry in Developing Countries: A Discussion of Issues', *World Development*, 10(11).

Anderson, K. (1983), 'Prospects for Trade Growth among Pacific Basin Countries', *Developing Economies*, 21(4).

Ariff, M. (1972), *Export Trade and the West Malaysian Economy—An Enquiry into the Economic Implications of Export Instability*, Faculty of Economics and Administration, University of Malaya, Kuala Lumpur.

——— (1975), 'Protection for Manufactures in Peninsular Malaysia', *Hitotsubashi Journal of Economics*, 15(2).

——— (1976), 'Industrialisation', in M. Ariff et. al., *Performance and Perspectives of the Malaysian Economy*, Institute of Developing Economies, Tokyo.

——— (1980), 'Malaysia's Trade and Industrialisation Strategy with Special Reference to ASEAN Industrial Co-operation', in R. Garnaut (ed.), *ASEAN in a Changing Pacific and World Economy*, Australian National University, Canberra.

——— (1981), *Malaysia and ASEAN Economic Cooperation*, Institute of Southeast Asian Studies, Singapore.

——— (1984), 'Export-oriented Industrialization in Malaysia: Policies and Responses', in P. van Dijck and H. Verbruggen (eds.), *Export-oriented Industrialization and Employment: Policies and Responses with Special Reference to ASEAN Countries*, Council for Asian Manpower Studies, Manila.

——— (1988), 'Multilateral Trade Negotiations: ASEAN Perspectives', in M. Ariff and L.H. Tan (eds.), *ASEAN Trade Policy Options*, Institute of Southeast Asian Studies, Singapore.

——— (1989a), 'The Changing Role of ASEAN in the Coming Decades: Post-Manila Perspectives', in M. Shinohara and F.C. Lo (eds.), *Global Adjustment and the Future of Asian–Pacific Economy*, Institute of Developing Economies, Tokyo, and Asian and Pacific Development Centre, Kuala Lumpur.

——— (1989b), 'Protection for Consumer Electronics in North America and Implications for Southeast and East Asia', in L.H. Tan and S.Y. Chia (eds.), *Trade, Protectionism and Industrial Adjustment in Consumer Electronics: Asian Responses to North America*, Institute of Southeast Asian Studies, Singapore.

—— (1989c), 'Export Processing Zones: The ASEAN Experience', in S. Y. Chia and C. Bifan (eds.), *ASEAN–China Economic Relations— Developments in ASEAN and China*, Institute of Southeast Asian Studies, Singapore.

—— (1990), 'Dynamic Comparative Advantage, International Trading Rules and Their Implications for the Industrializing Countries', paper submitted to the World Bank, Washington, DC (unpublished).

Ariff, M. and Hill, H. (1985), *Export-oriented Industrialisation: The ASEAN Experience*, Allen & Unwin, Sydney.

Ariff, M. and Semudram, M. (1987), 'Trade and Financing Strategies: A Case Study of Malaysia', Working Paper No. 21, Overseas Development Institute, London.

Arndt, H. W. (1989), 'The GATT System, Free Trade Areas and Regional Cooperation', in T. Fukuchi and M. Kagami (eds.), *Perspectives on the Pacific Basin Economy: A Comparison of Asia and Latin America*, The Asian Club Foundation and Institute of Developing Economies, Tokyo.

Asian Development Bank (ADB), *Key Indicators of Developing Member Countries of ADB*, Manila, various issues.

Balassa, B. (1965), 'Trade Liberalisation and Revealed Comparative Advantage', *Manchester School of Economics and Social Studies*, 33(2).

Baldwin, R. (1982), *The Inefficacy of Trade Policy*, Princeton University, Princeton.

Bhagwati, J. N. (1988), 'Export Promoting Strategy—Issues and Evidence', *Research Observer*, World Bank, Washington, DC.

Bowen, H. P. (1983), 'On the Theoretical Interpretation of Indices of Trade Intensity and Revealed Comparative Advantage', *Weltwirtschftliches Archiv*, 119(3).

Brown, A. J. (1949), *Applied Economics: Aspects of the World Economy in War and Peace*, Allen & Unwin, London.

Chenery, H. B. (1960), 'Patterns of Industrial Growth', *American Economic Review*, September.

Cheong K. C. et al. (1981), *Comparative Advantage of Electronics and Wood-Processing Industries in Malaysia*, Institute of Developing Economies, Tokyo.

Chia, S. Y. (1988), 'Economic Prospects in the Asia–Pacific: An Asian View', in T. S. Lau and L. Suryadinata (eds.), *Moving into the Pacific Century: The Changing Regional Order in the Asia–Pacific*, Heinemann Asia, Singapore.

China, Republic of (1987), *Statistical Yearbook of the Republic of China 1987*.

Cline, W. R. (1982), 'Can the East Asian Model of Development be Generalized?', *World Development*, 10(2).

Drysdale, P. and Garnaut, R. (1982), 'Trade Intensities and the Analysis of Bilateral Trade Flows in a Many-Country World: A Survey', *Hitotsubashi Journal of Economics*, 22(2).

Ethier, J. (1982), 'National and International Returns to Scale in the Modern Theory of International Trade', *American Economic Review*, Vol. 72.

Fong, C. O. (1987), 'Technology Acquisition under Alternative Arrangements with Transnational Corporations: Selected Industrial Case Studies in Malaysia', ESCAP/UNCTC Publications Series B. No. 11, Bangkok.

Fong, C. O. et al. (1988), 'Direct Foreign Investment and Technological Development', Report submitted to the Committee on Action Plan for Industrial Technology Development, Kuala Lumpur (unpublished).

Gan, W. B. (1989), 'Macroeconomic Policy, Real Exchange Rate and International Competitiveness—The Malaysian Experience', Faculty of Economics and Administration, University of Malaya, Kuala Lumpur (unpublished).

GATT (1980), 'The Tokyo Round Multilateral Trade Negotiations—II: Supplementary Report', GATT, Geneva.

Girling, R. H. (1985), *Multinational Institutions and the Third World*, Praeger Publishers, New York.

Golt, S. (1974), *The GATT Negotiations 1973–75, Guide to the Issues*, British North American Institute, London.

Gordon, B. K. (1988), 'Pacific Futures for the USA', in T. S. Lau and L. Suryadinata (eds.), *Moving into the Pacific Century: The Changing Regional Order in the Asia–Pacific*, Heinemann Asia, Singapore.

Grubel, H. G. and Lloyd, P. J. (1975), *Intra-industry Trade: The Theory and Measurement of International Trade in Differentiated Products*, Macmillan, London.

Hai, H. and Ng, F. A. (1982), 'Trade among ASEAN Countries', in S. H. Saw and H. Hai (eds.), *Growth and Direction of ASEAN Trade*, Singapore University Press, Singapore.

Hill, H. (1990), 'Role and Effects of Foreign Investment on Industrial, Technological Development, Product Development and Marketing', paper submitted to Economic Development Institute (EDI), World Bank, Washington, DC (unpublished).

Hill, H. and Johns, B. (1984), 'The Role of Direct Foreign Investment in Developing East Asian Countries', Australian National University, Canberra (unpublished).

Hirata, A. and Nohara, T. (1989), 'Changing Patterns in International Division of Labour in Asia and the Pacific', in M. Shinohara and F. C. Lo (eds.), *Global Adjustment and the Future of Asian–Pacific Economy*, Institute of Developing Economies, Tokyo, and Asian and Pacific Development Centre, Kuala Lumpur.

Hoffman, K. (1985), 'Clothing, Chips and Competitive Advantage—The Impact of Microelectronics on Trade and Production in the Garment Industry', *World Development*, 13(3).

Hoffman, K. and Rush, H. (1987), *Microelectronics and Clothing*, Praeger, New York.

Hoffman, L. and Tan, T. N. (1971), 'Pattern of Growth and Structural Change in West Malaysia's Manufacturing Industry 1959–68', *Kajian Ekonomi Malaysia*, December.

Hufbauer, G. (1989), 'A View of the Forest', in B. Balassa (ed.), *Subsidies and Countervailing Measures—Critical Issues for the Uruguay Round*, World Bank Discussion Papers 55, World Bank, Washington, DC.

International Monetary Fund (IMF), *Direction of Trade Statistics* (annual) and *Yearbook*, various issues, Washington, DC.

Japan External Trade Organisation (JETRO) (1990), *Tradescope*, 10(1), January, Tokyo.

Kalirajan K. P. (1989), 'A Simultaneous Determination of Market Concentration and Industry Performance in West Malaysian Manufacturing', Working Paper No. 89/4, National Centre for Development Studies, Australian National University, Canberra.

Kojima, K. (1964), 'The Pattern of International Trade among Advanced Countries', *Hitotsubashi Journal of Economics*, 5(1).

——— (1971), *Japan and a Pacific Free Trade Area*, Macmillan, London.

——— (1977), *Japan and a New World Economic Order*, Charles E. Tuttle and Co., Tokyo.

_____ (1990), *Japanese Direct Investment Abroad*, International Christian University, Tokyo.

Krause, L. B. (1982), *US Economic Policy towards the Association of Southeast Asian Nations: Meeting the Japanese Challenge*, Brookings Institution, Washington, DC.

Krause, L. B. and Sundberg, M. (1989), 'Inter-relationship between the World and Pacific Economic Performance', paper submitted to the Eighteenth Pacific Trade and Development Conference, Kuala Lumpur, 11–14 December (unpublished).

Krueger, A. O. (1978), *Foreign Trade Regimes and Economic Development: Liberalization Attempts and Consequences*, Ballinger, Cambridge, Mass., for the National Bureau of Economic Research.

Langhammer, R. and Gross, M. (1986), 'EC Foreign Investment in ASEAN and Its Impact on Trade', CEPS Working Documents, No. 8 (Political), Brussels.

Lary, H. B. (1968), *Imports of Manufactures from Less Developed Countries*, Columbia University Press, New York, for the National Bureau of Economic Research.

Leamer, E. L. and Stern, R. M. (1970), *Quantitative International Economics*, Allyn and Bacon, Boston.

Lee, K. F. (1990), 'Export Expansion and Industrial Growth—The Malaysian Experience 1968–1986', Masters thesis, Faculty of Economics and Administration, University of Malaya, Kuala Lumpur (unpublished).

Lee, K. H. (1986), 'Malaysia: The Structure and Causes of Manufacturing Sector Protection', in C. Findlay and R. Garnaut (eds.), *The Political Economy of Manufacturing Protection: Experiences of ASEAN and Australia*, Allen & Unwin, Sydney.

Lester, M. (1981), 'Case Study: The Transfer of Managerial and Technological Skills in the Malaysian Electronics Industry', paper presented at Training Workshop on Negotiating Technology Transfer with Transnational Corporations, Kuala Lumpur, 12–16 January (unpublished).

Lin, S. Y. (1989), 'Exchange Rate Regimes and Practices: The Case of Malaysia', paper presented at the Eighteenth Pacific Trade and Development Conference', Kuala Lumpur, 11–14 December (unpublished).

Lo, F. C. et al. (1989), 'Structural Interdependency and the Outlook for the Asian–Pacific Economy towards the Year 2000', in M. Shinohara and F. C. Lo (eds.), *Global Adjustment and the Future of the Asian–Pacific Economy*, Institute of Developing Economies, Tokyo, and Asian and Pacific Development Centre, Kuala Lumpur.

Lorenz, D. (1989), 'Inter-Regional Trade and Pacific Cooperation: Problems and Prospects', in W. Klenner (ed.), *Trends of Economic Development in Asia*, Springer Verlag Berlin, Heidelberg.

Malaysia (1981), *Fourth Malaysia Plan 1981–1985*, Kuala Lumpur.

_____ (1983), *Mid-Term Review of Fourth Malaysia Plan 1981–1985*, Kuala Lumpur.

_____ (1986a), *Fifth Malaysia Plan 1986–1990*, Kuala Lumpur.

_____ (1986b), *Industrial Master Plan 1986–1995*, Kuala Lumpur.

_____ (1989), *Mid-Term Review of the Fifth Malaysia Plan 1986–1990*, Kuala Lumpur.

Malaysia, Bank Negara Malaysia, *Annual Report*, various issues, Kuala Lumpur.

_____ *Quarterly Economic Bulletin*, various issues.

Malaysia, Department of Statistics, *External Trade Statistics*, various issues.

Malaysia, Economic Planning Unit (1978), 'Structure of Protection', Economic Planning Unit, Prime Minister's Department, Kuala Lumpur (unpublished).

Malaysia, Ministry of Finance, *Economic Report*, various issues.

Malaysian Industrial Development Authority (MIDA) (1989), *Malaysia: Investment in the Manufacturing Sector*, Kuala Lumpur, August.

Mendl, W. (1983), 'Japan–China: The Economic Nexus', in N. Akao (ed.), *Japan's Economic Security*, New York.

Mody, A. and Wheeler, D. (1989), 'Emerging Patterns of International Competition in Selected Industrial Product Groups', Industries Series Paper No. 2, World Bank, Washington, DC.

Montes, M. F. (1990), 'Resource Gaps and External Financing in the Asia–Pacific Countries', Pacific Trade and Development Conference Secretariat, Canberra (unpublished).

Naya, S. et al. (1989a), *ASEAN–US Initiative: Assessment and Recommendations for Improved Economic Relations*, East–West Center and Institute of Southeast Asian Studies, Honolulu-Singapore.

_____ (1989b), 'Pacific Economic Cooperation in the Global Context: Macroeconomic Structural Issues of Trade, Finance, and the Adjustment Process', East–West Center, Honolulu (mimeograph).

Nurkse, R. (1959), *Patterns of Trade and Development*, Wicksell Lectures, Almquist & Wicksell, Stockholm.

O'Connor, D. (1989), 'Microelectronics-based Innovations: Strategic Implications for Selected Industries in the Second-tier Newly Industrialising Economies (NIEs) of Southeast Asia', OECD Development Centre, Paris.

Organization for Economic Cooperation and Development (OECD), *Geographical Distribution of Financial Flows to Developing Countries*, various issues, Paris.

Patrick, H. (1981), 'US–Chinese Economic Relations in the Asian–Pacific Context', *The World Economy*, Vol. 4.

Phongpaichit, P. (1990), *The New Wave of Japanese Investment in ASEAN*, Institute of Southeast Asian Studies, Singapore.

Porter, M. (1989), *The Competitive Advantage of Nations and Their Firms*, Maxwell Macmillan, New York.

Power, J. H. (1971), 'The Structure of Protection in West Malaysia', in B. Balassa (ed.), *The Structure of Protection in Developing Countries*, Johns Hopkins University Press, Baltimore.

Prebisch, R. (1950), *The Economic Development of Latin America and Its Principal Problems*, United Nations, New York.

Ranis, G. (1985), 'Can the East Asian Model of Development Be Generalized? A Comment', *World Development*, 13(4).

Rasiah R. (1988), 'The Assembly Line in Transition: Implications and New Dimensions for the Electronics Industry in Penang', paper presented at the Seminar on Changing Dimensions in the Electronics Industry in Malaysia, 14–15 March, Penang (unpublished).

_____ (1989), 'Growth and Significance of Textile and Garment Industry in Penang', paper submitted to Seminar on Textile Industry, 11–12 August, Penang (unpublished).

Rasmussen, E. (1988), 'Economic Prospects in the Asia–Pacific: An American View', in T. S. Lau and L. Suryadinata (eds.), *Moving into the Pacific Century: The Changing Regional Order in the Asia–Pacific*, Heinemann Asia, Singapore.

Richardson, J.D. (1971), 'Constant Market Share Analysis of Export Growth', *Journal of International Economics*, 1(2).

Rieger, H. C. (1985), *ASEAN Co-operation and Intra-ASEAN Trade*, Institute of Southeast Asian Studies, Singapore.

Rostow, W. W. (1986), *The United States and the Regional Organization of Asia and the Pacific 1965–1985*, University of Texas Press, Austin.

Saham, J. (1980), *British Industrial Investment in Malaysia 1963–1971*, Oxford University Press, Kuala Lumpur.

Salih, K. et al. (1988), 'Trade Policy Options for Malaysia', in M. Ariff and L. H. Tan (eds.), *ASEAN Trade Policy Options*, Institute of Southeast Asian Studies, Singapore.

Scalapino, R. A. (1987), *Major Power Relations in Northeast Asia*, University Press of America, New York.

Schott, J. J. (1989), 'More Free Trade Areas?', in J. J. Schott (ed.), *Free Trade Areas and U.S. Trade Policy*, Institute for International Economics, Washington, DC.

Semudram, M. (1985), 'The Management of the Malaysian Ringgit', Institute of Strategic and International Studies (ISIS) Malaysia, Kuala Lumpur (mimeograph).

Singh, M. S. (1989), 'Malaysia's Manufacturing Corridor: Subnational Industrial Transformation and Regional Development in the Central, North and South Growth Centres Through the Internationalisation of Capital', United Nations Centre for Regional Development, Nagoya (unpublished).

Spence, A. M. (1981), 'The Learning Curve and Competition', *Bell Journal of Economics*, 12(1).

Takenaka, H. (1989), 'The Japanese Economy and the Economic Development of the Pacific Region', paper submitted to the Eighteenth Pacific Trade and Development Conference, Kuala Lumpur, 11–14 December (unpublished).

Tan, A. H. H. (1988), 'American Influence on Asian–Pacific Trade and Development', in T. S. Lau and L. Suryadinata (eds.), *Moving into the Pacific Century: The Changing Regional Order in the Asia–Pacific*, Heinemann Asia, Singapore.

Tyers, R. and Phillips, P. (1984), *Australia, ASEAN and Pacific Basin Merchandise Trade: Factor Composition and Performance in the 1970s*, ASEAN–Australia Economic Papers No. 13, ASEAN–Australia Joint Research Project, Kuala Lumpur–Canberra.

United Nations Industrial Development Organization (UNIDO) (1982), *Changing Pattern of Trade in World Industry: An Empirical Study on Revealed Comparative Advantage*, New York.

_____ (1988), *Industry and Development: Global Report 1988/89*, Vienna.

United Nations, *Commodity Trade Statistics*, various issues.

United States Department of Commerce, *Survey of Current Business*, various issues, Washington, DC.

Vernon, R. (1979), 'The Product Life Cycle Hypothesis in a New International Environment', *Oxford Bulletin of Economics and Statistics*, 41(4).

Wagner, N. (1989), *ASEAN and the EC: European Investment in ASEAN*, Institute of Southeast Asian Studies, Singapore.

World Bank (1955), *The Economic Development of Malaya*, Johns Hopkins University Press, Baltimore.

_____ (1989a), *Malaysia—Matching Risks and Rewards in a Mixed Economy Program*, Vols. I, II, and III, A World Bank Country Study, Washington, DC.

_____ (1989b), *World Development Report 1989*, Washington, DC.

Wong, J. (1984), *The Political Economy of China's Changing Relations with Southeast Asia*, London.

Index